ESTATE PUBL~~ICATIONS~~

LEICESTERSHIRE & RUTLAND

Street maps with index
Administrative Districts
Population Gazetteer
Road Map with index
Postcodes

C000217642

COUNTY RED BOOKS

This atlas is intended for those requiring street maps of the historical and commercial centres of towns within the county. Each locality is normally presented on one or two pages and although, with many small towns, this space is sufficient to portray the whole urban area, the maps of large towns and cities are for centres only and are not intended to be comprehensive. Such coverage in Super and Local Red Books (see page 2).

Every effort has been made to verify the accuracy of information in this book but the publishers cannot accept responsibility for expense or loss caused by any error or omission. Information that will be of assistance to the user of these maps will be welcomed.

The representation of a road, track or footpath on the maps in this atlas is no evidence of the existence of a right of way.

Street plans prepared and published by ESTATE PUBLICATIONS, Bridewell House, TENTERDEN, KENT, and based upon the ORDNANCE SURVEY mapping with the permission of the Controller of H. M. Stationery Office.

The Publishers acknowledge the co-operation of the local authorities of towns represented in this atlas.

Estate Publications 447 D   ISBN 0 86084 997 X   © Crown Copyright 398713

COUNTY RED BOOK

LEICESTERSHIRE
& RUTLAND

contains street maps for each town centre

SUPER & LOCAL RED BOOKS

are street atlases with comprehensive local coverage

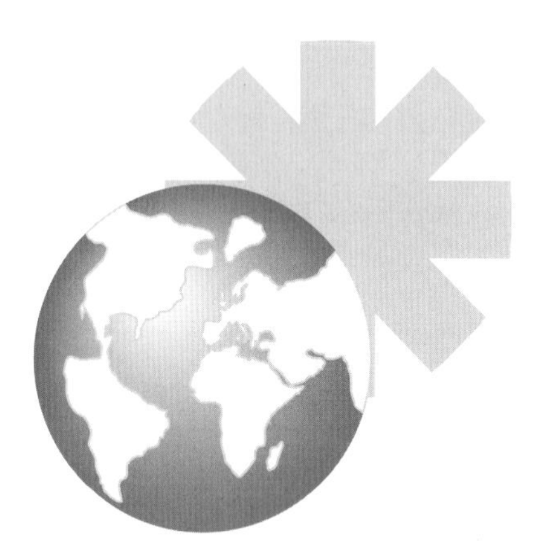

LEICESTER, LOUGHBOROUGH

including: Anstey, Blaby, Evington, Groby, Humberstone, Narborough, Oadby, Sileby, Syston, Wigston etc.

CONTENTS

LEGEND TO STREET MAPS

One-Way Street	→	Post Office	●
Pedestrianized	▨	Public Convenience	C
Car Park	P	Place of Worship	+

Scale of street plans: 4 Inches to 1 mile (unless otherwise stated on the map).

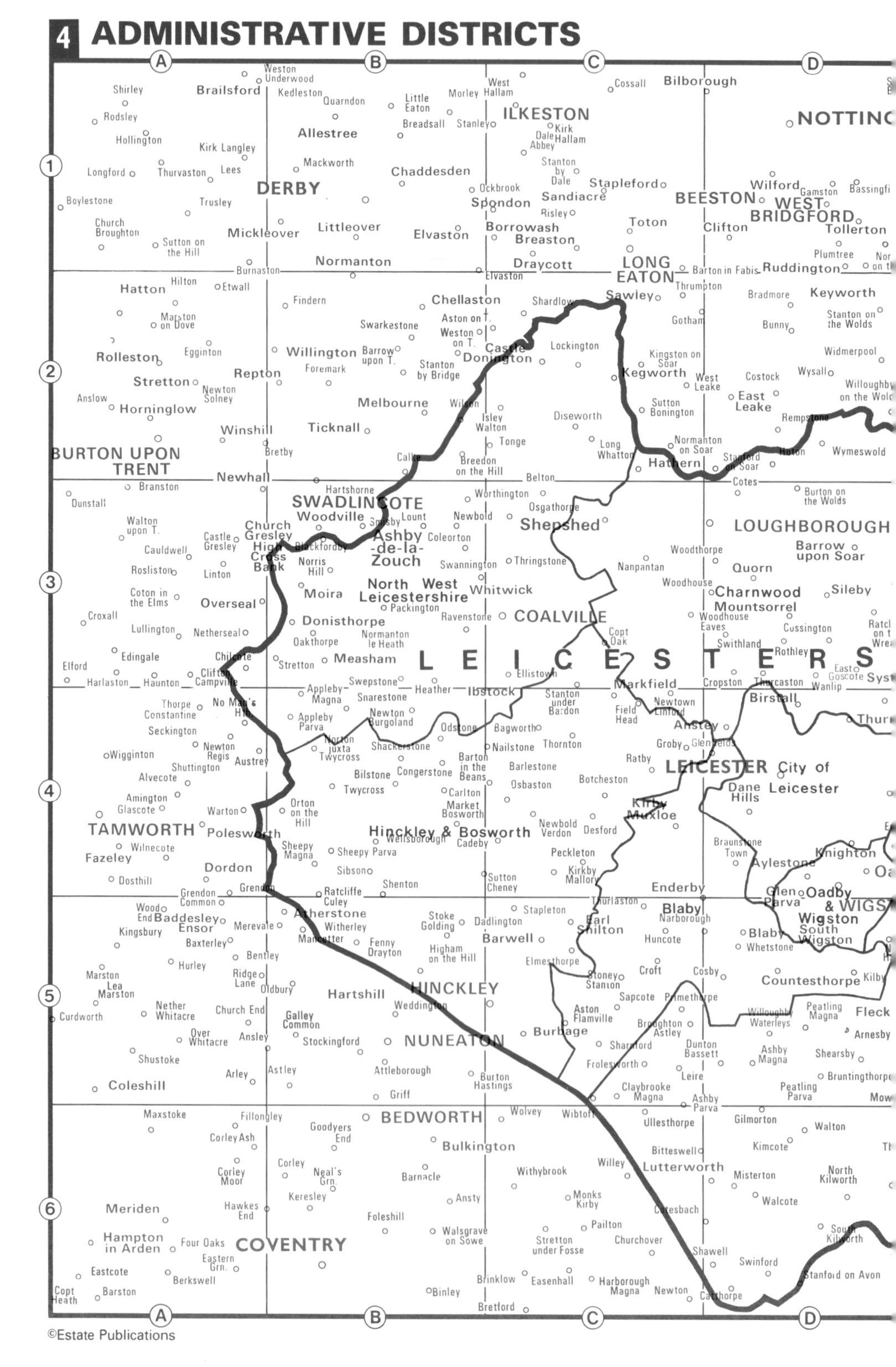

4
ADMINISTRATIVE DISTRICTS
A
B
C
D
1
2
3
4
5
6
Weston Underwood
Shirley
Brailsford
Kedleston
Quarndon
Little Eaton
Morley
West Hallam
Cossall
Bilborough
Rodsley
Breadsall
Stanley
ILKESTON
NOTTING
Hollington
Allestree
Kirk Hallam
Dale Abbey
Kirk Langley
Mackworth
Stanton by Dale
Longford
Thurvaston
Lees
Chaddesden
Stapleford
Wilford
Gamston
Bassingfi
DERBY
Ockbrook
Boylestone
Trusley
Spondon
Sandiacre
BEESTON
WEST BRIDGFORD
Church Broughton
Mickleover
Littleover
Elvaston
Borrowash
Risley
Toton
Clifton
Tollerton
Sutton on the Hill
Breaston
Plumtree
Normanton
Draycott
LONG EATON
Burnaston
Elvaston
Barton in Fabis
Ruddington
Hatton
Hilton
Etwall
Thrumpton
Bradmore
Keyworth
Findern
Chellaston
Shardlow
Sawley
Marston on Dove
Aston on T.
Gotham
Bunny
Stanton on the Wolds
Swarkestone
Weston on T.
Lockington
Rolleston
Egginton
Willington
Barrow upon T.
Castle Donington
Kingston on Soar
Widmerpool
Foremark
Stanton by Bridge
Kegworth
West Leake
Costock
Wysall
Stretton
Repton
Newton Solney
East Leake
Willoughby on the Wold
Anslow
Horninglow
Melbourne
Wilson
Sutton Bonington
Isley Walton
Diseworth
Rempstone
Winshill
Ticknall
Tonge
Normanton on Soar
BURTON UPON TRENT
Bretby
Long Whatton
Wymeswold
Calke
Breedon on the Hill
Hathern
Stanford on Soar
Hoton
Newhall
Belton
Cotes
Branston
Hartshorne
Worthington
Dunstall
SWADLINCOTE
Burton on the Wolds
Woodville
Lount
Newbold
Osgathorpe
Walton upon T.
Smisby
Shepshed
LOUGHBOROUGH
Church Gresley
Castle Gresley
Ashby -de-la- Zouch
Coleorton
Cauldwell
Blackfordby
Woodthorpe
Barrow upon Soar
High Cross Bank
Norris Hill
Swannington
Thringstone
Nanpantan
Quorn
Rosliston
Linton
Whitwick
Woodhouse
Sileby
North West Leicestershire
Charnwood
Moira
Coton in the Elms
Overseal
Packington
Mountsorrel
Croxall
Ravenstone
COALVILLE
Woodhouse Eaves
Donisthorpe
Cossington
Lullington
Netherseal
Copt Oak
Oakthorpe
Normanton le Heath
Swithland
Rothley
Edingale
Chilcote
L E I C E S T E R S
Stretton
Measham
Elford
Clifton Campville
Ellistown
East Goscote
Harlaston
Haunton
Appleby Magna
Swepstone
Heather
Markfield
Cropston
Thurcaston
Wanlip
Ibstock
Stanton under Bardon
Snarestone
No Man's Heath
Field Head
Newtown Linford
Thorpe Constantine
Birstall
Appleby Parva
Newton Burgoland
Odstone
Bagworth
Anstey
Seckington
Glenfields
Norton juxta Twycross
Shackerstone
Nailstone
Thornton
Groby
Newton Regis
Wigginton
Austrey
Ratby
LEICESTER
City of Leicester
Shuttington
Barton in the Beans
Barlestone
Bilstone
Congerstone
Botcheston
Alvecote
Twycross
Osbaston
Dane Hills
Carlton
Amington
Glascote
Market Bosworth
Kirby Muxloe
Orton on the Hill
Warton
Newbold Verdon
TAMWORTH
Polesworth
Hinckley & Bosworth
Desford
Braunstone Town
Wellsborough
Cadeby
Knighton
Wilnecote
Sheepy Magna
Sheepy Parva
Peckleton
Aylestone
Fazeley
Dordon
Kirkby Mallory
Sibson
Sutton Cheney
Oadby
Dosthill
Shenton
Enderby
Glen Parva
Oadby & Wigston
Grendon Common
Grendon
Ratcliffe Culey
Thurlaston
Wood End
Baddesley Ensor
Atherstone
Stapleton
Blaby
Stoke Golding
Earl Shilton
Narborough
Wigston
Witherley
Dadlington
Kingsbury
Merevale
Mancetter
Fenny Drayton
Barwell
Huncote
South Wigston
Baxterley
Higham on the Hill
Whetstone
Bentley
Hurley
Elmesthorpe
Marston
Ridge Lane
Cosby
Lea Marston
Oldbury
Hartshill
HINCKLEY
Croft
Countesthorpe
Kilby
Stoney Stanton
Sapcote
Primethorpe
Nether Whitacre
Church End
Weddington
Curdworth
Galley Common
Aston Flamville
Peatling Magna
Fleck
Broughton Astley
Willoughby Waterleys
Over Whitacre
Ansley
Stockingford
NUNEATON
Burbage
Arnesby
Sharnford
Shustoke
Dunton Bassett
Ashby Magna
Shearsby
Frolesworth
Leire
Arley
Astley
Attleborough
Burton Hastings
Bruntingthorpe
Coleshill
Claybrooke Magna
Peatling Parva
Griff
Ashby Parva
Mow
Maxstoke
Fillongley
Wolvey
Wibtoft
BEDWORTH
Ullesthorpe
Gilmorton
Walton
Goodyers End
Corley Ash
Kimcote
Bulkington
Bitteswell
Corley Moor
Corley
Neal's Grn.
Willey
Lutterworth
Withybrook
Misterton
North Kilworth
Barnacle
Keresley
Ansty
Monks Kirby
Walcote
Meriden
Hawkes End
Cotesbach
Foleshill
Pailton
South Kilworth
Walsgrave on Sowe
Stretton under Fosse
Churchover
Hampton in Arden
Four Oaks
COVENTRY
Shawell
Swinford
Eastern Grn.
Eastcote
Berkswell
Brinklow
Easenhall
Harborough Magna
Stanford on Avon
Copt Heath
Barston
Binley
Newton
Catthorpe
Bretford
©Estate Publications

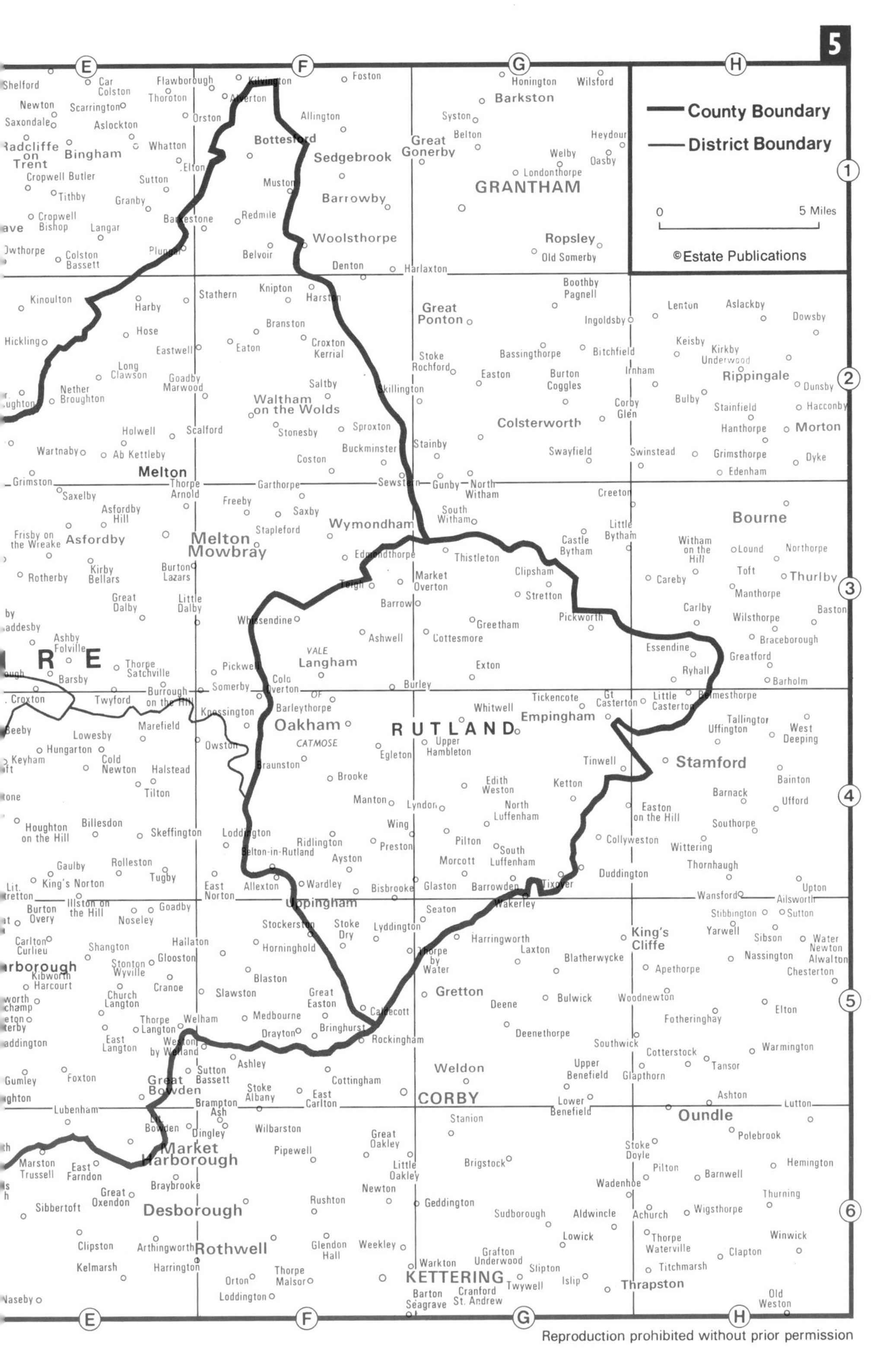
County Boundary
District Boundary
0
5 Miles
©Estate Publications
E
F
G
H
1
2
3
4
5
6
Shelford
Car Colston
Flawborough
Kilvington
Foston
Honington
Wilsford
Newton
Scarrington
Thoroton
Alverton
Barkston
Saxondale
Aslockton
Orston
Allington
Syston
Radcliffe on Trent
Bingham
Whatton
Bottesford
Sedgebrook
Great Gonerby
Belton
Heydour
Welby
Oasby
Cropwell Butler
Elton
Londonthorpe
Sutton
Muston
GRANTHAM
Tithby
Granby
Barrowby
Cropwell Bishop
Langar
Barkestone
Redmile
Woolsthorpe
Ropsley
Colston Bassett
Plungar
Belvoir
Old Somerby
Denton
Harlaxton
Boothby Pagnell
Kinoulton
Harby
Stathern
Knipton
Harston
Great Ponton
Lenton
Aslackby
Dowsby
Ingoldsby
Hose
Branston
Hickling
Eastwell
Eaton
Croxton Kerrial
Keisby
Kirkby Underwood
Stoke Rochford
Bassingthorpe
Bitchfield
Long Clawson
Goadby Marwood
Easton
Burton Coggles
Irnham
Rippingale
Dunsby
Nether Broughton
Saltby
Waltham on the Wolds
Skillington
Corby Glen
Bulby
Stainfield
Hacconby
Holwell
Scalford
Stonesby
Sproxton
Colsterworth
Hanthorpe
Morton
Wartnaby
Ab Kettleby
Coston
Buckminster
Stainby
Swayfield
Swinstead
Grimsthorpe
Dyke
Melton
Edenham
Grimston
Thorpe Arnold
Garthorpe
Sewstern
Gunby
North Witham
Creeton
Saxelby
Freeby
Saxby
Asfordby Hill
South Witham
Bourne
Stapleford
Wymondham
Little Bytham
Frisby on the Wreake
Asfordby
Melton Mowbray
Castle Bytham
Witham on the Hill
Lound
Northorpe
Edmondthorpe
Thistleton
Kirby Bellars
Burton Lazars
Clipsham
Toft
Thurlby
Rotherby
Market Overton
Careby
Teigh
Manthorpe
Great Dalby
Little Dalby
Stretton
Barrow
Carlby
Baston
Pickworth
Wilsthorpe
Whissendine
Greetham
Gaddesby
Ashby Folville
Ashwell
Cottesmore
Braceborough
Essendine
Greatford
VALE
Langham
Exton
Ryhall
Thorpe Satchville
Pickwell
Barsby
Cold Overton
Barholm
Somerby
Burley
Croxton
Twyford
Burrough on the Hill
OF
Barleythorpe
Whitwell
Tickencote
Gt Casterton
Little Casterton
Belmesthorpe
Knossington
Empingham
Tallington
Beeby
Marefield
Oakham
RUTLAND
Uffington
West Deeping
Lowesby
CATMOSE
Upper Hambleton
Owston
Hungarton
Egleton
Keyham
Cold Newton
Halstead
Braunston
Tinwell
Stamford
Brooke
Edith Weston
Bainton
Tilton
Ketton
Barnack
Manton
Lyndon
North Luffenham
Easton on the Hill
Ufford
Billesdon
Houghton on the Hill
Skeffington
Loddington
Wing
Southorpe
Ridlington
Pilton
Collyweston
Preston
South Luffenham
Wittering
Belton-in-Rutland
Ayston
Gaulby
Rolleston
Morcott
Thornhaugh
Tugby
Duddington
King's Norton
East Norton
Allexton
Wardley
Bisbrooke
Glaston
Barrowden
Tixover
Upton
Lit. Stretton
Illston on the Hill
Wansford
Ailsworth
Burton Overy
Goadby
Uppingham
Wakerley
Noseley
Seaton
Stibbington
Sutton
Stockerston
Stoke Dry
Lyddington
King's Cliffe
Yarwell
Carlton Curlieu
Hallaton
Harringworth
Sibson
Water Newton
Shangton
Horninghold
Thorpe by Water
Laxton
Stonton Wyville
Glooston
Blatherwycke
Nassington
Alwalton
Kibworth Harcourt
Blaston
Apethorpe
Chesterton
Church Langton
Cranoe
Slawston
Great Easton
Gretton
Bulwick
Woodnewton
Deene
Caldecott
Elton
Thorpe Langton
Welham
Medbourne
Fotheringhay
Bringhurst
Deenethorpe
East Langton
Drayton
Rockingham
Southwick
Warmington
Weston by Welland
Cotterstock
Tansor
Ashley
Weldon
Upper Benefield
Glapthorn
Sutton Bassett
Gumley
Foxton
Great Bowden
Cottingham
Stoke Albany
East Carlton
Ashton
Brampton Ash
CORBY
Lower Benefield
Lutton
Lubenham
Oundle
Stanion
Lit. Bowden
Dingley
Wilbarston
Great Oakley
Polebrook
Stoke Doyle
Market Harborough
Pipewell
Marston Trussell
East Farndon
Little Oakley
Brigstock
Pilton
Hemington
Barnwell
Wadenhoe
Braybrooke
Newton
Thurning
Great Oxendon
Sibbertoft
Rushton
Geddington
Desborough
Sudborough
Aldwincle
Achurch
Wigsthorpe
Lowick
Thorpe Waterville
Winwick
Clipston
Arthingworth
Rothwell
Glendon Hall
Weekley
Grafton Underwood
Clapton
Kelmarsh
Harrington
Thorpe Malsor
Warkton
Slipton
Titchmarsh
Orton
KETTERING
Twywell
Islip
Thrapston
Loddington
Barton Seagrave
Cranford St. Andrew
Old Weston
Naseby
R E

GAZETTEER INDEX TO ROAD MAP
with Populations

County of Leicestershire population 836,032
County of Rutland population 31,489

LEICESTERSHIRE Districts:

Blaby	82,700
Charnwood	141,806
Harborough	67,607
Hinckley & Bosworth	96,201
Leicester	270,493
Melton	45,112
North West Leicestershire	80,566
Oadby & Wigston	51,547

Ab Kettleby 544		9 E2
Allexton 38		9 F4
Anstey 6,192		8 C4
Appleby Magna 971		8 B4
Appleby Parva		8 B4
Arnesby 317		8 D5
Asfordby 3,086		9 E3
Asfordby Hill		9 E3
Ashby Folville		9 E3
Ashby Magna 290		8 D5
Ashby Parva 219		8 C5
Ashby Woulds 2,813		*
Ashby-de-la-Zouch 12,083		8 B3
Ashwell 237		9 F3
Aston Flamville 159		8 C5
Aylestone		8 D4
Ayston 38		9 F4
Bagworth 1,715		8 C4
Bardon 28		*
Barkby 337		8 D4
Barkby Thorpe 46		*
Barkestone		9 F2
Barlestone 2,288		8 C4
Barleythorpe 153		9 F4
Barrow 60		9 F3
Barrow upon Soar 4,773		8 D3
Barrowden 436		9 G4
Barsby		9 E3
Barton in the Beans		8 B4
Barwell		8 C5
Beaumont Chase 3		*
Beeby 81		9 E4
Belmisthorpe		9 H4
Belton 780		8 C3
Belton-in-Rutland 309		9 F4
Belvoir 281		9 F2
Billesdon 679		9 E4
Bilstone		8 B4
Birstall 11,770		8 D4
Bisbrooke 192		9 F4
Bittesby 12		*
Bitteswell 354		8 C6
Blaby 6,538		8 D5
Blaston 49		9 F5
Bottesford 2,981		9 F1
Branston		9 F2
Braunston 344		9 F4
Braunstone 12,945		8 D4
Breedon on the Hill 863		8 B2
Bringhurst 45		9 F5
Brooke 47		9 F4
Broughton and Old Dalby 1,336		9 E2
Broughton Astley 6,487		8 C5
Bruntingthorpe 389		8 D5
Buckminster 383		9 F2
Burbage 14,420		8 C5

Burley 286		9 F3
Burrough on the Hill		9 E4
Burton & Dalby 863		*
Burton Lazars		9 E3
Burton on the Wolds 940		8 D3
Burton Overy 259		9 E5
Butcheston		8 C4
Cadeby 161		8 B4
Caldecott 250		9 F5
Carlton 256		8 B4
Carlton Curlieu 42		9 E5
Castle Donington 6,313		8 C2
Catthorpe 179		*
Charley 208		8 C3
Chilcote 94		8 B3
Church Langton		9 E5
Claybrooke Magna 502		8 C5
Claybrooke Parva 220		*
Clipsham 91		9 G3
Coalville 31,126		8 C3
Cold Newton 59		9 E4
Cold Overton and Knossington 333		9 F4
Coleorton 851		8 B3
Congerstone		8 B4
Copt Oak		8 C3
Cosby 3,390		8 D5
Cossington 488		
Coston		9 F2
Cotes 41		8 D3
Cotesbach 195		8 C6
Cottesmore 2,487		9 G3
Countesthorpe 6,161		8 D5
Cranoe 32		9 E5
Croft 1,629		8 C5
Cropston and Thurcaston 2,012		8 D3
Croxton Kerrial 463		9 F2
Cussington		8 D3
Dadlington		8 C5
Dalby and Burton 863		*
Dane Hills		8 D4
Desford 3,565		8 C4
Diseworth		8 C2
Donisthorpe and Oakthorpe 2,041		8 B3
Drayton 147		9 F5
Dunton Bassett 777		8 D5
Earl Shilton		8 C5
East Goscote 3,038		8 D3
East Langton 344		9 E5
East Norton 97		9 F4
Eastwell		9 E2
Eaton 563		9 F2
Edith Weston 1,262		9 G4
Edmondthorpe		9 F3
Egleton 71		9 F4
Ellistown		8 C3
Elmesthorpe 508		8 C5
Empingham 824		9 G4
Enderby 5,767		8 C4
Essendine 210		9 H3
Evington		8 D4
Exton 557		9 G3
Fenny Drayton		8 B5
Field Head		8 C4

Fleckney 4,295		8 D5
Foxton 463		9 E5
Freeby 267		9 F3
Frisby 20		*
Frisby on the Wreake and Kirby 855		9 E3
Frolesworth 206		8 C5
Gaddesby 699		9 E3
Garthorpe 93		9 F3
Gaulby 88		9 E4
Gilmorton 859		8 D6
Glaston 156		9 G4
Glenfields 9,335		8 C4
Glen Parva 5,365		8 D4
Glooston 45		9 E5
Goadby 43		9 E5
Goadby Marwood		9 F2
Great Bowden		9 E5
Great Casterton 585		9 G4
Great Dalby		9 E3
Great Easton 538		9 F5
Great Glen 3,071		9 E5
Greetham 580		9 G3
Grimston 291		9 E2
Groby 7,321		8 C4
Gumley 118		9 E5
Gunthorpe 28		*
Hallaton 511		9 F5
Halstead		9 E4
Hambleton 128		*
Harby, Hose and Clawson 2,148		9 E2
Harston		9 F2
Hathern 1,791		8 C2
Heather 928		8 B4
Higham on the Hill 715		8 B5
Hinckley 58,531		8 B5
Hoby with Rotherby 531		9 E3
Holwell		9 E2
Horn 12		*
Horninghold 69		9 F5
Hose, Harby and Clawson 2,148		9 E2
Hoton 307		8 D2
Houghton on the Hill 1,681		9 E4
Humberstone		8 D4
Huncote 1,855		8 C5
Hungarton 239		9 E4
Husbands Bosworth 912		8 D6
Ibstock 5,493		8 B4
Illston on the Hill 181		9 E5
Isley cum Langley 78		*
Isley Walton		8 C2
Kegworth 3,405		8 C2
Ketton 1,708		9 G4
Keyham 147		9 E4
Kibworth Beauchamp 3,550		9 E5
Kibworth Harcourt 817		9 E5
Kilby 875		8 D5
Kimcote and Walton 526		8 D6
King's Norton 53		9 E4
Kirby Bellars and Frisby 855		9 E3
Kirby Muxloe 4,519		8 C4
Kirkby Mallory		8 C4
Knaptoft 40		*

Place	Ref.
Knighton	8 D4
Knipton	9 F2
Knossington and Cold Overton 333	9 F4
Langham 1,095	9 F3
Laughton 91	9 E5
Launde 18	*
Leicester 270,493	8 C4
Leicester Forest East 4,921	*
Leicester Forest West 43	*
Leighfield 14	*
Leire 571	8 C5
Little Bowden	9 E6
Little Casterton 77	9 H4
Little Dalby	9 E3
Little Stretton 61	9 E4
Lockington-Hemington 452	8 C2
Loddington 62	9 F4
Long Clawson, Hose and Harby 2,148	9 E2
Long Whatton 1,574	8 C2
Loughborough 48,664	8 D3
Lount	8 B3
Lowesby 85	9 E4
Lubbesthorpe 77	*
Lubenham 1,150	9 E6
Lutterworth 7,380	8 C6
Lyddington 396	9 F5
Lyndon 85	9 G4
Manton 352	9 F4
Marefield 19	9 E4
Market Bosworth 2,019	8 B4
Market Harborough 16,563	9 E6
Market Overton 450	9 F3
Markfield 4,053	8 C3
Measham 4,044	8 B3
Medbourne 405	9 F5
Melton Mowbray 24,312	9 E3
Misterton 436	8 D6
Moira	8 B3
Morcott 345	9 G4
Mountsorrel 6,033	8 D3
Mowsley 223	8 D5
Muston	9 F2
Nailstone 547	8 C4
Nanpantan	8 C3
Narborough 7,613	8 C5
Nevill Holt 44	*
Newbold	8 B3
Newbold Verdon 3,426	8 C4
Newton Burgoland	8 B4
Newton Harcourt	8 D5
Newtown Linford 971	8 C4
Normanton 28	*
Normanton le Heath 114	8 B3
North Kilworth 537	8 D6
North Luffenham 548	9 G4
Norton juxta Twycross	8 B4
Noseley 38	9 E5
Oadby 19,579	8 D4
Oakham 8,691	9 F4
Oakthorpe and Donisthorpe 2,041	8 B3
Odstone	8 B4
Old Dalby and Broughton 1,336	9 E2
Orton on the Hill	8 B4
Osbaston 259	8 C4
Osgathorpe 369	8 C3
Owston and Newbold 88	9 F4
Packington 764	8 B3
Peatling Magna 178	8 D5
Peatling Parva 165	8 D5
Peckleton 985	8 C4
Pickwell	9 F3
Pickworth 216	9 G3
Pilton 19	9 G4
Potters Marston 28	*
Preston 175	9 F4
Prestwold 82	*
Primethorpe	8 C5
Queniborough 2,387	8 D3
Quorn 4,614	8 D3
Ragdale	9 E3
Ratby 3,601	8 C4
Ratcliffe Culey	8 B5
Ratcliffe on the Wreake 133	8 D3
Ravenstone with Snibstone 1,874	8 B3
Rearsby 874	9 E3
Redmile 697	9 F2
Ridlington 174	9 F4
Rolleston 43	9 E4
Rotherby with Hoby 531	9 E3
Rothley 3,141	8 D3
Ryhall 1,661	9 H3
Saddington 225	9 E5
Saltby	9 F2
Sapcote 2,628	8 C5
Saxby	9 F3
Saxelby	9 E3
Scalford 608	9 E2
Scraptoft 1,148	8 D4
Seagrave 426	*
Seaton 178	9 G5
Sewstern	9 F3
Shackerstone 679	8 B4
Shangton 101	9 E5
Sharnford 1,111	8 C5
Shawell 151	8 D6
Shearsby 205	8 D5
Sheepy Magna with Sheepy Parva 1,136	8 B4
Shenton	8 B4
Shepshed 12,961	8 C3
Sibson	8 B4
Sileby 6,702	8 D3
Skeffington 178	9 E4
Slawston 111	9 F5
Smeeton Westerby 346	9 E5
Smisby	8 B3
Snarestone 265	8 B4
Somerby 768	9 F3
South Croxton 226	9 E4
South Kilworth 386	8 D6
South Luffenham 458	9 G4
South Wigston	8 D5
Sproxton 459	9 F2
Stanton under Bardon 604	8 C4
Stapleford	9 F3
Stapleton	8 C5
Stathern 552	9 E2
Staunton Harold 116	*
Stockerston 33	9 F5
Stoke Dry 37	9 F5
Stoke Golding 1,607	8 B5
Stonesby	9 F2
Stoney Stanton 3,113	8 C5
Stonton Wyville 27	9 E5
Stoughton 217	8 D4
Strathern 552	*
Stretton 384	9 G3
Stretton en le Field 36	8 B3
Stretton Magna 12	*
Sutton Cheney 475	8 C4
Swannington 1,195	8 B3
Swepstone 558	8 B4
Swinford 496	8 D6
Swithland 212	8 D3
Syston 10,900	8 D3
Teigh 43	9 F3
Theddingworth 203	8 D6
Thistleton 108	9 G3
Thornton	8 C4
Thorpe Arnold	9 E3
Thorpe by Water 41	9 G5
Thorpe Langton 136	9 E5
Thorpe Satchville	9 E3
Thringstone	8 C3
Thrussington 512	8 D3
Thurcaston and Cropston 2,012	8 D3
Thurlaston 652	8 C5
Thurmaston 9,146	8 D4
Thurnby 2,838	8 D4
Tickencote 54	9 G4
Tilton 508	9 E4
Tinwell 5	9 G4
Tixover 103	9 G4
Tonge	8 C2
Tugby and Keythorpe 281	9 E4
Tur Langton 166	*
Twycross 739	8 B4
Twyford & Thorpe 577	9 E4
Ullesthorpe 864	8 C6
Ulverscroft 91	*
Upper Hambleton	9 G4
Uppingham 3,140	9 F5
Walcote	8 D6
Waltham on the Wolds 798	9 F2
Walton on the Wolds 253	*
Walton and Kimcote 526	8 D6
Wanlip 181	8 D3
Wardley 28	9 F4
Wartnaby	9 E2
Welham 30	9 E5
Wellsborough	8 B4
West Langton 51	*
Westrill and Starmore 12	*
Whatborough 13	*
Whetstone 4,032	8 D5
Whissendine 1,177	9 F3
Whitwell 37	9 G4
Whitwick	8 B3
Wigston 35,439	8 D5
Wigston Parva 34	*
Willoughby Waterleys 223	8 D5
Wilson	8 C2
Wing 312	9 F4
Wistow 249	*
Withcote 36	*
Witherley 1,513	8 B5
Woodhouse 2,215	8 D3
Woodhouse Eaves	8 C3
Woodthorpe	8 C3
Worthington 1,406	8 B3
Wymeswold 1,063	8 D2
Wymondham 588	9 F3

Population figures are based upon the 1991 census and relate to the local authority area or parish as constituted at that date Boundaries of the districts are shown on pages 4-5. Places with no population figure form part of a larger local authority area or parish.

Population figures in bold type.

*Place not included on map due to limitation of space

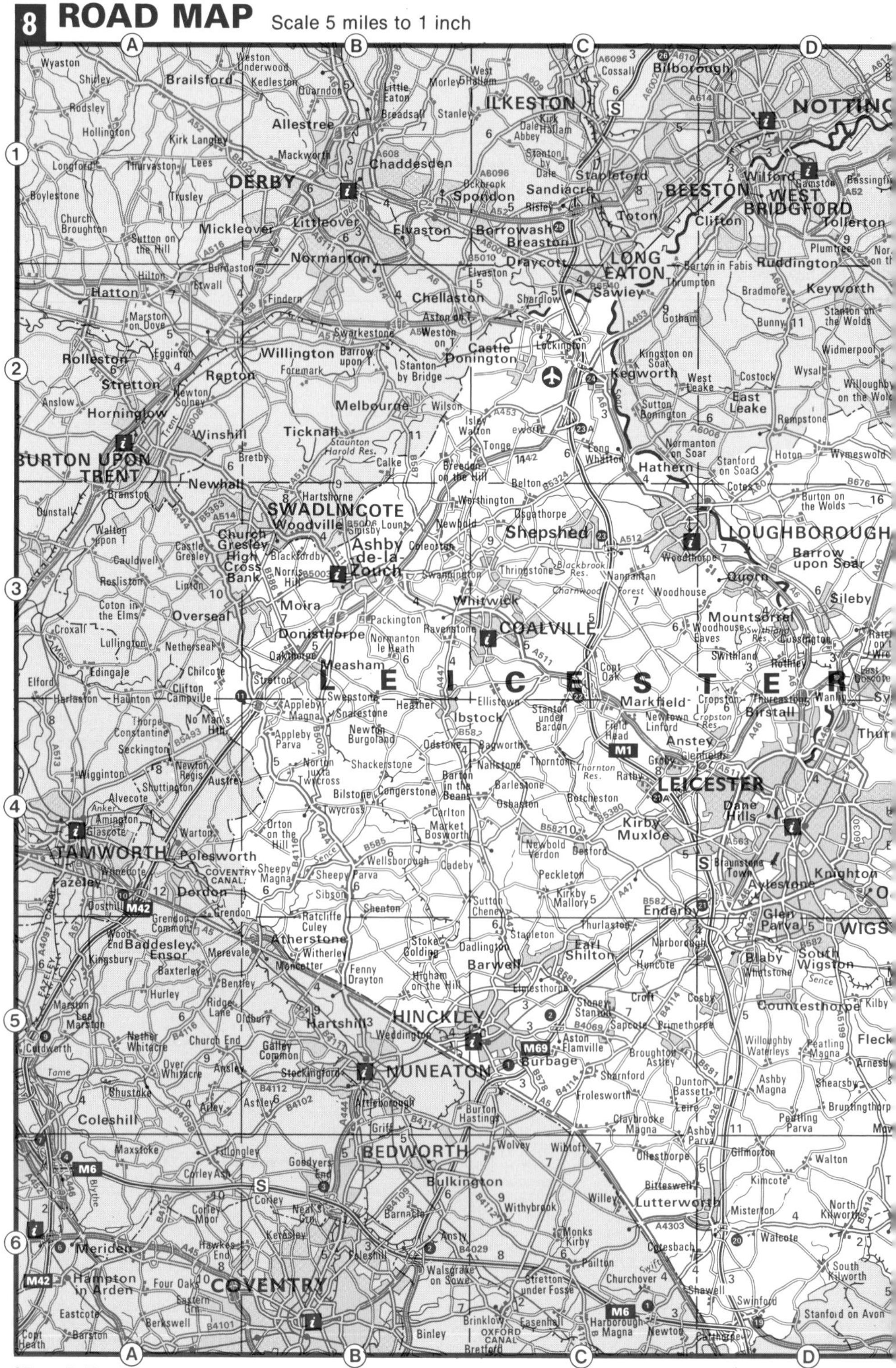

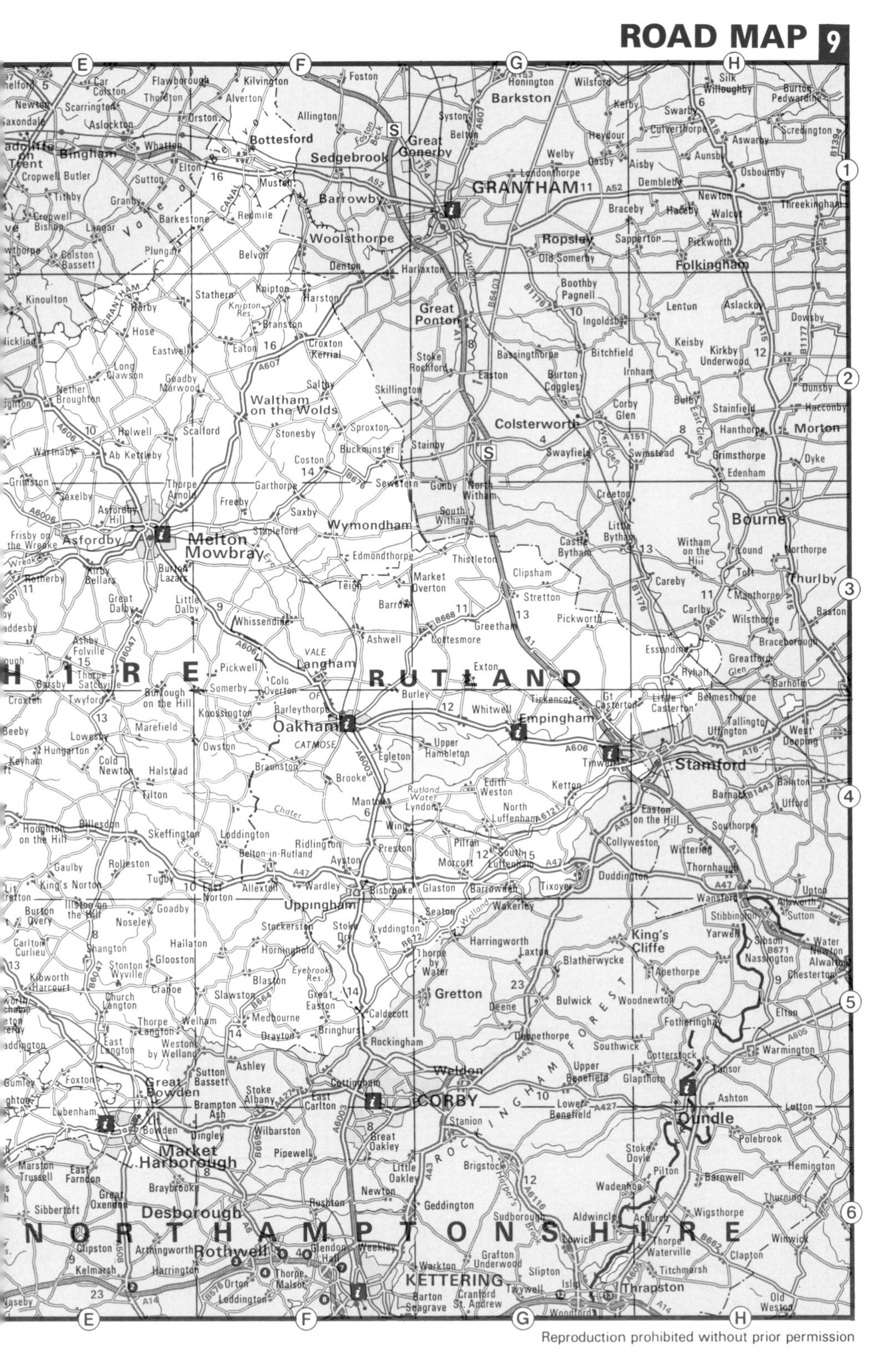
E
F
G
H
1
2
3
4
5
6
Foston
Honington
Barkston
Wilsford
Silk Willoughby
Burton Pedwardine
Car Colston
Flawborough
Kilvington
Alverton
Thoroton
Newton
Scarrington
Aslockton
Orston
Allington
Syston
Belton
Kelby
Swarby
Culverthorpe
Aswarby
Scredington
Heydour
Aisby
Aunsby
Bottesford
Sedgebrook
Great Gonerby
Welby
Oasby
Bingham
Whatton
Elton
Cropwell Butler
Sutton
Muston
Londonthorpe
Osbournby
Dembleby
GRANTHAM
Barrowby
Newton
Threekingham
Tithby
Granby
Redmile
Braceby
Haceby
Walcot
Cropwell Bishop
Langar
Barkestone
Woolsthorpe
Ropsley
Sapperton
Pickworth
Colston Bassett
Plungar
Belvoir
Old Somerby
Folkingham
Denton
Harlaxton
Vale of Belvoir
CANAL
Kinoulton
Harby
Stathern
Knipton
Knipton Res.
Harston
Great Ponton
Boothby Pagnell
Lenton
Aslackby
Dowsby
Hose
Branston
Ingoldsby
Eastwell
Eaton
Croxton Kerrial
Stoke Rochford
Bassingthorpe
Bitchfield
Keisby
Kirkby Underwood
Long Clawson
Goadby Marwood
Saltby
Easton
Burton Coggles
Irnham
Dunsby
Nether Broughton
Waltham on the Wolds
Skillington
Corby Glen
Bulby
Stainfield
Hacconby
Colsterworth
Hanthorpe
Morton
Holwell
Scalford
Stonesby
Sproxton
Buckminster
Stainby
Swayfield
Swinstead
Grimsthorpe
Dyke
Wartnaby
Ab Kettleby
Coston
West Glen
East Glen
Edenham
Grimston
Thorpe Arnold
Garthorpe
Sewstern
Gunby
North Witham
Creeton
Saxelby
Freeby
Asfordby Hill
Saxby
South Witham
Bourne
Frisby on the Wreake
Asfordby
Melton Mowbray
Stapleford
Wymondham
Little Bytham
Castle Bytham
Witham on the Hill
Northorpe
Lound
Edmondthorpe
Thistleton
Toft
Thurlby
Rotherby
Kirby Bellars
Burton Lazars
Teigh
Market Overton
Clipsham
Careby
Great Dalby
Little Dalby
Barrow
Stretton
Carlby
Manthorpe
Baston
Whissendine
Greetham
Pickworth
Wilsthorpe
Braceborough
Ashby Folville
Ashwell
Cottesmore
Essendine
Greatford
Thorpe Satchville
VALE
Langham
Exton
Ryhall
Pickwell
RUTLAND
Barholm
Barsby
Burrough on the Hill
Somerby
Cold Overton
OF
Burley
Tickencote
Gt Casterton
Little Casterton
Belmesthorpe
Croxton
Twyford
Knossington
Barleythorpe
Whitwell
Empingham
Tallington
Uffington
West Deeping
Beeby
Lowesby
Marefield
Oakham
CATMOSE
Owston
Egleton
Upper Hambleton
Tinwell
Stamford
Hungarton
Cold Newton
Halstead
Braunston
Brooke
Edith Weston
Ketton
Keyham
Tilton
Rutland Water
Manton
Lyndon
North Luffenham
Barnack
Bainton
Ufford
Chater
Easton on the Hill
Southorpe
Houghton on the Hill
Billesdon
Skeffington
Loddington
Ridlington
Wing
Preston
Pilton
Collyweston
Wittering
Eye Brook
Belton-in-Rutland
Ayston
Morcott
South Luffenham
Thornhaugh
Gaulby
Rolleston
Tugby
King's Norton
East Norton
Allexton
Wardley
Uppingham
Bisbrooke
Glaston
Barrowden
Tixover
Duddington
Wansford
Upton
Ailsworth
Burton Overy
Illston on the Hill
Goadby
Noseley
Seaton
Wakerley
Welland
Stibbington
Sutton
Stockerston
Stoke Dry
Lyddington
Yarwell
Carlton Curlieu
Hallaton
Shangton
Horninghold
Harringworth
King's Cliffe
Sibson
Water Newton
Stonton Wyville
Glooston
Thorpe by Water
Laxton
Blatherwycke
Nassington
Alwalton
Kibworth Harcourt
Eyebrook Res.
Blaston
Apethorpe
Chesterton
Cranoe
Slawston
Great Easton
Gretton
Church Langton
Medbourne
Caldecott
Deene
Bulwick
Woodnewton
Elton
Thorpe Langton
Welham
Drayton
Bringhurst
Fotheringhay
East Langton
Weston by Welland
Rockingham
Deenethorpe
Southwick
Warmington
ROCKINGHAM FOREST
Ashley
Weldon
Cotterstock
Tansor
Sutton Bassett
Upper Benefield
Glapthorn
Foxton
Great Bowden
Cottingham
Stoke Albany
CORBY
Ashton
Lubenham
Brampton Ash
East Carlton
Lower Benefield
Lutton
Bowden
Dingley
Stanion
Oundle
Wilbarston
Great Oakley
Polebrook
Market Harborough
Pipewell
Stoke Doyle
Marston Trussell
East Farndon
Little Oakley
Brigstock
Pilton
Hemington
Braybrooke
Newton
Harper's Brook
Wadenhoe
Barnwell
Great Oxendon
Sibbertoft
Rushton
Geddington
Thurning
Desborough
Sudborough
Aldwincle
Achurch
Wigsthorpe
NORTHAMPTONSHIRE
Lowick
Clipston
Arthingworth
Rothwell
Glendon Hall
Weekley
Grafton Underwood
Thorpe Waterville
Winwick
Kelmarsh
Harrington
Warkton
Slipton
Titchmarsh
Clapton
Orton
Thorpe Malsor
KETTERING
Islip
Loddington
Twywell
Thrapston
Barton Seagrave
Cranford St. Andrew
Woodford
Old Weston
A52
A1
A15
A607
A606
A6006
A47
A43
A427
A6003
A6121
A16
A605
A14
A6
A6116
A151
B1176
B6403
B1177
B1394
B668
B672
B671
B664
B6047
B1443
B662
B676
B5

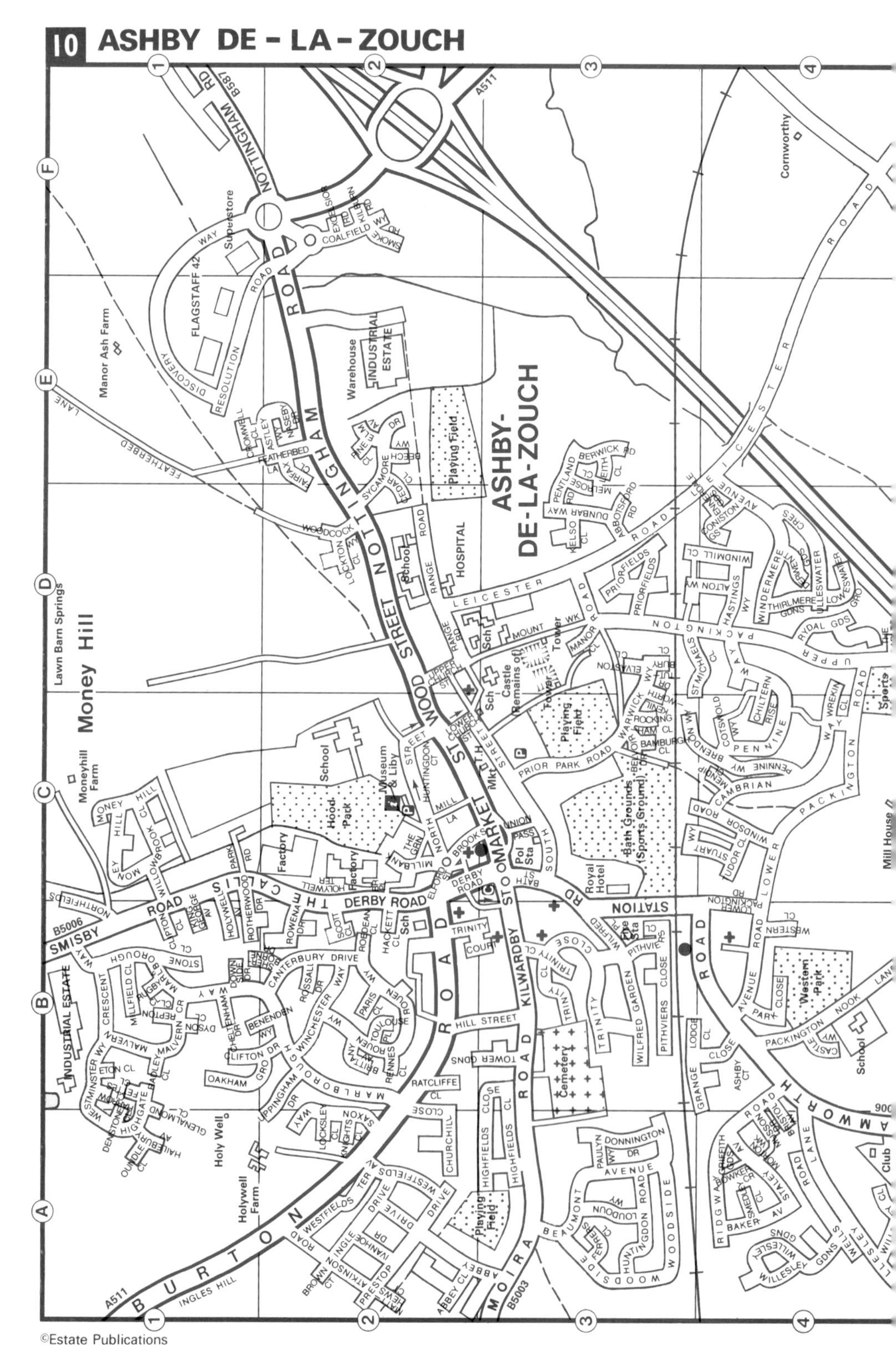
ASHBY-DE-LA-ZOUCH
Money Hill
NOTTINGHAM ROAD
WOOD STREET
MARKET ST
DERBY ROAD
BURTON ROAD
LEICESTER ROAD
PACKINGTON ROAD
STATION RD
KILWARDBY STREET
TAMWORTH ROAD
MOIRA ROAD
SMISBY ROAD
Hood Park
Bath Grounds (Sports Ground)
Western Park
Cemetery
Playing Field
Hospital
Industrial Estate
Castle (Remains of)
Manor Ash Farm
Moneyhill Farm
Holywell Farm
Holy Well
Lawn Barn Springs
Cornworthy
Mill House
Superstore
FLAGSTAFF 42
Royal Hotel
Museum & Liby
Pol Sta

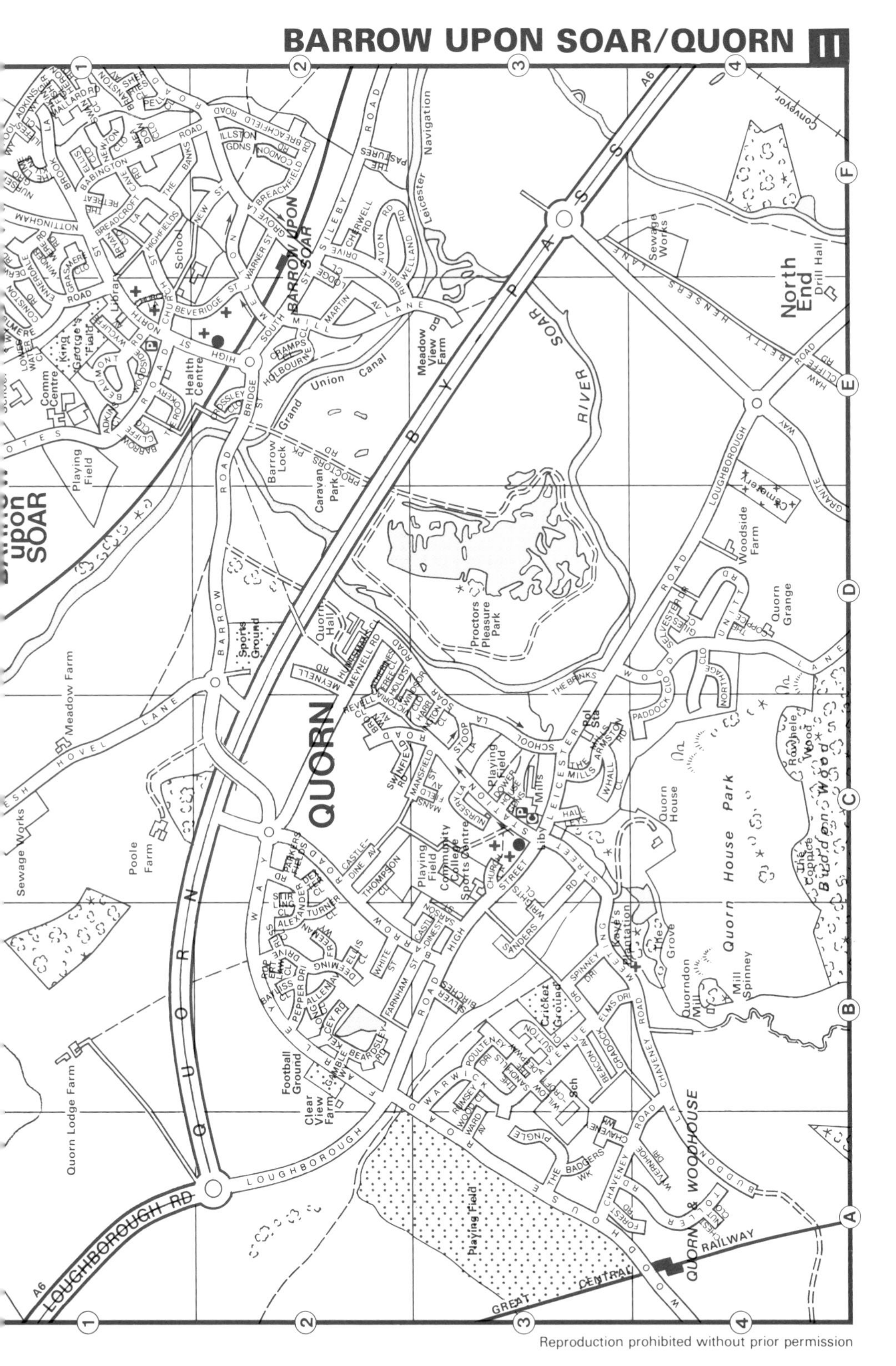
BARROW UPON SOAR
upon SOAR
QUORN
QUORN & WOODHOUSE
North End
Quorn House Park
Proctors Pleasure Park
RIVER SOAR
Grand Union Canal
Leicester Navigation
BY PASS
A6
LOUGHBOROUGH RD
GREAT CENTRAL RAILWAY
Sewage Works
Poole Farm
Meadow Farm
Quorn Lodge Farm
Clear View Farm
Football Ground
Playing Field
Cricket Ground
Quorn Hall
Sports Ground
Health Centre
Comm Centre
King George's Field
Library
School
Barrow Lock
Caravan Park
Meadow View Farm
Drill Hall
Cemetery
Woodside Farm
Quorn Grange
Buddon Wood
The Coppice
Mill Spinney
Quorndon Mill
The Grove
Kaye's Plantation
Quorn House
Community College Sports Centre
Conveyor

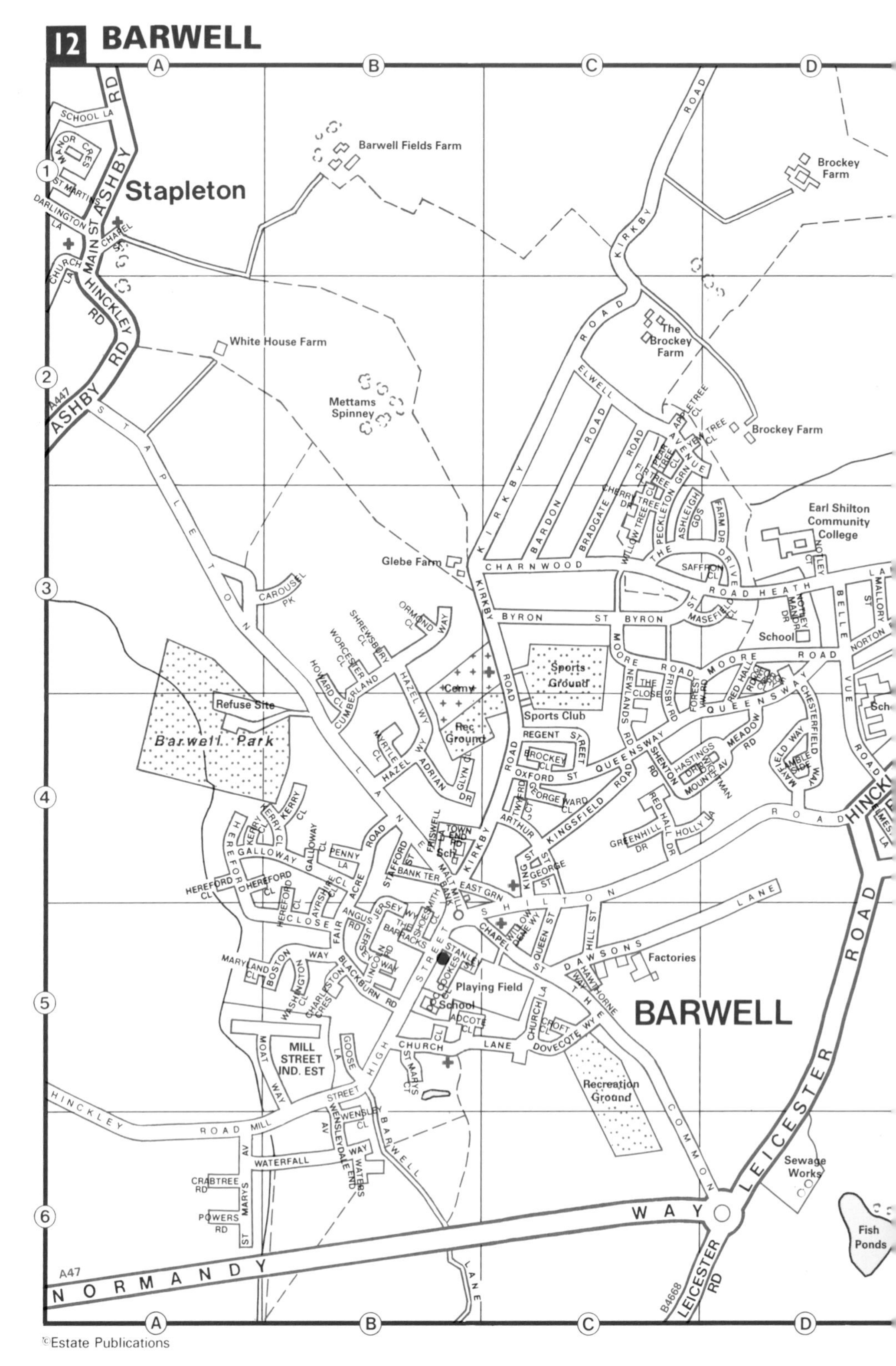

Stapleton

BARWELL

Barwell Fields Farm

Brockey Farm

White House Farm

The Brockey Farm

Brockey Farm

Earl Shilton Community College

Mettams Spinney

Glebe Farm

Refuse Site

Barwell Park

School

Sports Ground

Sports Club

Rec Ground

Cem

CAROUSEL PK

MILL STREET IND. EST

Playing Field

School

Factories

Recreation Ground

Sewage Works

Fish Ponds

MILL STREET IND. EST

NORMANDY WAY

LEICESTER ROAD

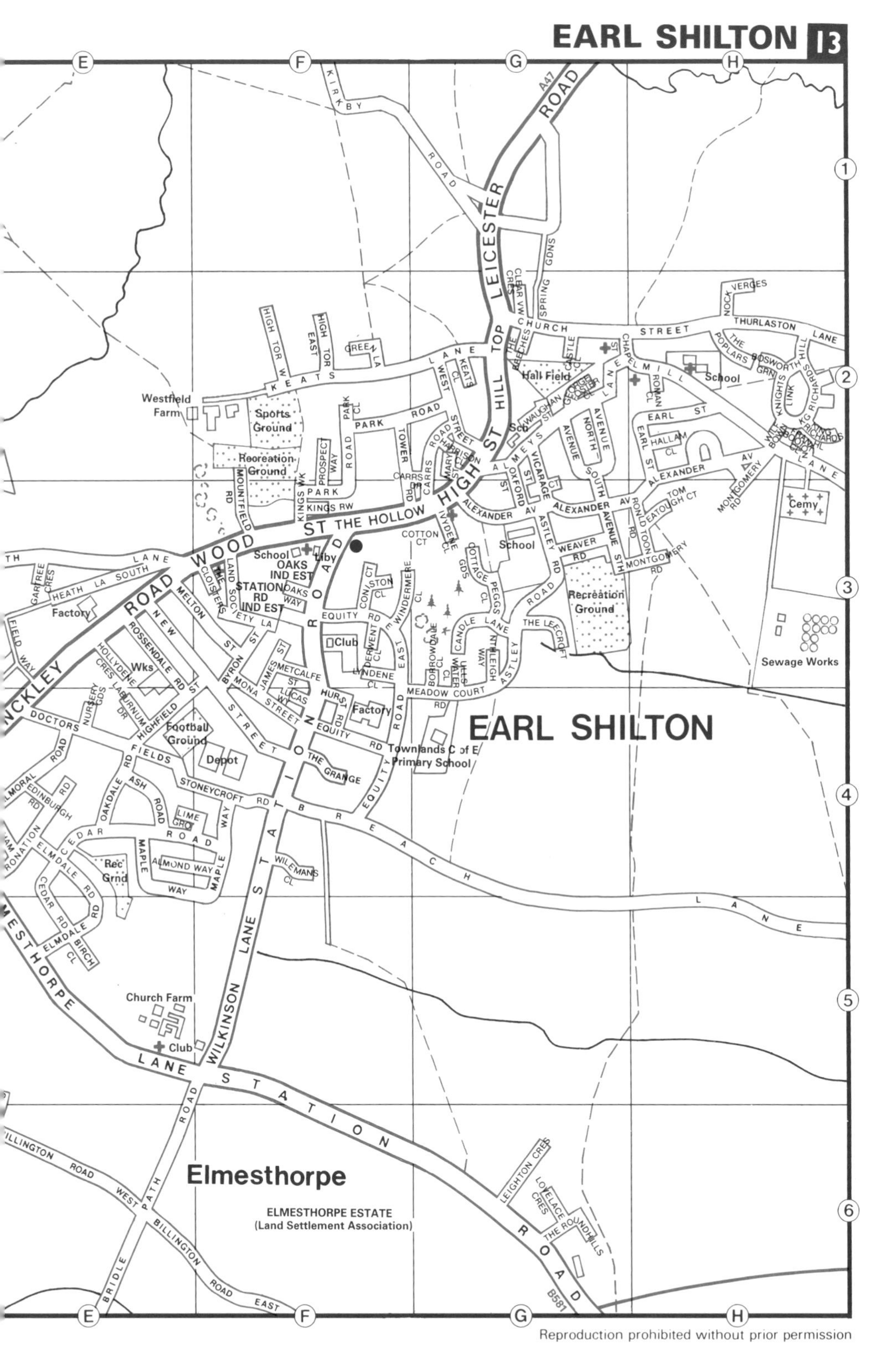
EARL SHILTON
Elmesthorpe
ELMESTHORPE ESTATE
(Land Settlement Association)
Westfield Farm
Sports Ground
Recreation Ground
Hall Field
School
Cemy
Sewage Works
Recreation Ground
Factory
Wks
Football Ground
Depot
Club
Townlands C of E Primary School
Rec Grnd
Church Farm
OAKS IND EST
STATION RD IND EST
Liby
LEICESTER ROAD
WOOD ROAD
HINCKLEY ROAD
HIGH ST
THE HOLLOW
KEATS LANE
CHURCH STREET
THURLASTON LANE
CHAPEL ST
MILL LANE
ALEXANDER AV
STATION ROAD
BREACH LANE
WILKINSON LANE
ELMESTHORPE LANE
BILLINGTON ROAD WEST
BILLINGTON ROAD EAST
BRIDLE PATH ROAD
KIRKBY ROAD
EQUITY ROAD
B581
A47

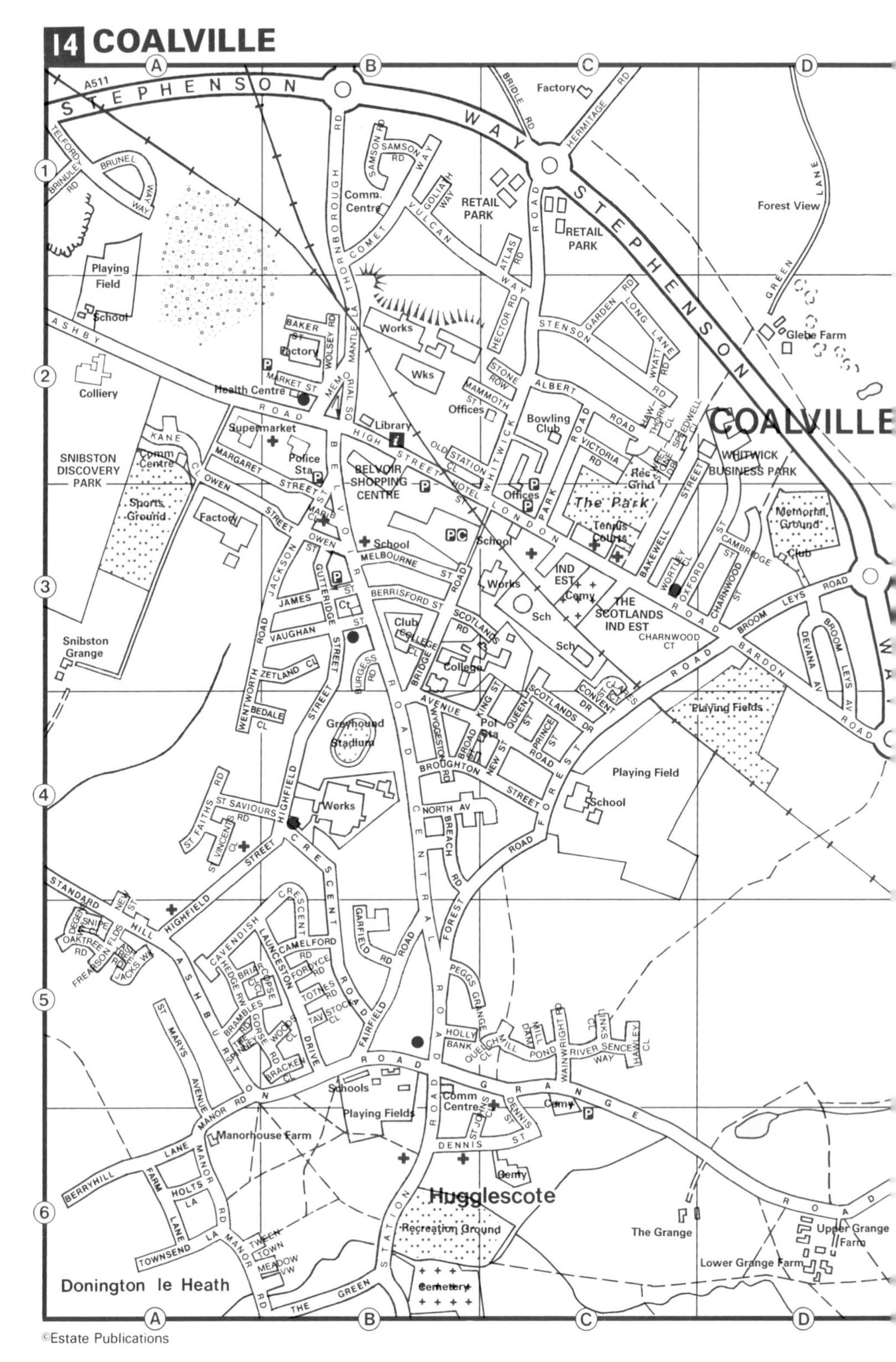

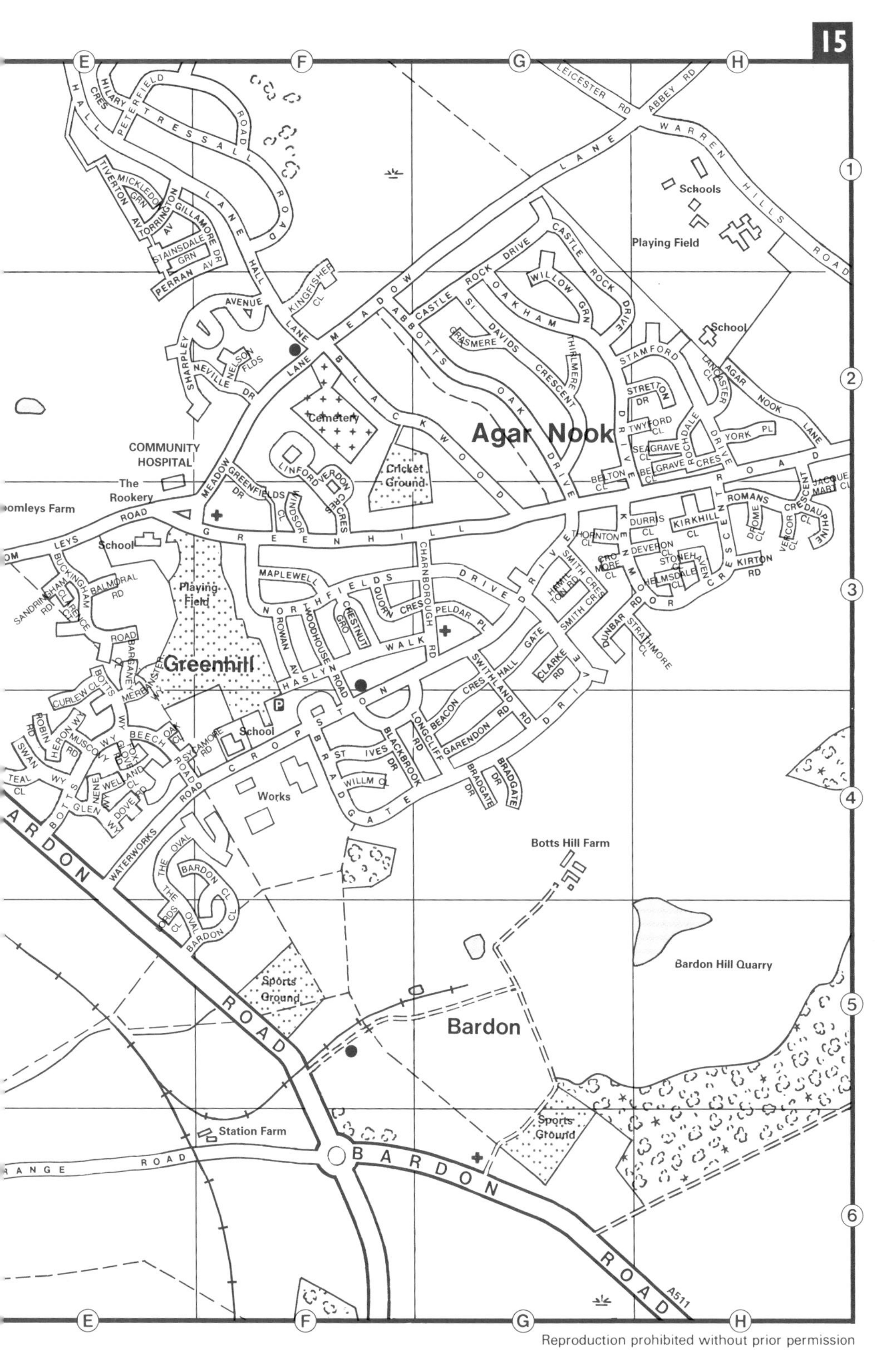

E F G H

LEICESTER RD ABBEY RD

HALL GRN HILARY CRES PETERFIELD TRESSALL ROAD

LANE WARREN HILLS ROAD

Schools

1

MICKLEDON GILLAMORE AV TORRINGTON AV TIVERTON AV STAINSDALE GRN PERRAN AV HALL LANE ROAD

Playing Field

CASTLE ROCK DRIVE WILLOW GRN OAKHAM HILLMERE CASTLE ROCK DRIVE

School

SHARPLEY AVENUE NEVILLE DR KINGFISHER CL

MEADOW LANE BLACKWOOD

ABBOTTS LANE CASTLE GRASMERE ST DAVIDS CRESCENT OAK DRIVE STAMFORD STRETTON DR LANCASTER

AGAR NOOK LANE

2

COMMUNITY HOSPITAL

The Rookery

omleys Farm

ROAD

LEYS

School

BUCKINGHAM RD BALMORAL RD SANDRINGHAM RD PRINCE ROAD MARGARET

Cemetery

Cricket Ground

Agar Nook

TWYFORD CL SEAGRAVE ROCHDALE YORK PL

MEADOW DR GREENFIELDS DR LINFORD VERDON WINSOR CL CRES

GREENHILL

Playing Field

MAPLEWELL NORTHFIELDS ROWAN AV WOODHOUSE CRO CHESTNUT GRO QUORN CRES PELDAR PL WALK HASLYN ROAD

CHARNBOROUGH DRIVE

BELTON CC BELGRAVE CRES ROMANS DURRIS CL KIRKHILL CL CROME VELCOR DAU AVE JACQUE MART CL DEVERON CL STONEH AVEN HELMSDALE R KIRTON RD DUNBAR STRATHMORE

THORNTON CL HENRY TON RD SMITH CRES SMITH CRES

RIVER DRIVE

3

Greenhill

School

SWAN WY TEAL CL ROBIN CL CURLEW CL BOTTS RD HERON WY MUSCOVY WY NENE WY WELLAND DOVE CL GLEN BEECH RD MERISTER SYCAMORE RD CROP WY ROAD

ST IVES DR WILLM CL BLACKBROOK LONGCLIFFE GARENDON RD BRADGATE BEACON CRES SWITHLAND RD CLARKE RD BRADGATE HALL GATE

Works

4

WATERWORKS THE OVAL THE OVAL BARDON CL BARDON CL

Botts Hill Farm

BARDON

ROAD

Sports Ground

Bardon Hill Quarry

5

Station Farm

Bardon

Sports Ground

RANGE ROAD

BARDON ROAD

A511

6

E F G H

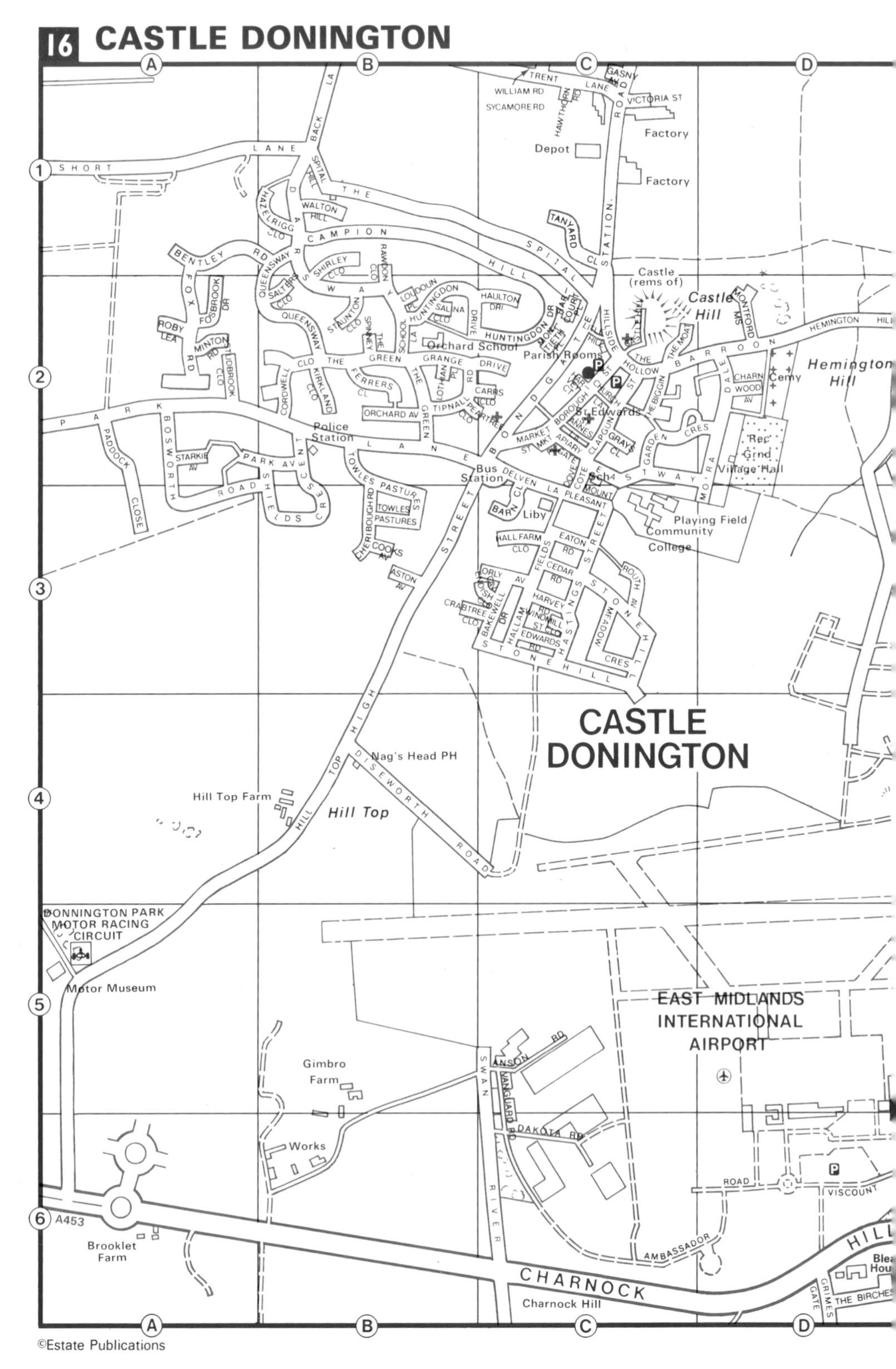

CASTLE
DONINGTON

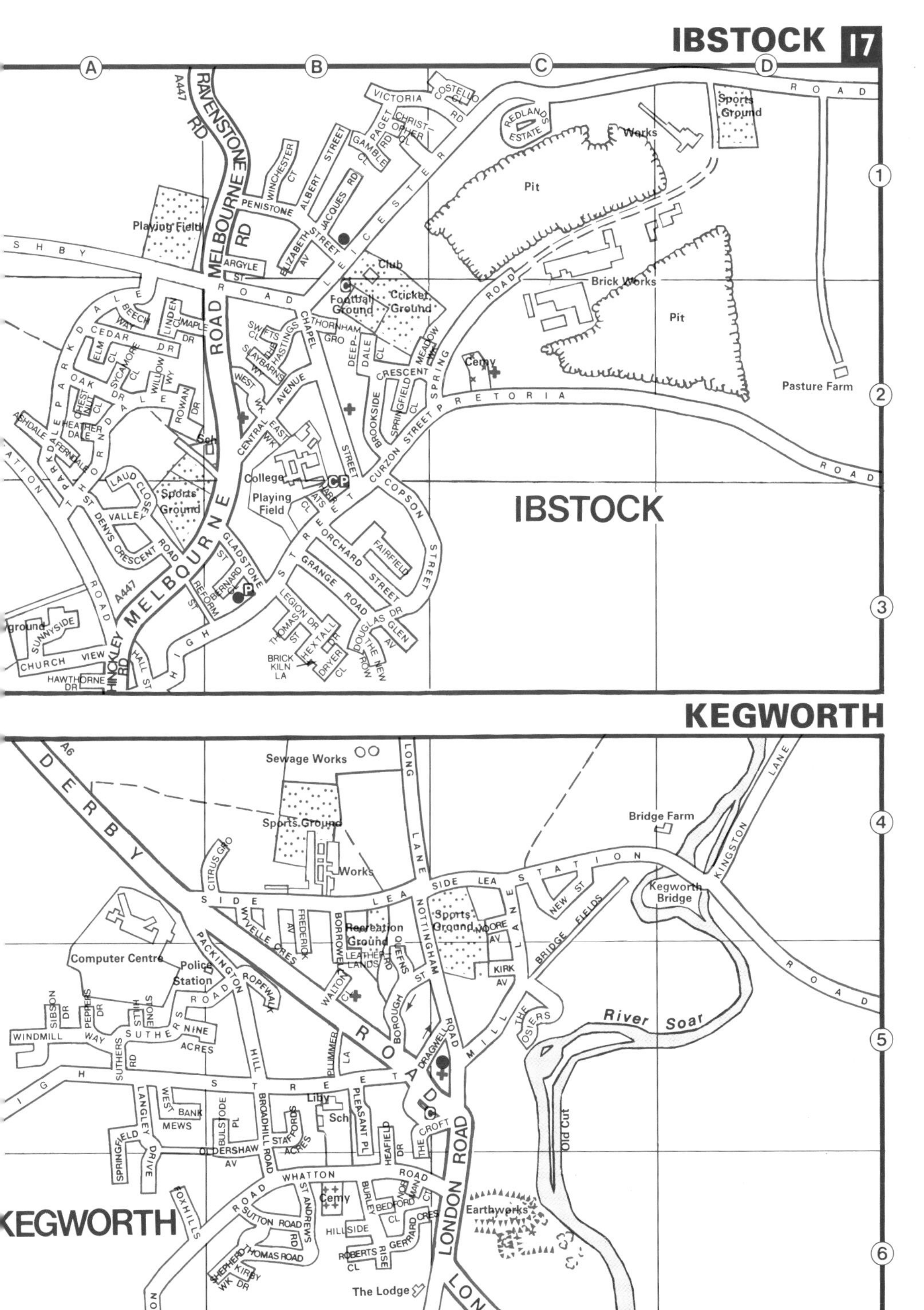
IBSTOCK
KEGWORTH
Playing Field
Pit
Works
Sports Ground
Brick Works
Club
Football Ground
Cricket Ground
Cemy
Pasture Farm
College
Playing Field
Sch
Sports Ground
Sewage Works
Bridge Farm
Kegworth Bridge
River Soar
Old Cut
Computer Centre
Police Station
Recreation Ground
Liby
Earthworks
The Lodge
DERBY ROAD
LONDON ROAD
STATION ROAD
KINGSTON LANE
MELBOURNE ROAD
LEICESTER ROAD
PRETORIA ROAD
HIGH STREET

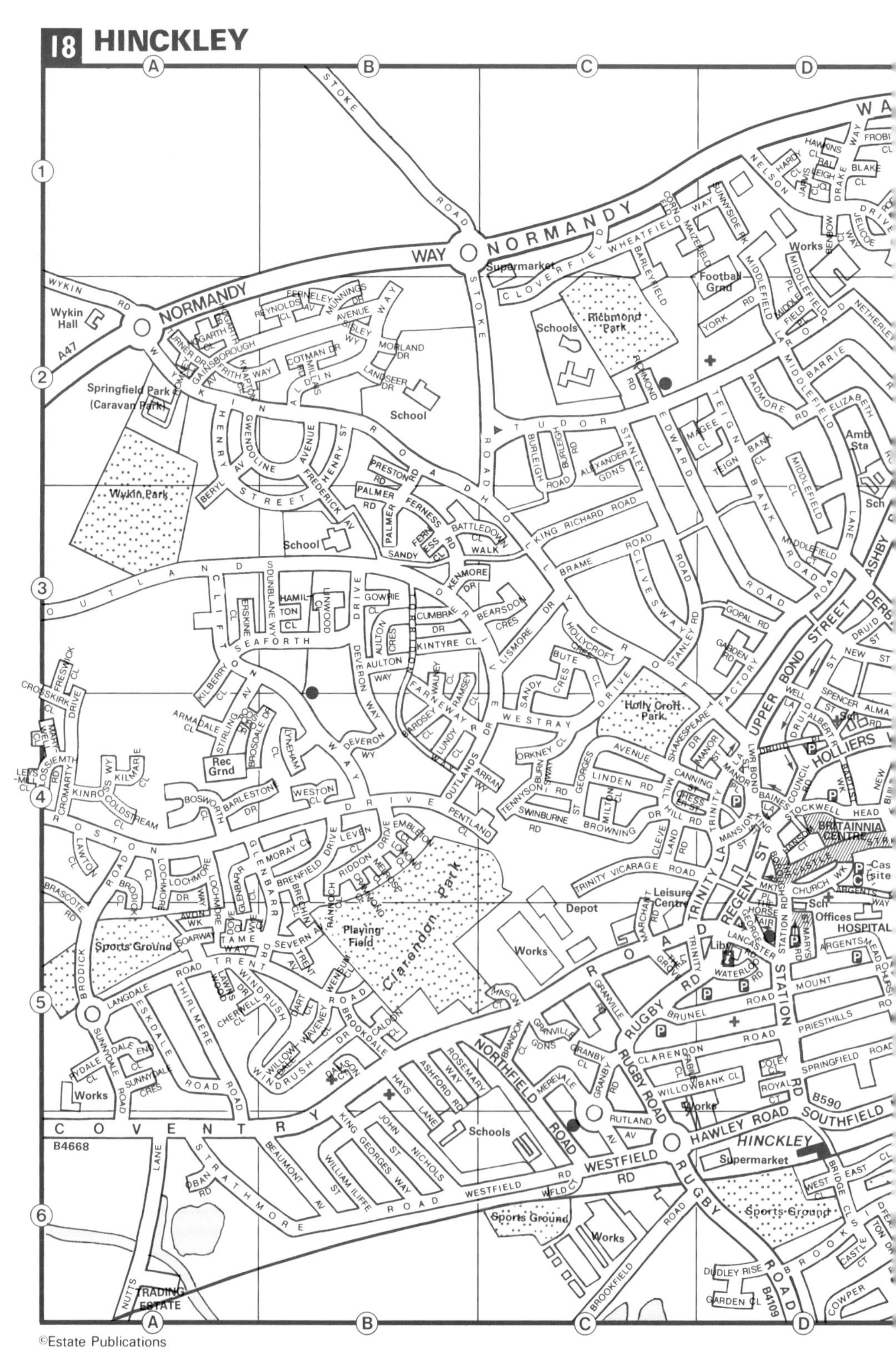
18
HINCKLEY
A
B
C
D
1
2
3
4
5
6
NORMANDY WAY
STOKE ROAD
WYKIN RD
Wykin Hall
A47
Springfield Park (Caravan Park)
Wykin Park
School
Schools
Supermarket
Richmond Park
Football Grnd
Works
CLOVERFIELD
WHEATFIELD WAY
BARLEYFIELD
MAIZEFIELD
SUNNYSIDE PK
YORK RD
MIDDLEFIELD LA
MIDDLEFIELD PL
NETHERLEY RD
NELSON DRIVE
HAWKINS CL
HARDY CL
JARVIS CL
DRAKE CL
BLAKE CL
RALEIGH CL
BENBOW CL
JELLICOE WAY
FROBISHER
REYNOLDS AV
FERNELEY AV
MUNNINGS DR
AVENUE WAY
SISLEY WY
HOGARTH CL
TURNER DR
GAINSBOROUGH
FRITH WAY
KNAPTON
COTMAN DR
MILLAIS
ALDIN
MORLAND DR
LANDSEER DR
WYKIN LA
HENRY AV
GWENDOLINE AVENUE
HENRY ST
FREDERICK AV
BERYL AV
STREET
ROAD
TUDOR
HOLLY
PRESTON RD
PALMER RD
FERNESS RD
FERN ESS CL
BATTLEDOWN CL
WALK
SANDY
KENMORE DR
BURLEIGH ROAD
BURLEIGH RD
ALEXANDER GDNS
STANLEY
EDWARD
MAGEE CL
TEIGN BANK
TEIGN BANK CL
RADMORE RD
BARRIE
ELIZABETH
MIDDLEFIELD ROAD
MIDDLEFIELD CL
MIDDLEFIELD CT
Amb Sta
Sch
LANE
ASHBY
KING RICHARD ROAD
BRAME ROAD
CLIVESWAY
STANLEY RD
GOPAL RD
GARDEN RD
FACTORY
OUTLANDS
CLIFTON
DUNBLANE WY
ERSKINE CL
HAMIL-TON CL
LINWOOD CL
GOWRIE CL
DRIVE
CUMBRAE DR
TORRIDON
BEARSDON CRES
KINTYRE CL
LISMORE DR
SEAFORTH
DEVERON WAY
AULTON CRES
AULTON WAY
HOLLYCROFT CRES
BUTE CL
SANDY CRES
DRIVE
Holly Croft Park
KILBERRY CL
ARMADALE CL
STIRLING
BROSDALE DR
Rec Grnd
LYNEHAM CL
DEVERON WY
FARNEWAY
WALNEY
RAMSEY CL
BARDSEY CL
LUNDY CL
WESTRAY DR
ORKNEY CL
ARRAN WY
PENTLAND CL
UPPER BOND STREET
DERBY
DRUID ST
NEW ST
WELL LA
SPENCER
ALMA
ALBERT RD
HOLLIERS WALK
COUNCIL
STOCKWELL HEAD
BRITANNIA CENTRE
CASTLE ST
CHURCH WK
ARGENTS
Sch Offices
HOSPITAL
FRESHWICK CL
CROSSKIRK CL
DRIVE
MARTWELL
LEYS MILL CL
LOSSIEMOUTH
CROMARTY
KINROSS WY
KILMARIE CL
COLDSTREAM
BOSWORTH CL
BARLESTONE DR
WESTON CL
TENNYSON RD
BURNS WAY
SWINBURNE RD
ST GEORGES AVENUE
LINDEN RD
MILTON CL
BROWNING
MILL HILL RD
CANNING ST
MANOR ST
CRESS ST
TRINITY LA
MANSION ST
KING ST
LWR BOND
BAINES LA
HANSOM CT
ROSTON DRIVE
LAWTON CL
LOCHMORE CL
LOCHMORE DR
LOCHMORE WAY
BRODICK CL
GLENBARR
MORAY CL
BRENFIELD DRIVE
LEVEN CL
EMBLETON CL
LOMOND
RIDDON CL
MELROSE
CRANMOND
BRECHIN CL
BRASCOTE RD
AVON WK
DOVE CL
TAME WAY
SOARWAY
Sports Ground
SEVERN AV
TRENT AV
RANNOCH
Playing Field
Clarendon Park
WINDRUSH DR
TRENT ROAD
LAWNS WOOD
CHERWELL CL
DART CL
WENSUM CL
ROAD
BROOKDALE DR
CALDON CL
WAVENEY CL
WILLOWDALE
WINDRUSH
BRODICK
LANGDALE
ESKDALE ROAD
THIRLMERE ROAD
RYDALE CL
DALE END
SUNNYDALE RD
SUNNYDALE CRES
Works
DAMSON CT
TRINITY VICARAGE ROAD
CLEVELAND RD
Leisure Centre
MARCHANT RD
Depot
Works
REGENT ST
TRINITY LA
THE GROVE
THE HORSE FAIR
MKT PL
LANCASTER RD
GEORGE ST
Liby
WATERLOO RD
STATION RD
ST MARYS RD
ARGENTS MEAD
MOUNT RD
PRIESTHILLS ROAD
SPRINGFIELD ROAD
RUGBY RD
BRUNEL ROAD
GRANVILLE RD
GRANVILLE GDNS
MASON CT
CLARENDON ROAD
FABIS CL
COLEY CL
ROYAL CT
WILLOWBANK CL
BRANDON CL
GRANBY CL
GRANBY RD
MEREVALE
RUGBY ROAD
NORTHFIELD ROAD
ROSEMARY WAY
ASHFORD RD
HAYS LANE
Schools
RUTLAND AV
Works
HAWLEY ROAD
SOUTHFIELD
B590
HINCKLEY
Supermarket
COVENTRY
B4668
LANE
STRATHMORE ROAD
OBAN RD
BEAUMONT AV
WILLIAM ILIFFE ST
KING GEORGES WAY
JOHN ST
NICHOLS
WESTFIELD RD
WESTFIELD
WFLD CT
Sports Ground
Works
RUGBY ROAD
BROOKFIELD
DUDLEY RISE
GARDEN CL
B4109
WEST CL
BRIDGE
EAST
BROOKSIDE
Sports Ground
CASTLE CT
COWPER
TON
NUTTS
TRADING ESTATE
©Estate Publications

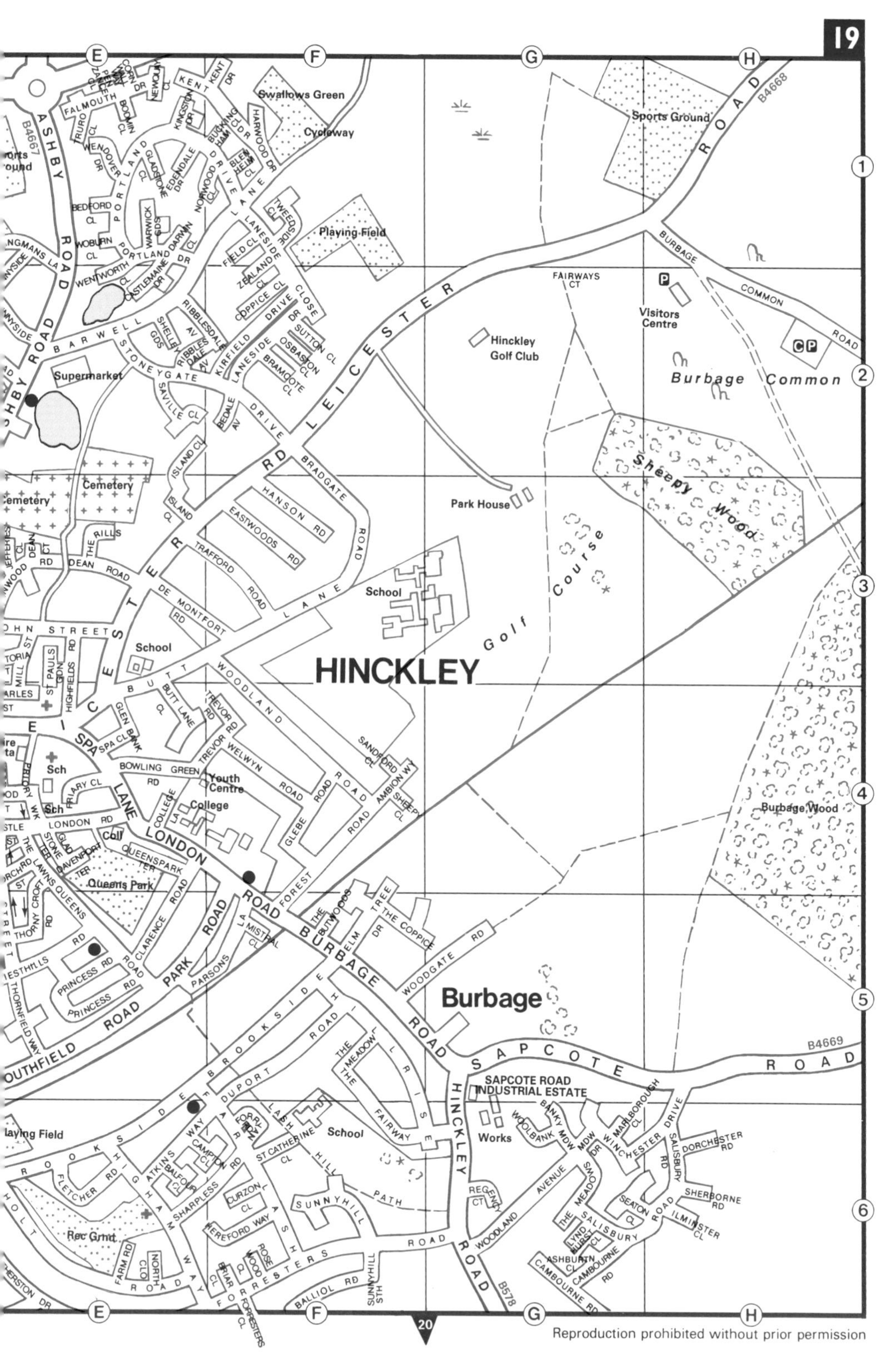
HINCKLEY
Burbage
Burbage Common
Sheepy Wood
Burbage Wood
Golf Course
Hinckley Golf Club
Visitors Centre
Park House
Sports Ground
Swallows Green
Cycleway
Playing Field
Supermarket
Cemetery
School
Youth Centre
College
Queens Park
SAPCOTE ROAD INDUSTRIAL ESTATE
Works
Rec Grnd
LEICESTER RD
ASHBY ROAD
B4667
B4668
B4669
B578
BURBAGE COMMON ROAD
SAPCOTE ROAD
HINCKLEY ROAD
BURBAGE ROAD
LONDON ROAD
SPA LANE
BUTT LANE
WOODLAND ROAD
BRADGATE ROAD
BARWELL LANE
STONEYGATE DRIVE
FORRESTERS ROAD
BROOKSIDE
HIGHAM WAY
SOUTHFIELD ROAD
PARK ROAD
WOODGATE RD
WOODLAND AVENUE
SALISBURY ROAD
WINCHESTER DRIVE
DE MONTFORT RD
TRAFFORD ROAD
HANSON RD
EASTWOODS RD
GLEBE ROAD
WELWYN ROAD
SANDFORD RD
CLARENCE ROAD
PRINCESS RD
Reproduction prohibited without prior permission

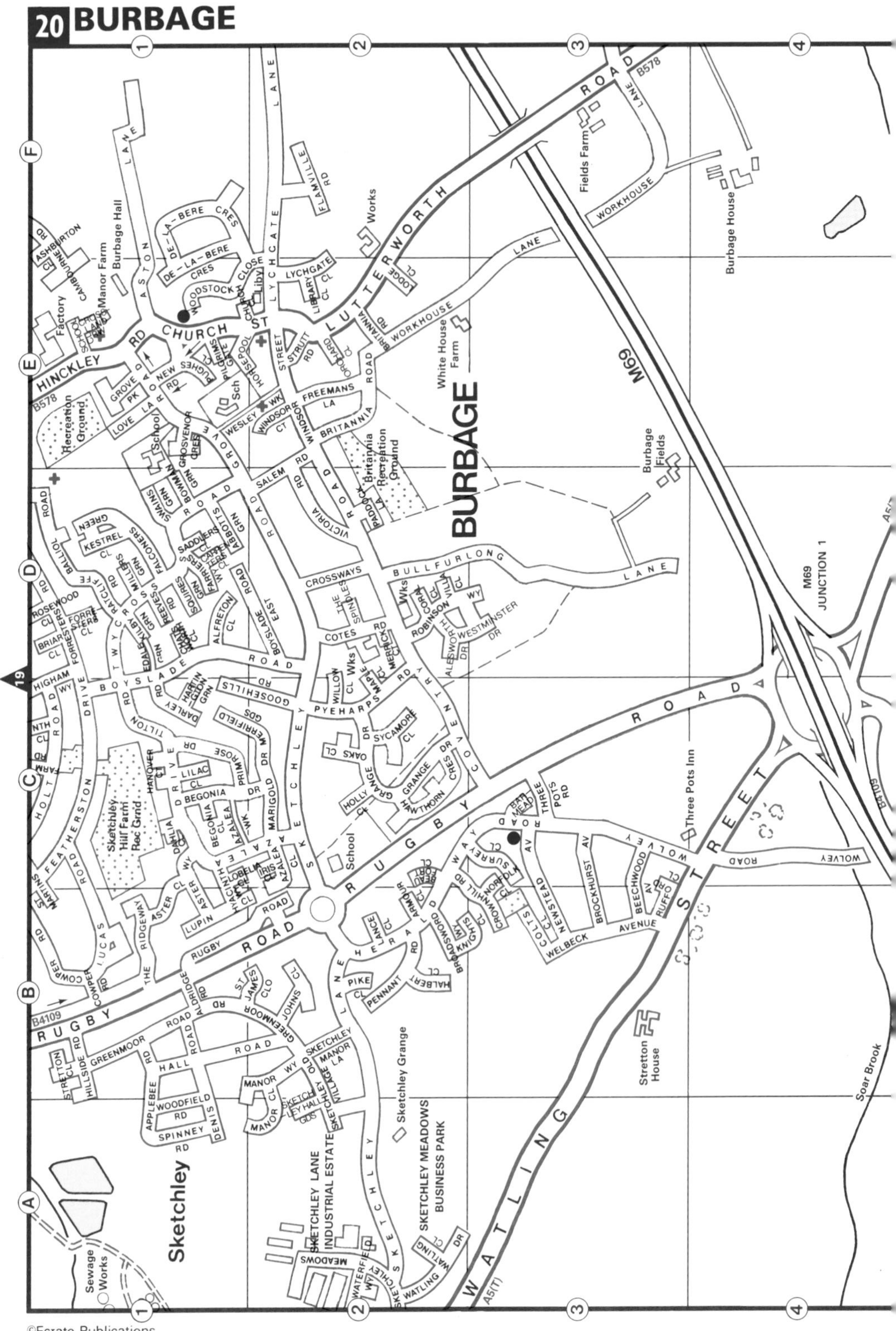
BURBAGE
Sketchley
M69
M69 JUNCTION 1
A5(T)
B578
B4109
HINCKLEY RD
CHURCH ST
LUTTERWORTH ROAD
ASTON LANE
LYCHGATE LANE
WORKHOUSE LANE
BULLFURLONG LANE
RUGBY ROAD
COVENTRY RD
WATLING STREET
WOLVEY ROAD
SKETCHLEY LANE
SKETCHLEY RD
BOYSLADE ROAD
BOYSLADE EAST
SALEM RD
VICTORIA ROAD
BRITANNIA ROAD
FEATHERSTON DRIVE
FORRESTERS RD
TWYCROSS RD
HOLT FARM RD
HIGHAM WY
GREENMOOR ROAD
HALL ROAD
ALDRIDGE RD
BALLIOL ROAD
Burbage Hall
Manor Farm
Factory
Recreation Ground
Britannia Recreation Ground
Sketchley Hill Farm Rec Grnd
White House Farm
Fields Farm
Burbage House
Burbage Fields
Three Pots Inn
Stretton House
Sketchley Grange
SKETCHLEY LANE INDUSTRIAL ESTATE
SKETCHLEY MEADOWS BUSINESS PARK
Sewage Works
Soar Brook
School
Works
Liby
Sch
Wks

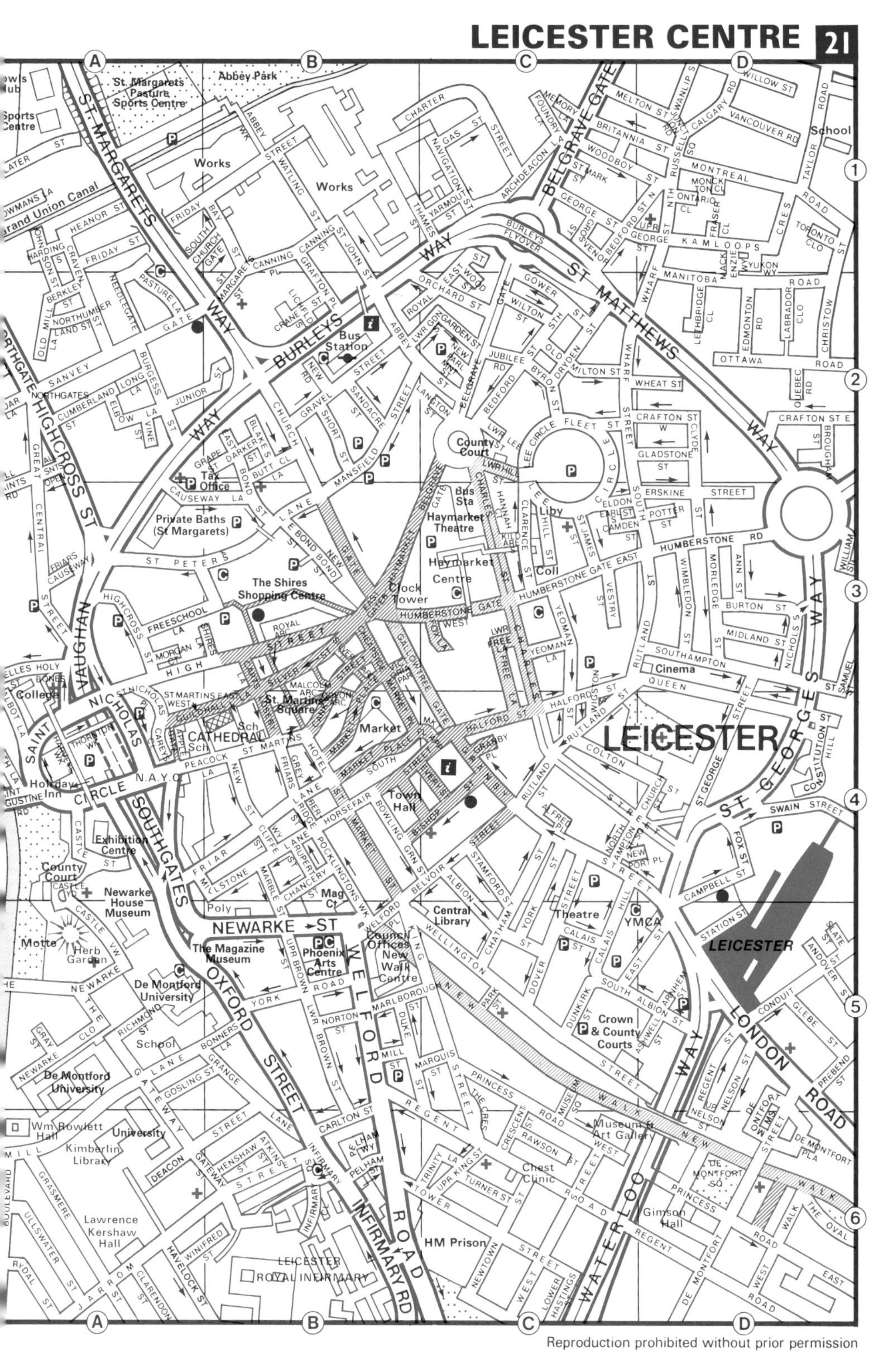
LEICESTER
St. Margarets Pasture Sports Centre
Abbey Park
Grand Union Canal
Works
Bus Station
County Court
Tax Office
Private Baths (St Margarets)
The Shires Shopping Centre
Haymarket Theatre
Haymarket Centre
Clock Tower
Liby
Coll
St Martins Square
Market
CATHEDRAL
Town Hall
Holiday Inn
Exhibition Centre
Newarke House Museum
Motte
Herb Garden
The Magazine Museum
Phoenix Arts Centre
Council Offices
New Walk Centre
Central Library
Theatre
YMCA
Cinema
Crown & County Courts
De Montford University
School
University
Kimberlin Library
Lawrence Kershaw Hall
Wm Rowlett Hall
LEICESTER ROYAL INFIRMARY
HM Prison
Chest Clinic
Museum & Art Gallery
Gimson Hall
BURLEYS WAY
ST MATTHEWS WAY
ST MARGARETS WAY
VAUGHAN WAY
HIGHCROSS ST
ST NICHOLAS CIRCLE
SOUTHGATES
OXFORD STREET
WELFORD ROAD
INFIRMARY RD
WATERLOO WAY
LONDON ROAD
ST GEORGES WAY
BELGRAVE GATE
HUMBERSTONE GATE
NEWARKE ST
CHARLES ST
GRANBY ST
HIGH ST
HUMBERSTONE RD
NEW WALK
PRINCESS ROAD
REGENT ROAD

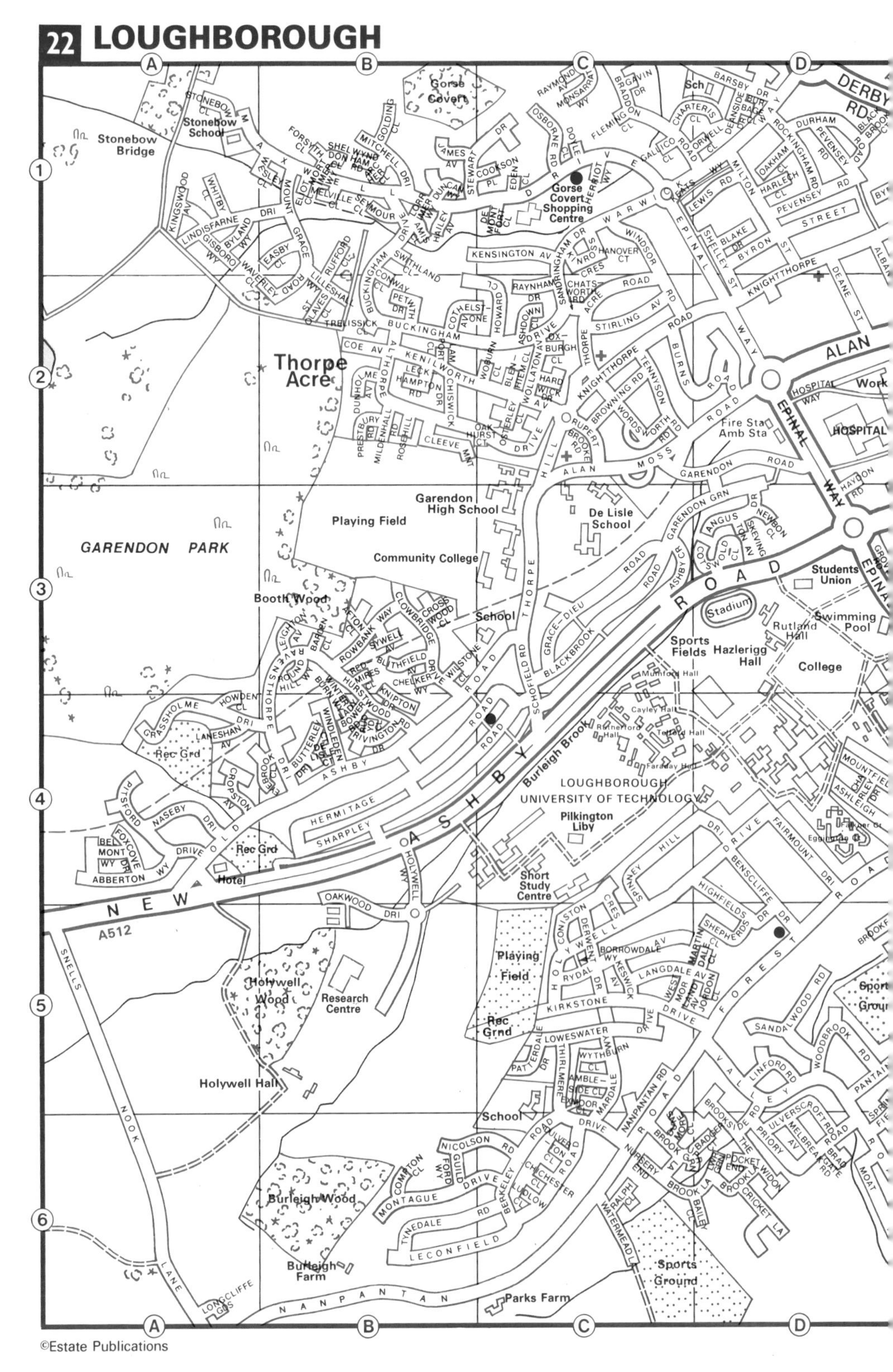

A
B
C
D
1
2
3
4
5
6
Stonebow Bridge
Stonebow School
Gorse Covert
Gorse Covert Shopping Centre
DERBY RD
Thorpe Acre
ALAN MOSS ROAD
HOSPITAL
Work
Fire Sta
Amb Sta
Garendon High School
De Lisle School
Playing Field
GARENDON PARK
Community College
Booth Wood
School
Students Union
Stadium
Swimming Pool
Rutland Hall
Sports Fields
Hazlerigg Hall
College
Mumford Hall
Cayley Hall
Rutherford Hall
Telford Hall
Faraday Hall
Burleigh Brook
LOUGHBOROUGH UNIVERSITY OF TECHNOLOGY
Pilkington Liby
Short Study Centre
ASHBY ROAD
NEW ASHBY ROAD
A512
Rec Grd
Hotel
Playing Field
Rec Grnd
Holywell Wood
Research Centre
Holywell Hall
School
Burleigh Wood
Burleigh Farm
Parks Farm
Sports Ground
NANPANTAN ROAD
FOREST ROAD
SNELLS NOOK LANE
EPINAL WAY
KNIGHTTHORPE ROAD
ALAN MOSS ROAD
GARENDON ROAD
THORPE HILL

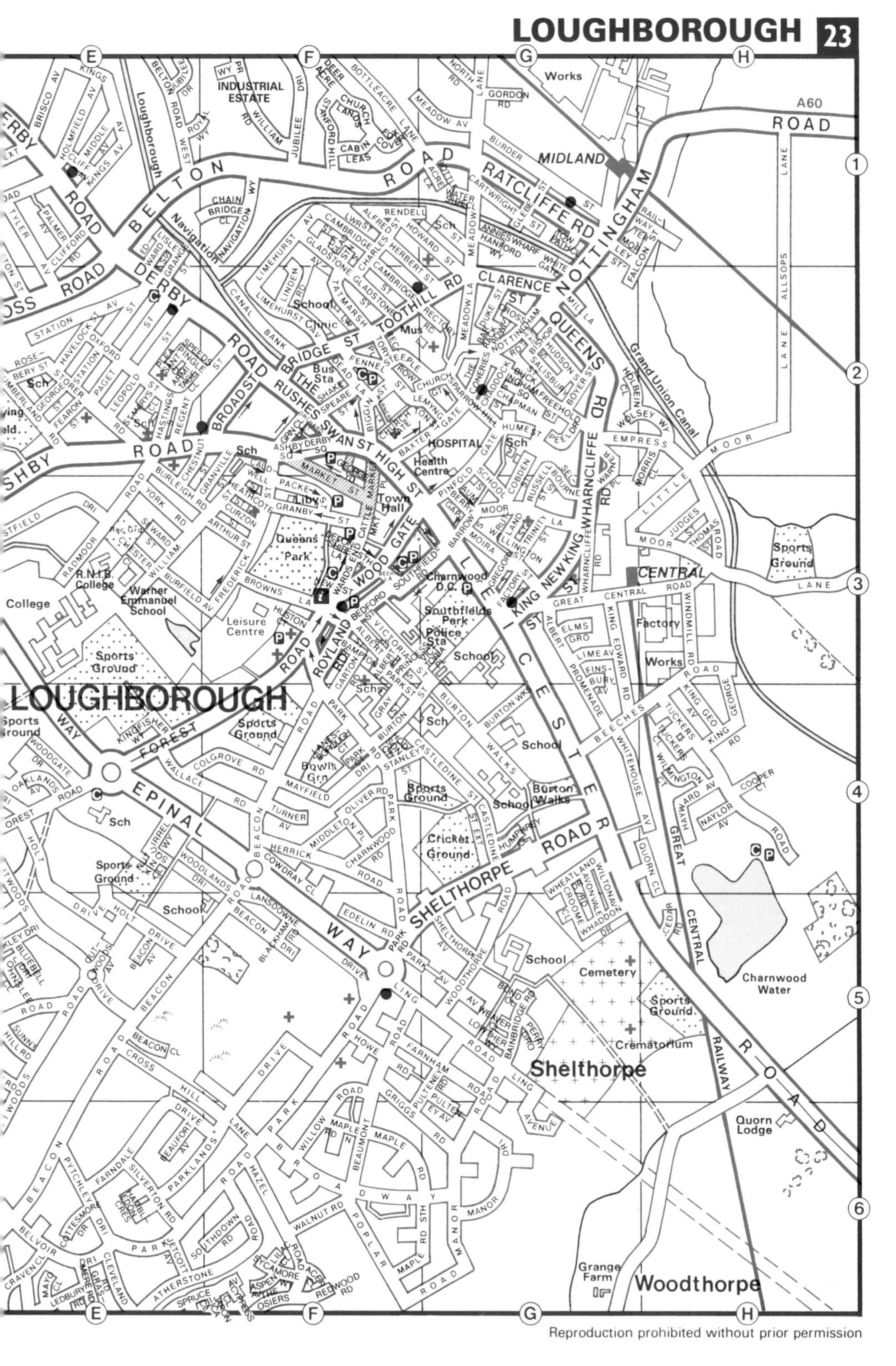
LOUGHBOROUGH
23
E
F
G
H
1
2
3
4
5
6
INDUSTRIAL ESTATE
Works
A60
MIDLAND
BELTON ROAD
RATCLIFFE RD
NOTTINGHAM RD
DERBY ROAD
ASHBY ROAD
Loughborough Navigation
Grand Union Canal
CLARENCE ST
TOOTHILL RD
QUEENS RD
BRIDGE ST
RUSHES
SWAN ST
HIGH ST
School
Clinic
Mus
Bus Sta
HOSPITAL
Health Centre
Town Hall
Liby
MARKET PL
Queens Park
WOOD GATE
Charnwood D.C.
Southfields Park
Police Sta
R.N.I.B. College
Warner Emmanuel School
College
Leisure Centre
Sports Ground
CENTRAL
Factory
KING EDWARD RD
WHARNCLIFFE RD
MOOR LANE
EMPRESS
LEICESTER ROAD
FOREST WAY
EPINAL WAY
SHELTHORPE ROAD
Bowls Grn
Cricket Ground
Burton Walks
Cemetery
Crematorium
Charnwood Water
GREAT CENTRAL RAILWAY
Shelthorpe
Quorn Lodge
Grange Farm
Woodthorpe
BEACON ROAD
PARK ROAD
BROADWAY
Reproduction prohibited without prior permission

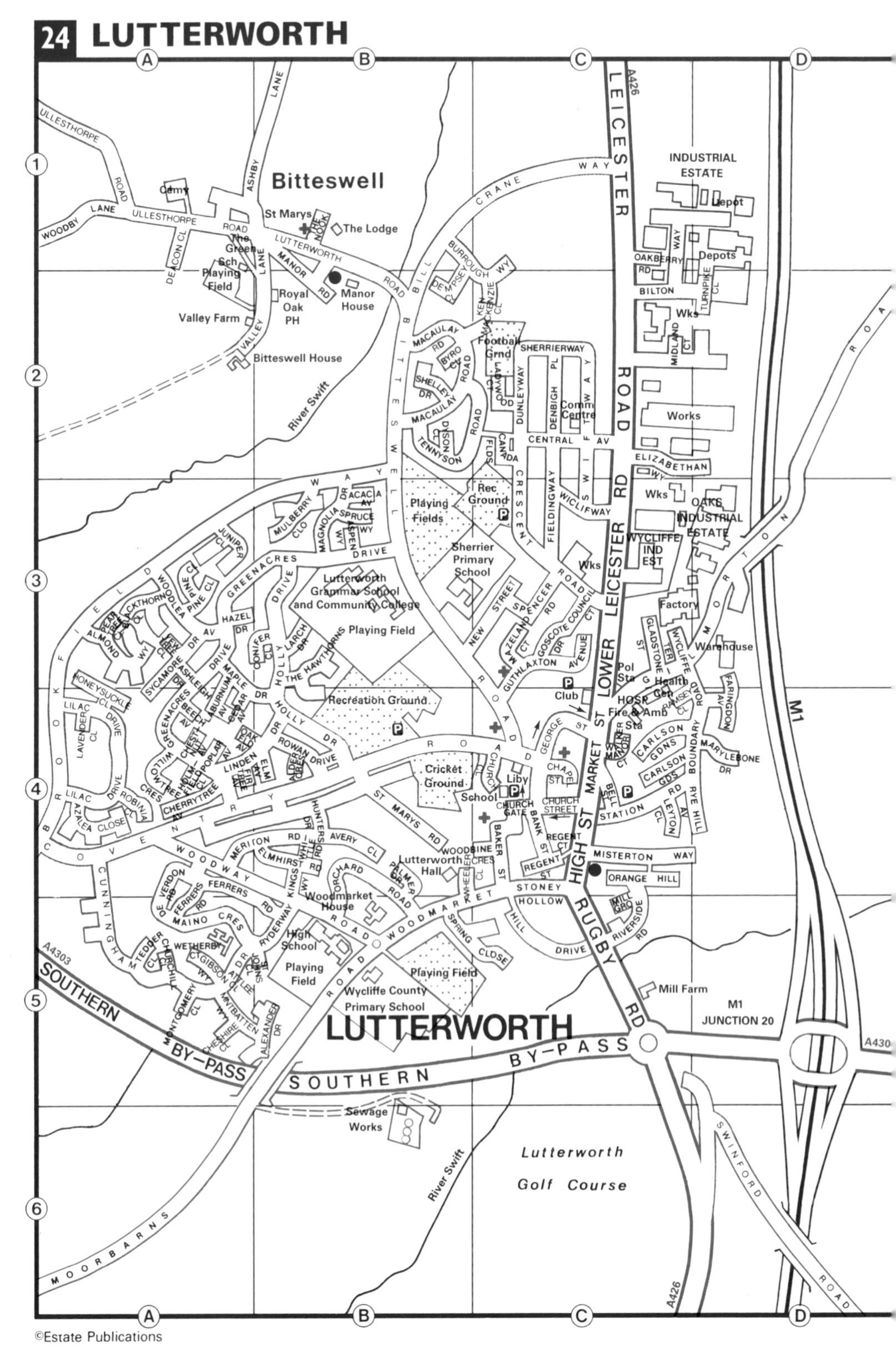

Bitteswell

LUTTERWORTH

Lutterworth Golf Course

M1 JUNCTION 20

SOUTHERN BY-PASS

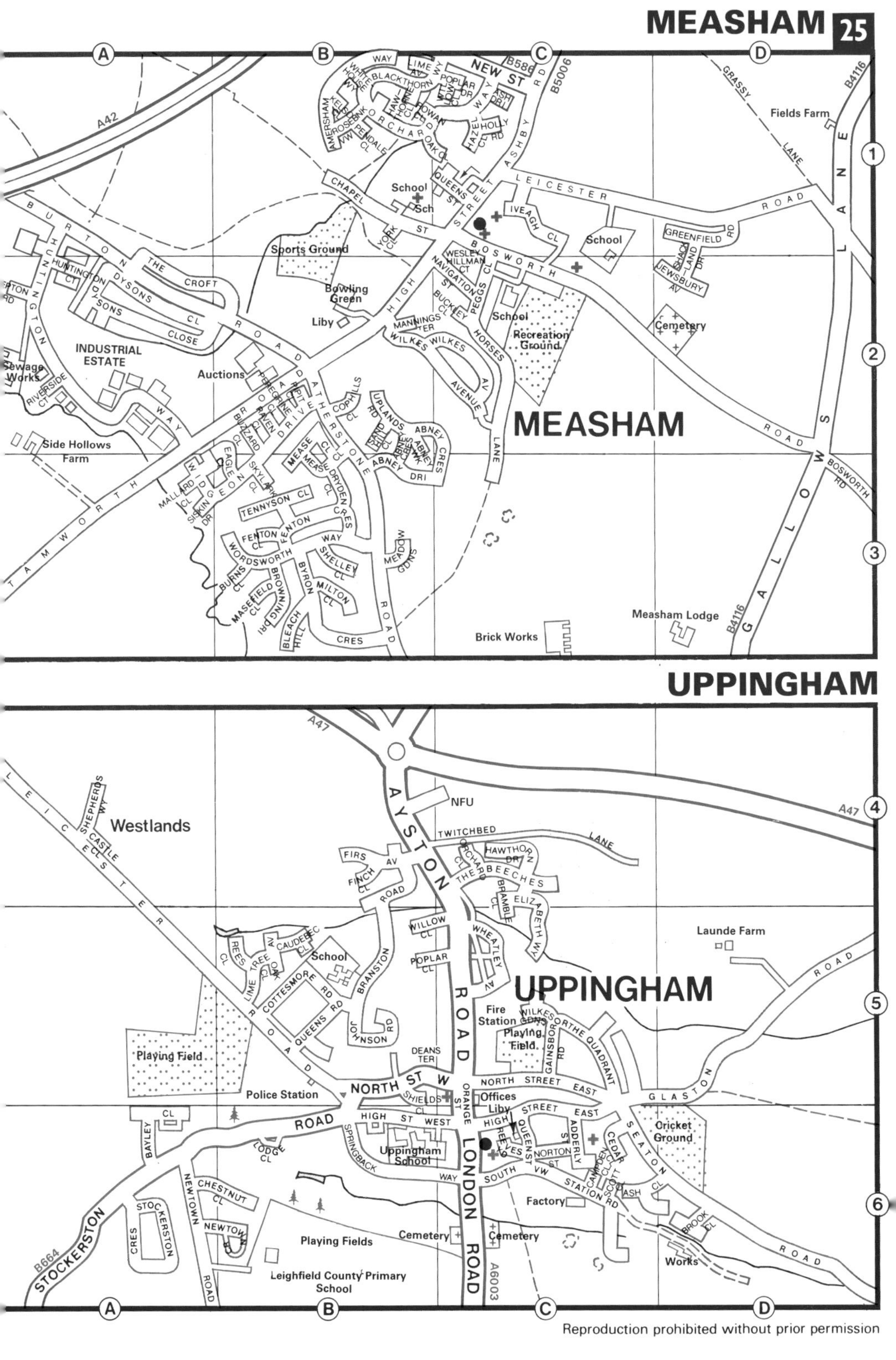
MEASHAM
25
A
B
C
D
1
2
3
A42
NEW ST
B586
B5006
B4116
GRASSY LANE
Fields Farm
LANE
WAY
LIME AV
WHITE HORSE WY
BLACKTHORN
POPLAR DR
ASH DR
HAWTHORNE CL
ROWAN
HAZEL WAY
HOLLY RD
AMERSHAM
ROSEBANK
PENDALE CL
ORCHARD
OAK CL
ASHBY RD
QUEENS ST
LEICESTER ROAD
CHAPEL ST
School
Sch
YORK CL
STREET
IVEAGH CL
School
GREENFIELD RD
SHACKLAND DR
JEWSBURY AV
BURTON ROAD
HUNTINGTON
HUNTINGTON CT
THE CROFT
DYSONS
DYSONS CLOSE
Sports Ground
Bowling Green
Liby
WESLEY HILLMAN CT
BOSWORTH
NAVIGATION ST
PEGGS CL
BUCKLEY
School
Recreation Ground
Cemetery
HIGH
MANNINGS TER
WILKES
WILKES AVENUE
HORSES
AV
INDUSTRIAL ESTATE
Sewage Works
RIVERSIDE CT
Auctions
WAY
PEREGRINE
DRIVE
ATHERSTONE
COPHILLS CL
UPLANDS RD
SAND
ABNEY CRES
ABNEY DRI
LANE
MEASHAM
ROAD
BOSWORTH RD
Side Hollows Farm
RAVEN
BUZZARD
EAGLE
SKYLARK CL
MEASE CL
DRYDEN CRES
WIDGEON
MALLARD
SISKIN DR
TAMWORTH
TENNYSON CL
FENTON CL
FENTON WAY
WORDSWORTH
SHELLEY CL
MEADOW GDNS
BURNS CL
MASEFIELD
BROWNING DRI
BYRON
MILTON CL
BLEACH HILL
CRES
ROAD
GALLOWS
B4116
Measham Lodge
Brick Works
UPPINGHAM
A47
AYSTON
NFU
A47
4
5
6
LEICESTER ROAD
SHEPHERDS WY
CASTLE CL
Westlands
TWITCHBED LANE
FIRS AV
FINCH CL
ROAD
ORCHARD CL
HAWTHORN DR
THE BEECHES
BRAMBLE CL
ELIZABETH WY
WILLOW CL
WHEATLEY AV
Launde Farm
REES CL
LIME TREE AV
OAK CL
CAUDEBEC
School
COTTESMORE RD
BRANSTON
POPLAR CL
ROAD
UPPINGHAM
QUEENS RD
JOHNSON RD
Fire Station
GDNS
WILKES
Playing Field
GAINSBOROUGH RD
THE QUADRANT
Playing Field
DEANS TER
NORTH ST W
NORTH STREET EAST
Police Station
SHIELDS
ORANGE ST
Offices
Liby
GLASTON
ROAD
CL
BAYLEY CL
HIGH ST WEST
HIGH STREET EAST
SEATON
Cricket Ground
SPRINGBACK
Uppingham School
REEVES
QUEEN ST
NORTON ST
ADDERLY ST
CEDAR
CAMPDEN CL
LODGE CL
WAY
SOUTH VW
STATION RD
SCOTT CL
ASH CL
LONDON
NEWTOWN
CHESTNUT CL
STOCKERSTON
CRES
NEWTOWN
Factory
BROOK CL
Playing Fields
Cemetery
Cemetery
ROAD
Works
B664
STOCKERSTON
Leighfield County Primary School
ROAD
A6003
ROAD
C
D

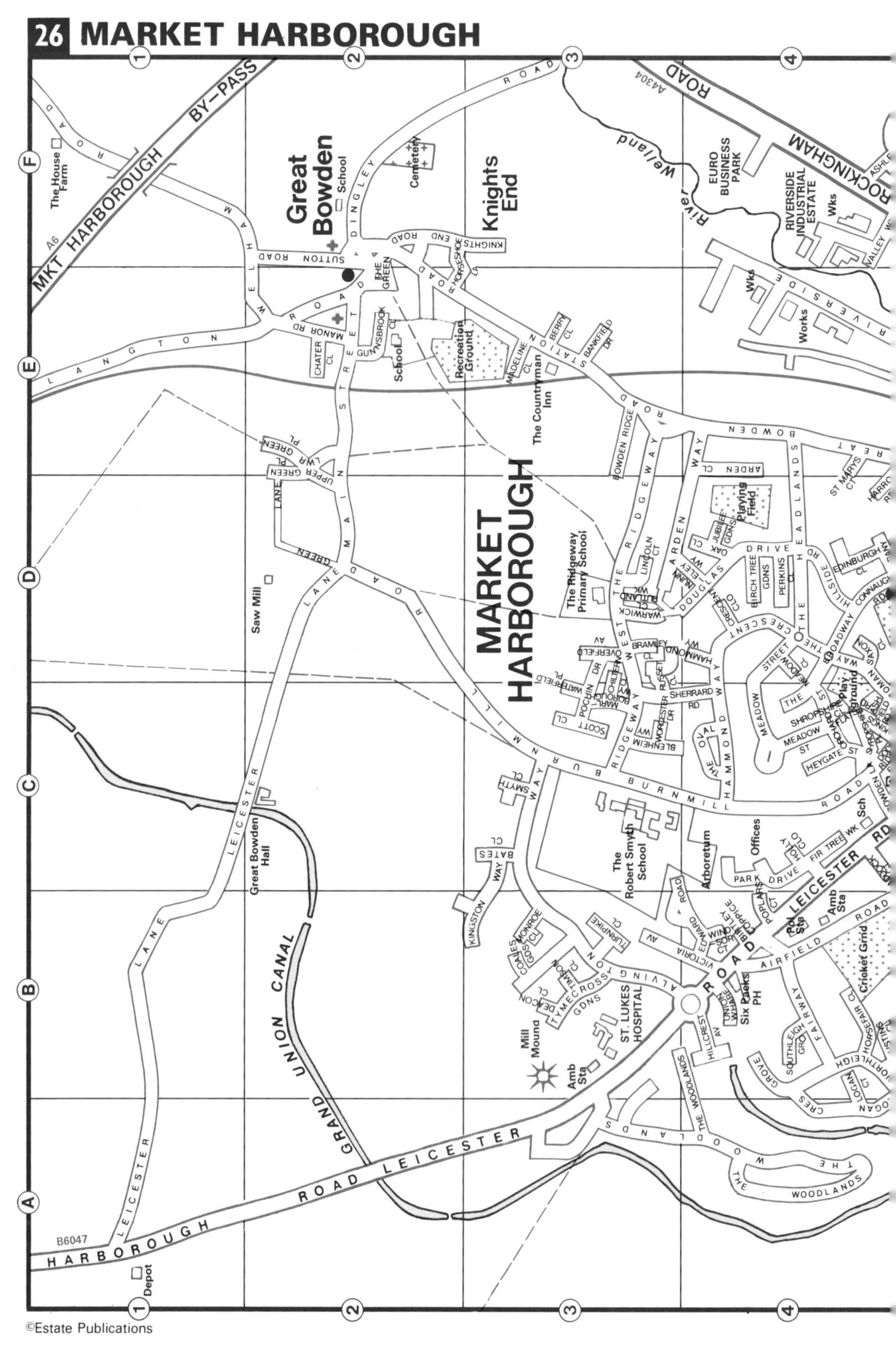
Great Bowden
Knights End
MARKET HARBOROUGH
MKT HARBOROUGH BY-PASS
A6
A4304
ROCKINGHAM ROAD
River Welland
EURO BUSINESS PARK
RIVERSIDE INDUSTRIAL ESTATE
The House Farm
School
Cemetery
Recreation Ground
The Countryman Inn
The Ridgeway Primary School
Playing Field
Saw Mill
Great Bowden Hall
The Robert Smyth School
Arboretum
Offices
Cricket Grid
Six Packs PH
ST. LUKES HOSPITAL
Mill Mound
Amb Sta
Pol Sta
Play Ground
GRAND UNION CANAL
LEICESTER ROAD
HARBOROUGH ROAD
B6047
Depot
BURNMILL ROAD
MAIN STREET
LANGTON ROAD
SUTTON ROAD
DINGLEY ROAD
BOWDEN ROAD
THE RIDGEWAY
THE WOODLANDS
AIRFIELD ROAD
STATION ROAD
RIVERSIDE
LEICESTER LANE
GREEN LANE

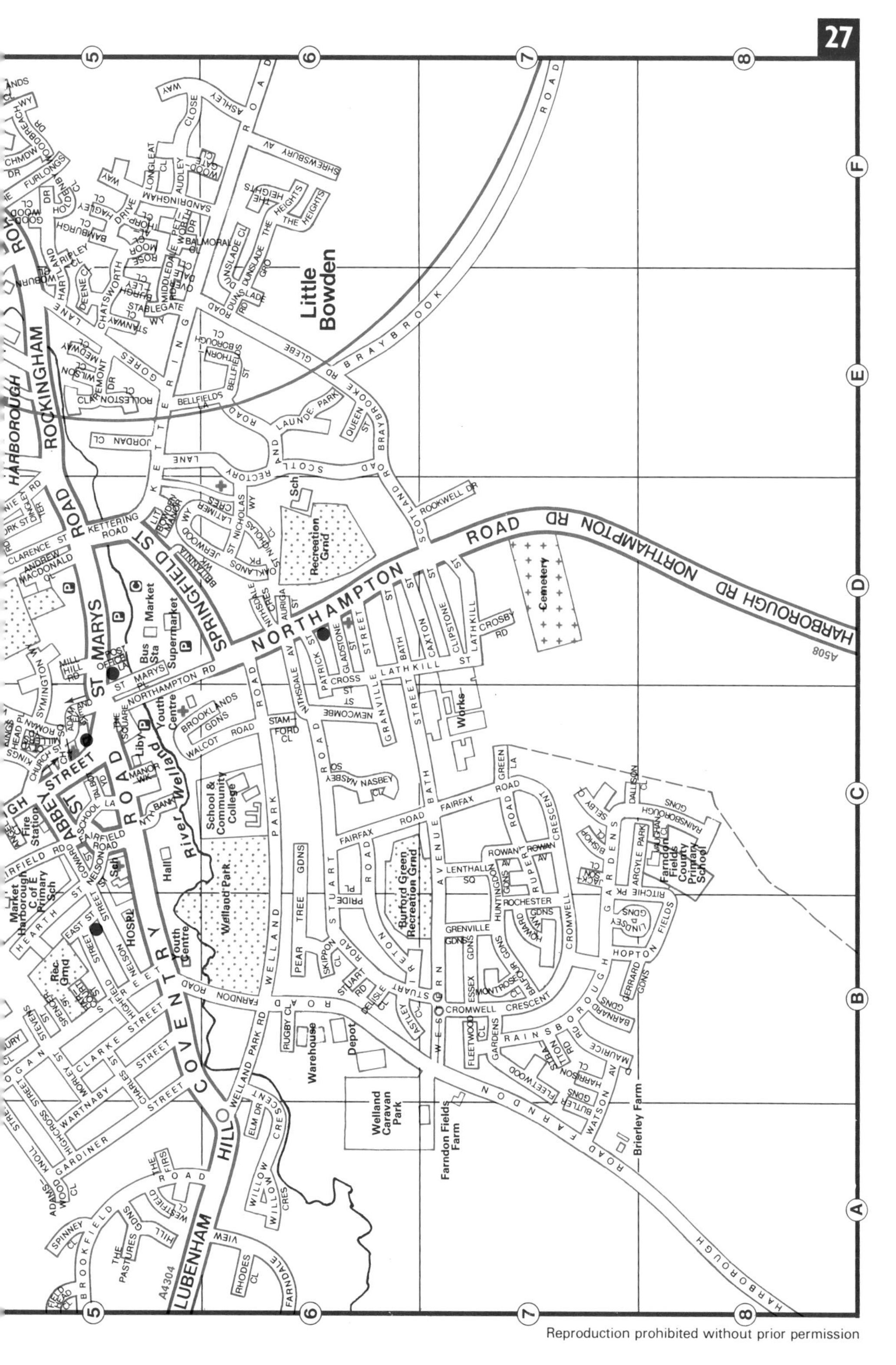
Little Bowden
NORTHAMPTON ROAD
NORTHAMPTON RD
HARBOROUGH RD
A508
ROCKINGHAM ROAD
HARBOROUGH
ST MARYS ROAD
SPRINGFIELD ST
KETTERING ROAD
COVENTRY ROAD
LUBENHAM HILL
A4304
FARNDON ROAD
BRAYBROOKE RD
GLEBE RD
SCOTLAND RD
WELLAND PARK RD
WESTERN AVENUE
FAIRFAX ROAD
STUART ROAD
RAINSBOROUGH GARDENS
ABBEY STREET
River Welland
Welland Park
Cemetery
Recreation Grnd
Burford Green Recreation Grnd
School & Community College
Farndon Fields County Primary School
Market Harborough C of E Primary Sch
Fire Station
Supermarket
Market
Bus Sta
Post Office
Youth Centre
Works
Warehouse
Depot
Welland Caravan Park
Farndon Fields Farm
Brierley Farm
Hall
Liby
Hospl

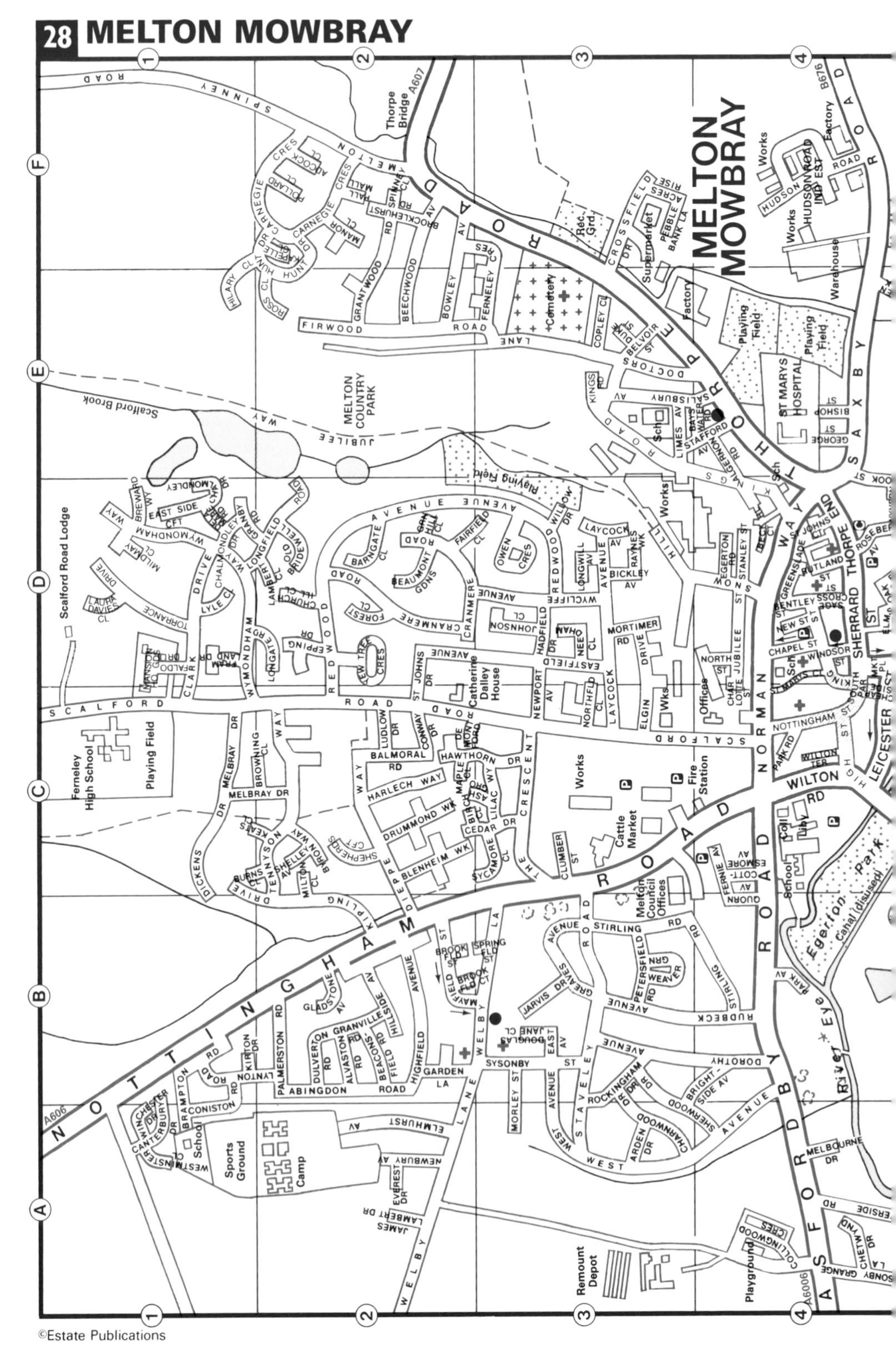
MELTON MOWBRAY
MELTON COUNTRY PARK
SCALFORD ROAD
NOTTINGHAM ROAD
NORMAN WAY
THORPE ROAD
SAXBY ROAD
ASFORDBY ROAD
WILTON RD
LEICESTER
Cattle Market
Fire Station
Melton Council Offices
Cemetery
ST MARYS HOSPITAL
Ferneley High School
Playing Field
Scalford Road Lodge
Sports Ground
Camp
Remount Depot
Catherine Dalley House
Egerton Park
River Eye
Scalford Brook
JUBILEE WAY
Supermarket
Factory
Warehouse
Works
HUDSON ROAD IND EST
Thorpe Bridge

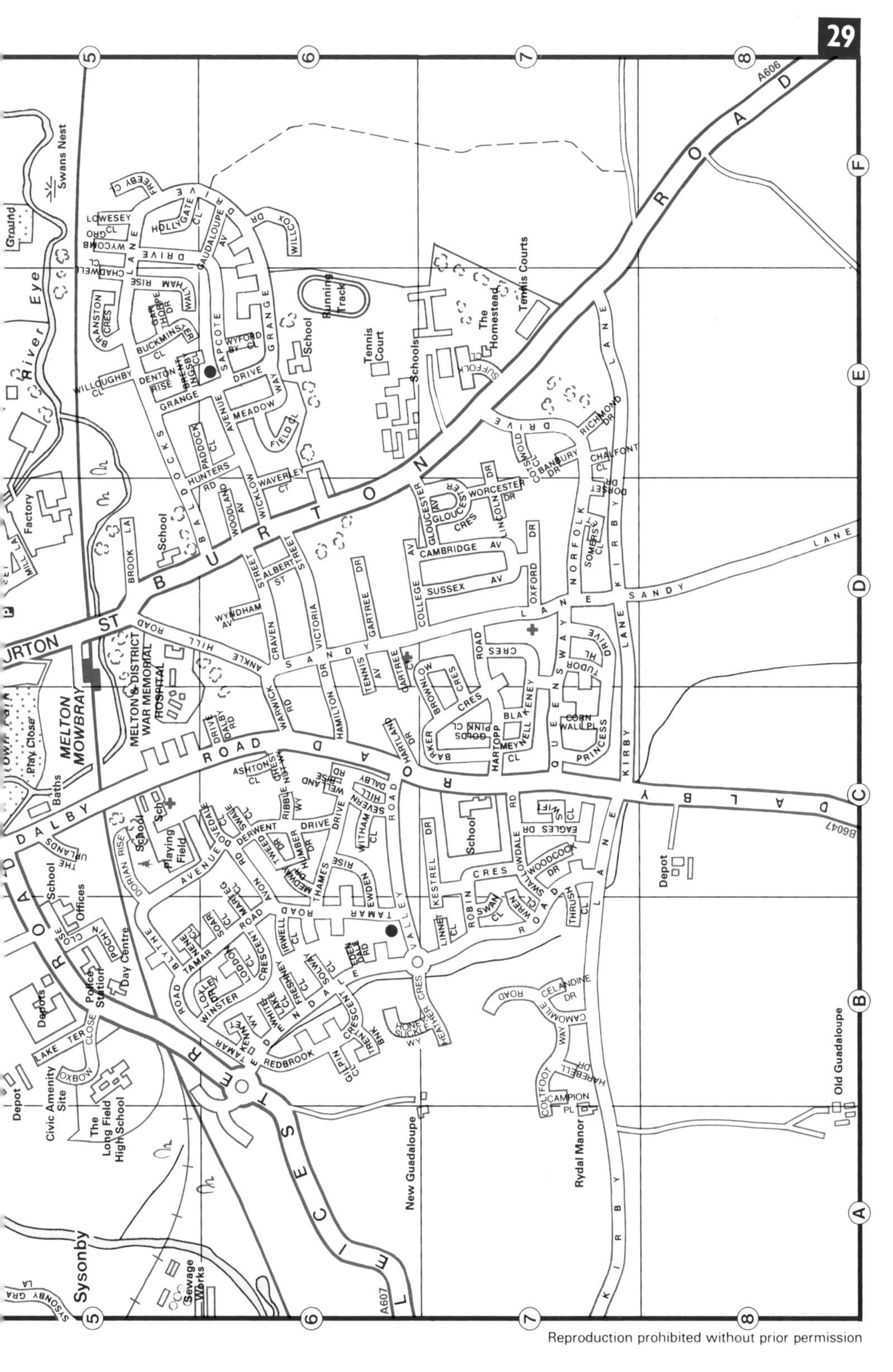
BURTON ROAD
A606
DALBY ROAD
B6047
LEICESTER ROAD
A607
BURTON ST
MELTON MOWBRAY
River Eye
Swans Nest
Factory
School
Schools
Running Track
Tennis Court
Tennis Courts
The Homestead
MELTON & DISTRICT WAR MEMORIAL HOSPITAL
Play Close
Baths
Playing Field
Offices
Day Centre
Police Station
Depots
Depot
Civic Amenity Site
The Long Field High School
Sewage Works
Sysonby
New Guadaloupe
Old Guadaloupe
Rydal Manor
KIRBY LANE
SANDY LANE
QUEENSWAY
NORFOLK DRIVE
BALDOCKS LANE
GAUDALOUPE AV
SAPCOTE DRIVE
GRANGE DRIVE
WICKLOW AV
WOODLAND AV
HUNTERS RD
PADDOCK CL
MEADOW WAY
WAVERLEY CT
BROOK LA
ALBERT ST
CRAVEN STREET
VICTORIA STREET
GARTREE DR
COLLEGE AV
CAMBRIDGE AV
SUSSEX AV
OXFORD DR
GLOUCESTER AV
WORCESTER DR
LINCOLN DR
COTSWOLD DR
BANBURY DR
RICHMOND DR
CHALFONT CL
DORSET DR
SOMERSET CL
ANKLE HILL
WYNDHAM AV
WARWICK RD
HAMILTON DR
TENNIS AV
BROWNLOW CRES
HARTOPP RD
BLAKENEY CRES
PRINCESS DRIVE
CORNWALL PL
TUDOR HL
HARTLAND DR
VALLEY ROAD
KESTREL DR
ROBIN CRES
SWAN CL
WREN CL
WOODCOCK DR
THRUSH CL
EAGLES DR
SWIFT CL
DOVEDALE AVENUE
DORIAN RISE
DERWENT DRIVE
HUMBER DR
TWEED DR
THAMES RISE
WITHAM CL
SEVERN HILL
WELLAND RISE
RIBBLE WY
ASHTON CL
TAMAR ROAD
AVON RD
CRESCENT ROAD
IRWELL CL
SOLWAY CL
DALE CRESCENT
REDBROOK
BLYTHE ROAD
WINSTER CL
LODDON CL
LAKE TER
OXBOW CLOSE
HEATHER CRES
CELANDINE DR
CAMOMILE WAY
COLTFOOT CL
CAMPION PL
HAREBELL DR
WILLOUGHBY CL
BUCKMINSTER CL
BRANSTON CRES
LOWESEY CL
WYFORD CL
HOLLYGATE CL
WILLCOX DR
THE UPLANDS

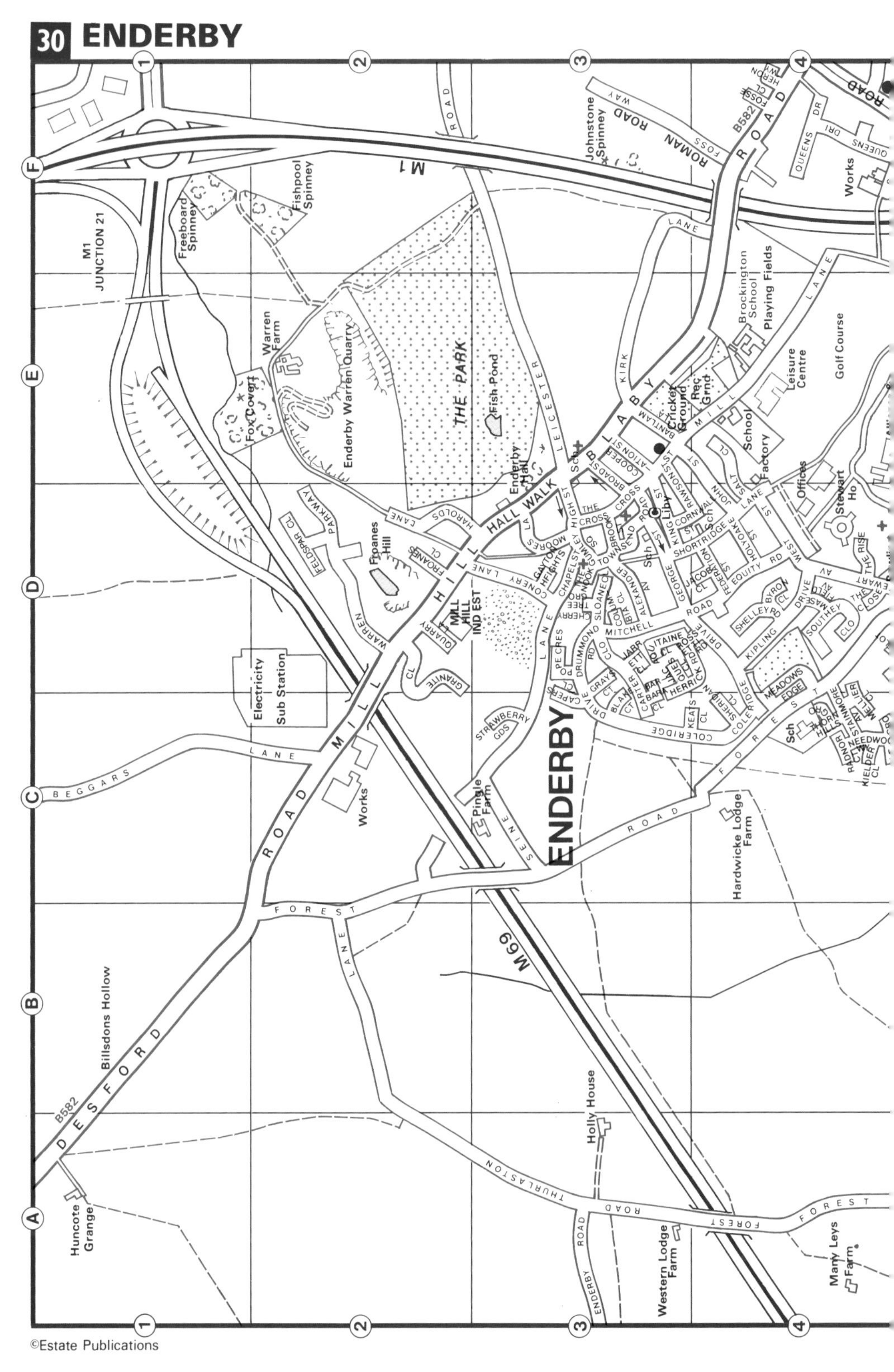
ENDERBY
M1
M1 JUNCTION 21
M69
THE PARK
Fish Pond
Enderby Hall
Enderby Warren Quarry
Warren Farm
Fox Covert
Freeboard Spinney
Fishpool Spinney
Johnstone Spinney
Froanes Hill
MILL HILL IND EST
Electricity Sub Station
Works
Pingle Farm
Hardwicke Lodge Farm
Holly House
Western Lodge Farm
Many Leys Farm
Huncote Grange
Billsdons Hollow
Brockington School
Playing Fields
Golf Course
Leisure Centre
School
Factory
Offices
Stewart Ho
Cricket Ground
Rec Grnd
Liby
Sch
DESFORD ROAD
B582
MILL ROAD
MILL HILL
BEGGARS LANE
FOREST LANE
FOREST ROAD
THURLASTON ROAD
ENDERBY ROAD
SEINE LANE
CONERY LANE
LEICESTER LANE
HALL WALK
BLABY ROAD
ROMAN ROAD
FOSS WAY
KIRK LANE
MILL LANE
WEST ST
HIGH ST
CROSS ST
TOWNSEND RD
KING ST
GEORGE ST
SHORTRIDGE ST
EQUITY RD
MITCHELL ROAD
COLERIDGE DRIVE
SHERIDAN CL
KEATS CL
HERRICK RD
KIPLING DRIVE
SHELLEY RD
BYRON CL
SOUTHEY CL
MEADOWS EDGE
STRAWBERRY GDS
GRANITE CL
QUARRY LA
WARREN LANE
PARKWAY
FELDSPAR CL
HAROLDS LANE
FROANES CL
ALEXANDER AV
DRUMMOND RD
CAPERS DRIVE
GAYTON HEIGHTS
CHAPEL ST
HOLYOAKE ST
JOHN ST
SALT CL
RAWSON ST
BANTLAM LA
COOPER LA
BROADS
HERON CL
FOSS CL
QUEENS DRI
QUEENS DR
THE RISE
NEEDWOOD
KIELDER CL
RADNOR CL
HILLS
©Estate Publications

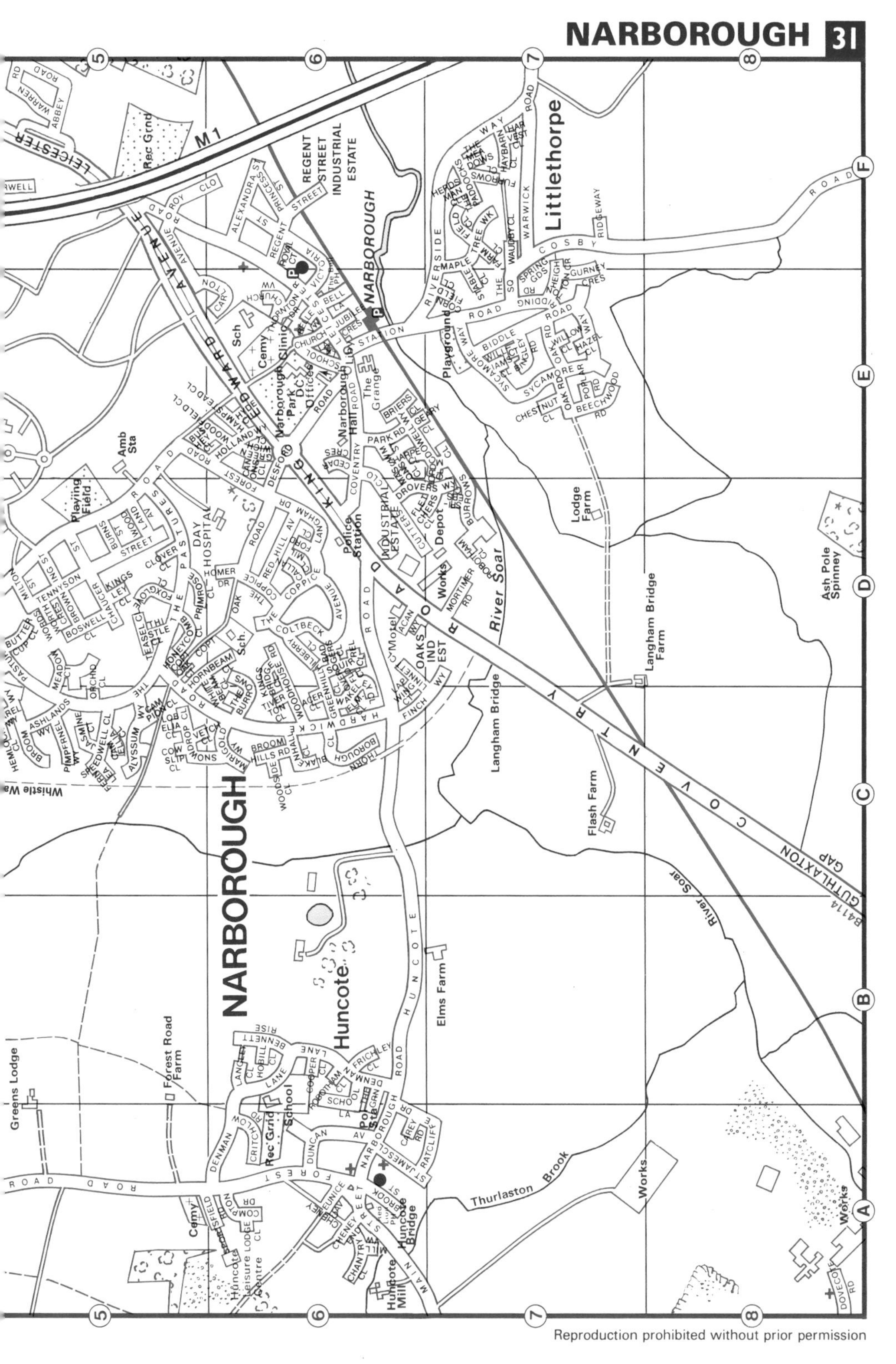
NARBOROUGH
Huncote
Littlethorpe
M1
River Soar
REGENT STREET INDUSTRIAL ESTATE
Lodge Farm
Langham Bridge Farm
Langham Bridge
Flash Farm
Ash Pole Spinney
Elms Farm
Forest Road Farm
Greens Lodge
Thurlaston Brook
Huncote Bridge
Huncote Mill
Huncote Leisure Centre
Works
Playing Field
Playground
Police Station
Day Hospital
B4114

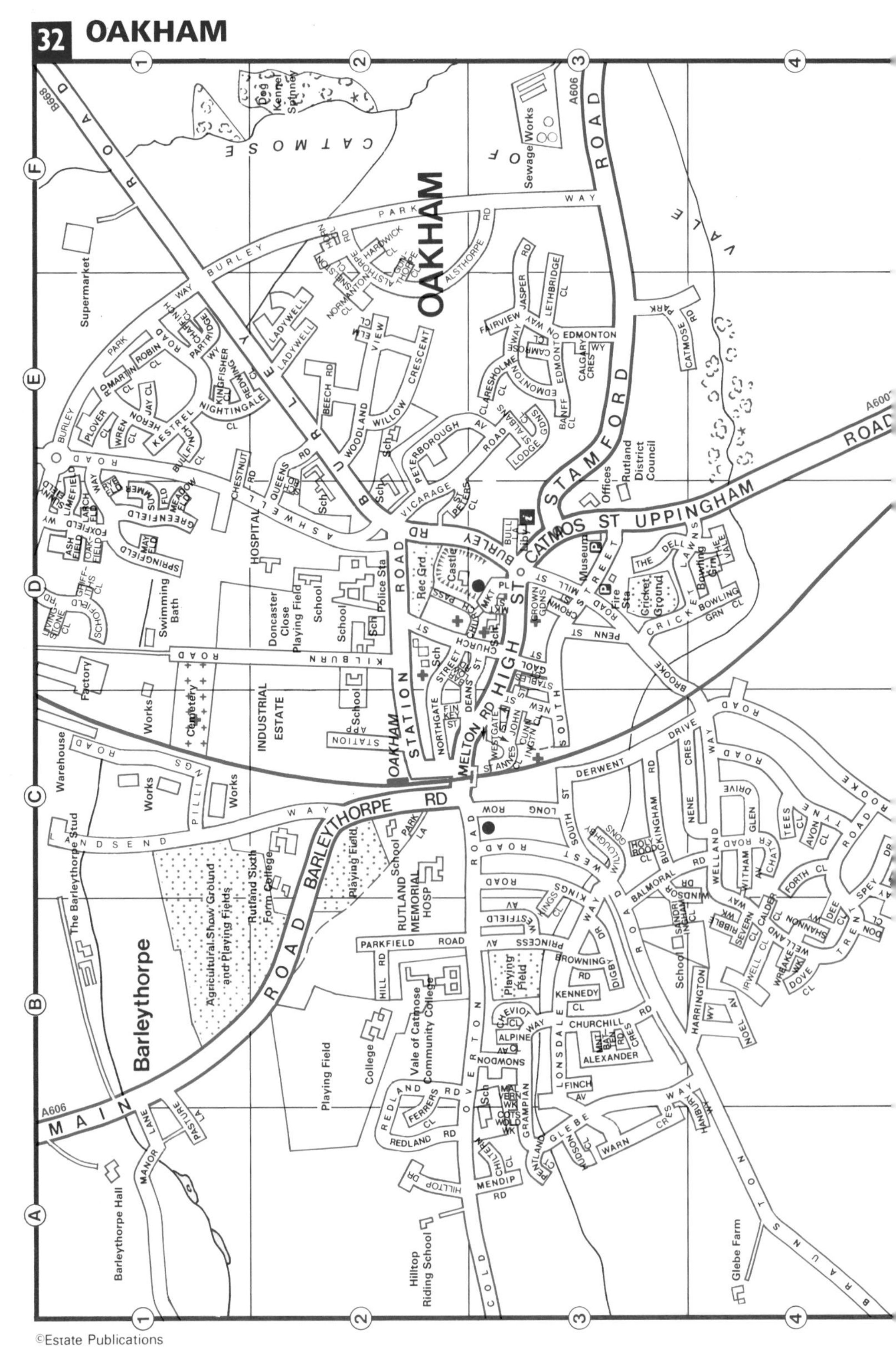
OAKHAM
CATMOSE
VALE OF CATMOSE
Barleythorpe
Supermarket
Sewage Works
Dog Kennel Spinney
Rutland District Council
Offices
Museum
Fire Sta
Cricket Ground
Bowling Grn
Castle
Rec Grd
Police Sta
School
Hospital
Doncaster Close Playing Field
Swimming Bath
Factory
Works
Cemetery
Industrial Estate
Warehouse
The Barleythorpe Stud
Agricultural Show Ground and Playing Fields
Rutland Sixth Form College
Playing Field
Rutland Memorial Hosp
Vale of Catmose Community College
College
Hilltop Riding School
Barleythorpe Hall
Glebe Farm
STAMFORD ROAD
UPPINGHAM ROAD
BURLEY ROAD
BARLEYTHORPE ROAD
MAIN ROAD
COLD OVERTON ROAD
BRAUNSTON ROAD
BROOKE ROAD
STATION ROAD
MELTON RD
HIGH ST
CATMOS ST
KILBURN ROAD
ASHWELL RD
BURLEY PARK WAY
LANDSEND WAY
PILLINGS ROAD
BALMORAL RD
WEST ROAD
SOUTH ST
LONG ROW
PARKFIELD ROAD
A606
A6003
B668

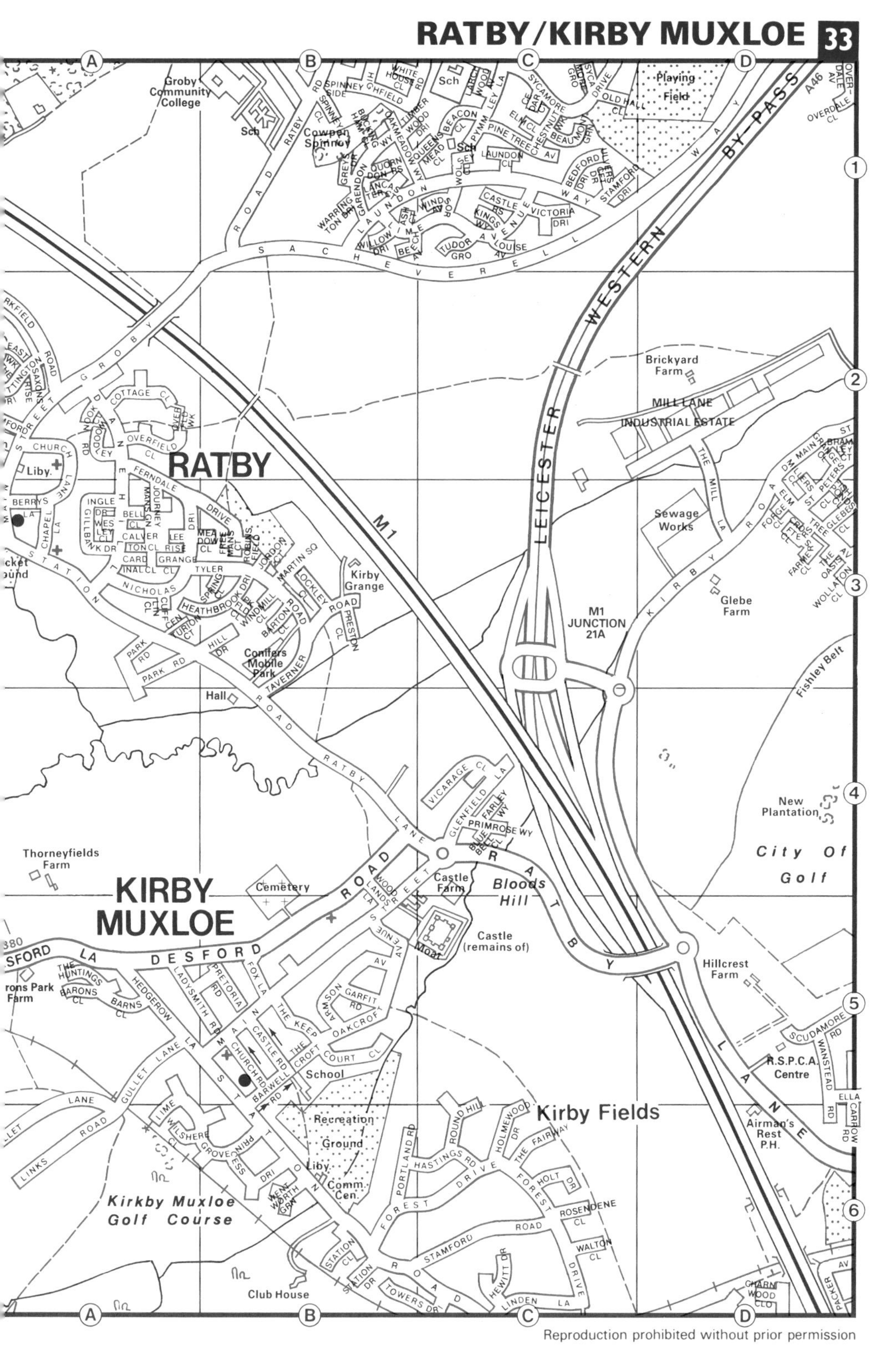
RATBY
KIRBY MUXLOE
Groby Community College
Cowpen Spinney
Playing Field
WESTERN BY-PASS
LEICESTER
M1
SACHEVERELL WAY
GROBY ROAD
Brickyard Farm
MILL LANE INDUSTRIAL ESTATE
Sewage Works
Kirby Grange
Glebe Farm
M1 JUNCTION 21A
Conifers Mobile Park
Fishley Belt
New Plantation
City Of Golf
Thorneyfields Farm
Cemetery
Castle Farm
Bloods Hill
Castle (remains of)
Moat
Hillcrest Farm
R.S.P.C.A. Centre
Airman's Rest P.H.
Kirby Fields
Recreation Ground
Comm. Cen.
School
Kirkby Muxloe Golf Course
Club House
DESFORD LA
RATBY LANE
STATION ROAD
FOREST DRIVE
STAMFORD ROAD
KIRBY ROAD
RATBY
LANE

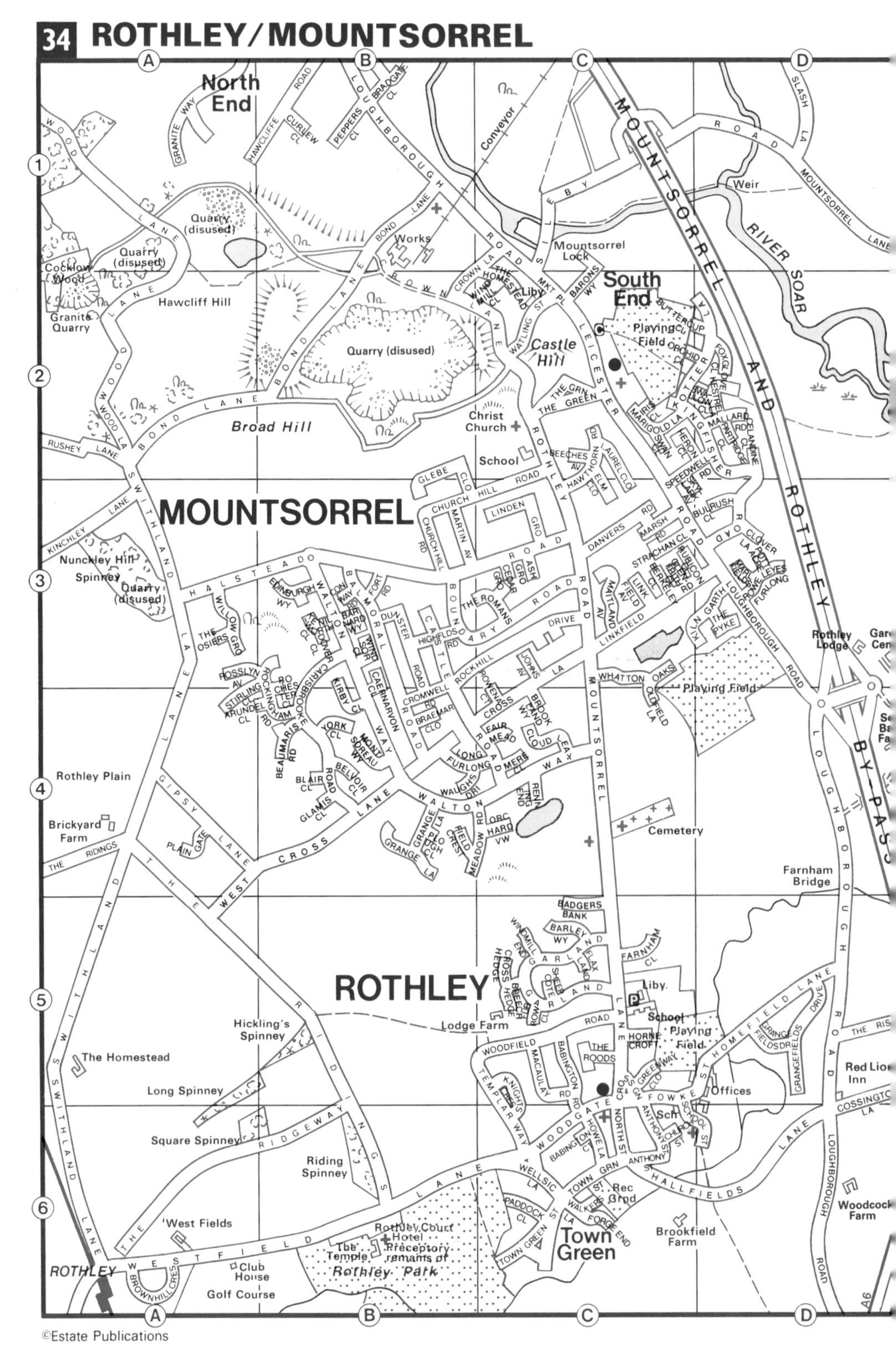
North End
Quarry (disused)
Cocklow Wood
Granite Quarry
Hawcliff Hill
Quarry (disused)
Works
Mountsorrel Lock
South End
Castle Hill
Playing Field
Broad Hill
Christ Church
School
MOUNTSORREL
Nunckley Hill Spinney
Rothley Plain
Brickyard Farm
Cemetery
Rothley Lodge
Playing Field
Farnham Bridge
ROTHLEY
Hickling's Spinney
The Homestead
Long Spinney
Square Spinney
Riding Spinney
Lodge Farm
Liby.
School
Playing Field
Offices
Red Lion Inn
West Fields
Rothley Court Hotel
The Temple
Preceptory remains of
Rothley Park
Club House
Golf Course
Town Green
Rec Grnd
Brookfield Farm
Woodcock Farm
Weir
RIVER SOAR
MOUNTSORREL AND ROTHLEY BY-PASS
ROTHLEY

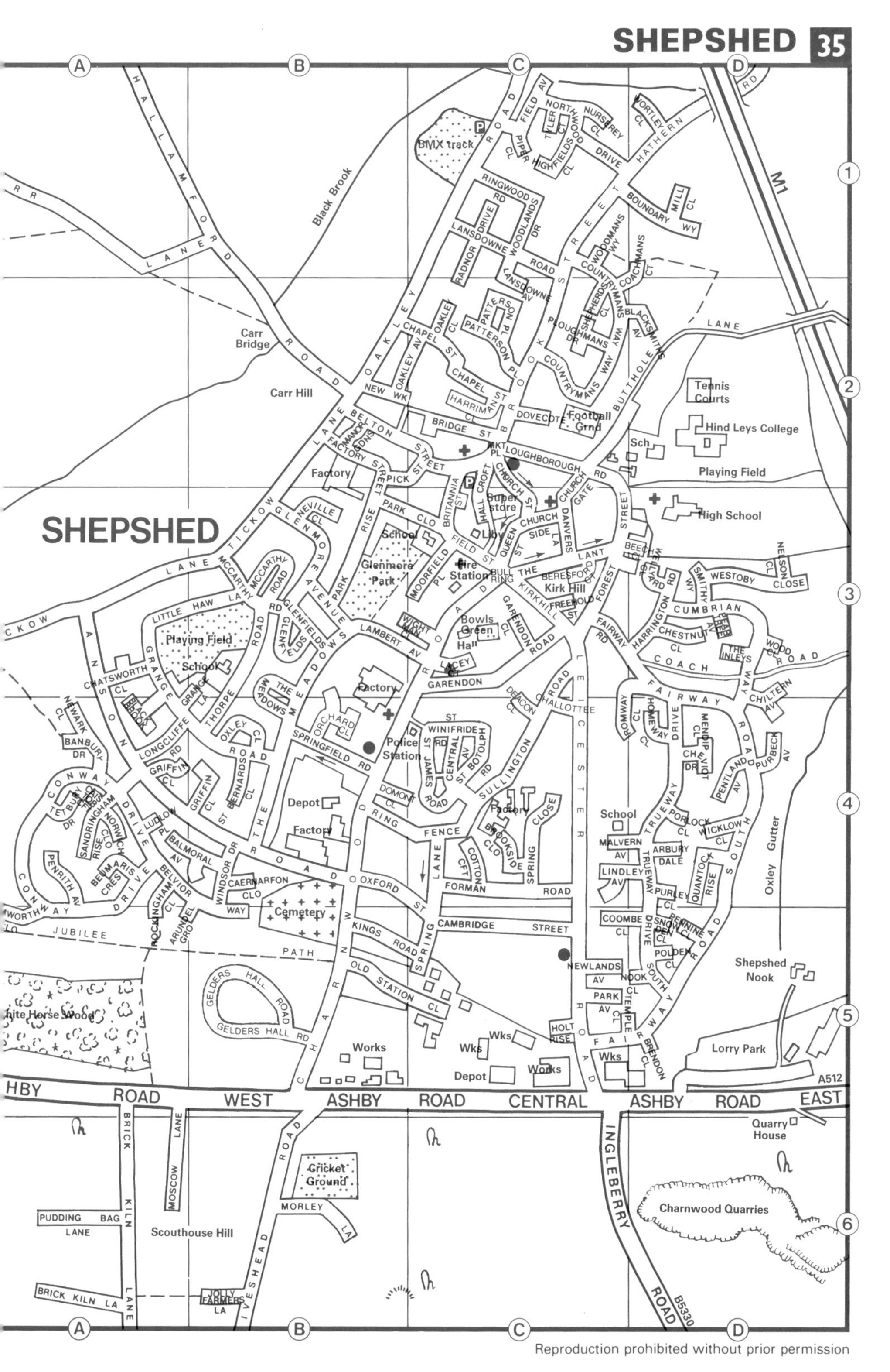
SHEPSHED
A
B
C
D
1
2
3
4
5
6
M1
BMX track
Black Brook
Carr Bridge
Carr Hill
HALLAMFORD ROAD
OAKLEY ROAD
FIELD AV
NORTHWOOD DRIVE
NURSERY CL
VORTLEY CL
HATHERN
TYLER CL
PIPER CL
HIGHFIELDS CL
RINGWOOD RD
WOODLANDS DR
DRIVE
LANSDOWNE ROAD
LANSDOWNE AV
RADNOR
PATTERSON PL
OAKLEY AV
CHAPEL ST
NEW WK
HARRIMAN CL
BRIDGE ST
BOUNDARY WY
MILL CL
WOODMANS WY
COACHMANS CT
COUNTRYMANS
SHEPHERDS CL
PLOUGHMANS DR
COUNTRYMANS WAY
BLACKSMITHS AV
BUTTHOLE LANE
DOVECOTE
Football Grnd
Tennis Courts
Hind Leys College
Sch
Playing Field
High School
BELTON STREET
MANOR GDNS
FACTORY STREET
Factory
PICK ST
MKT PL
LOUGHBOROUGH RD
CHURCH GATE
CHURCH ST
HALL CROFT
BRITANNIA ST
Super store
Liby
QUEEN ST
CHURCH SIDE LA
DANVERS
PARK CL
FIELD ST
School
Glenmore Park
MOORFIELD PL
Fire Station
BULL RING
THE KIRKHILL
BERESFORD CT
Kirk Hill
FREEHOLD ST
FOREST
STREET
BEECH CL
WELLYARD RD
SMITHY WY
WESTOBY CLOSE
NELSON CL
CUMBRIAN
HARRINGTON
CHESTNUT
THE INLEYS
WOOD CL
COACH ROAD
FAIRWAY RD
TICKOW LANE
McCARTHY ROAD
GLENMORE AVENUE
NEVILLE CL
LITTLE HAW LA
GLENFIELDS
Playing Field
School
GRANGE
THORPE ROAD
ANSON DRIVE
CHATSWORTH CL
BLACK BROOK
LONGCLIFFE RD
THE MEADOWS
LAMBERT AV
WIGHT MAN
Bowls Green
Hall
GARENDON ROAD
LACEY CT
GARENDON
Factory
ORCHARD CL
SPRINGFIELD RD
Police Station
WINIFRIDE ST
ST JAMES ROAD
CENTRAL AV
ST BOTOLPH RD
SULLINGTON
DEACON
CHALLOTTEE
LEICESTER ROAD
ROMWAY
HOMEWAY CL
DRIVE
MENDIP CL
CHEVIOT DR
CHILTERN AV
PENTLAND AV
PURBECK AV
ROAD
NEWARK CL
BANBURY DR
CONWAY DRIVE
TETBURY DR
SANDRINGHAM RISE
NORWICH CLO
PENRITH AV
BEAUMARIS CRES
OXLEY CL
ROAD
GRIFFIN CL
ST BERNARDS CL
LUDLOW PL
BALMORAL AV
BELVOIR CL
WINDSOR DR
CAERNARFON CLO
WAY
ROCKINGHAM CL
ARUNDEL GRO
Depot
Factory
DOMONT CL
RING FENCE
Factory
BROOKSIDE
SPRING CLOSE
COTTON CFT
FORMAN ROAD
OXFORD ST
Cemetery
CAMBRIDGE STREET
KINGS ROAD
SPRING LANE
School
MALVERN AV
TRUEWAY
PORLOCK CL
WICKLOW CL
ARBURY DALE
LINDLEY AV
QUANTOCK RISE
PURLEY CL
PENNINE CL
COOMBE CL
SNOWDEN CL
POLDEN CL
SOUTH ROAD
Oxley Gutter
JUBILEE PATH
White Horse Wood
GELDERS HALL ROAD
GELDERS HALL RD
OLD STATION CL
NEWLANDS AV
NOOK CL
PARK AV
TEMPLE CL
HOLT RISE
FAIRWAY
BRENDON CL
Shepshed Nook
Works
Wks
Depot
Works
Wks
Lorry Park
A512
ASHBY ROAD WEST
ASHBY ROAD CENTRAL
ASHBY ROAD EAST
BRICK KILN LANE
MOSCOW LANE
IVESHEAD ROAD
INGLEBERRY ROAD
B5330
Cricket Ground
MORLEY LA
Quarry House
Charnwood Quarries
PUDDING BAG LANE
Scouthouse Hill
BRICK KILN LA
JOLLY FARMERS LA

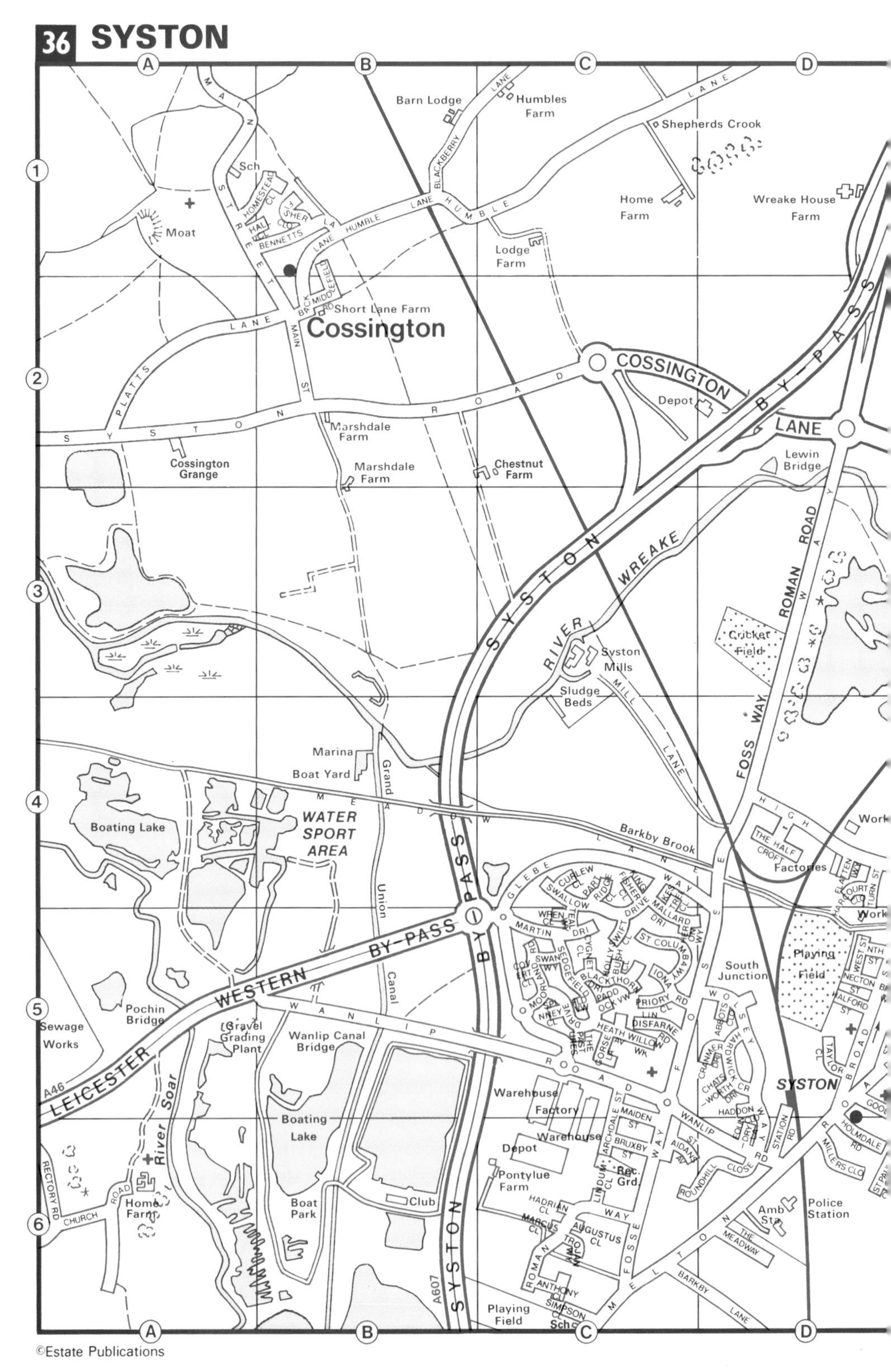
Cossington
Barn Lodge
Humbles Farm
Shepherds Crook
Home Farm
Wreake House Farm
Lodge Farm
Short Lane Farm
Moat
Sch
MAIN STREET
HOMESTEAD CL
HALL CL
BENNETTS
BACK LANE
HUMBLE LANE
BLACKBERRY LANE
PLATTS LANE
MAIN ST
SYSTON ROAD
COSSINGTON LANE
SYSTON BY-PASS
Depot
Marshdale Farm
Cossington Grange
Chestnut Farm
Lewin Bridge
ROMAN ROAD
FOSS WAY
RIVER WREAKE
Cricket Field
Syston Mills
Sludge Beds
MILL LANE
Marina
Boat Yard
Grand Union Canal
MEADOW LANE
Boating Lake
WATER SPORT AREA
Barkby Brook
HIGH ST
THE HALF CROFT
Factories
Works
GLEBE WAY
CURLEW CL
SWALLOW DRI
MALLARD DRI
MARTIN DRI
WREN CL
SWIFT CL
ST COLUMBA WAY
SEDGEFIELD DRI
BLACKTHORN DRI
IONA CL
PRIORY CL
LINDISFARNE RD
HEATH AV
WILLOW WK
South Junction
Playing Field
WESTERN BY-PASS
LEICESTER
A46
Pochin Bridge
Sewage Works
Gravel Grading Plant
WANLIP ROAD
Wanlip Canal Bridge
River Soar
Boating Lake
Boat Park
Club
Warehouse
Factory
Depot
Pontylue Farm
Rec. Grd.
HADRIAN CL
MARCUS CL
AUGUSTUS CL
TROJAN WAY
ANTHONY CL
SIMPSON CL
Playing Field
Sch
FOSSE WAY
ARCHDALE ST
MAIDEN ST
BRUXBY ST
LINDUM CL
WANLIP ST
AIDANS AV
ROUNDHILL CLOSE
WOLSEY WAY
ABBOTS CL
HARDWICK DRI
CRANMER DRI
CHATSWORTH DRI
HADDON CL
STATION RD
SYSTON
MELTON ROAD
THE MEADWAY
BARKBY LANE
Amb Sta
Police Station
HOLMDALE RD
MILLERS CL
TAYLOR CL
BROAD ST
WEST ST
NECTON ST
HALFORD ST
RECTORY RD
CHURCH ROAD
Home Farm
A607
SYSTON BY-PASS

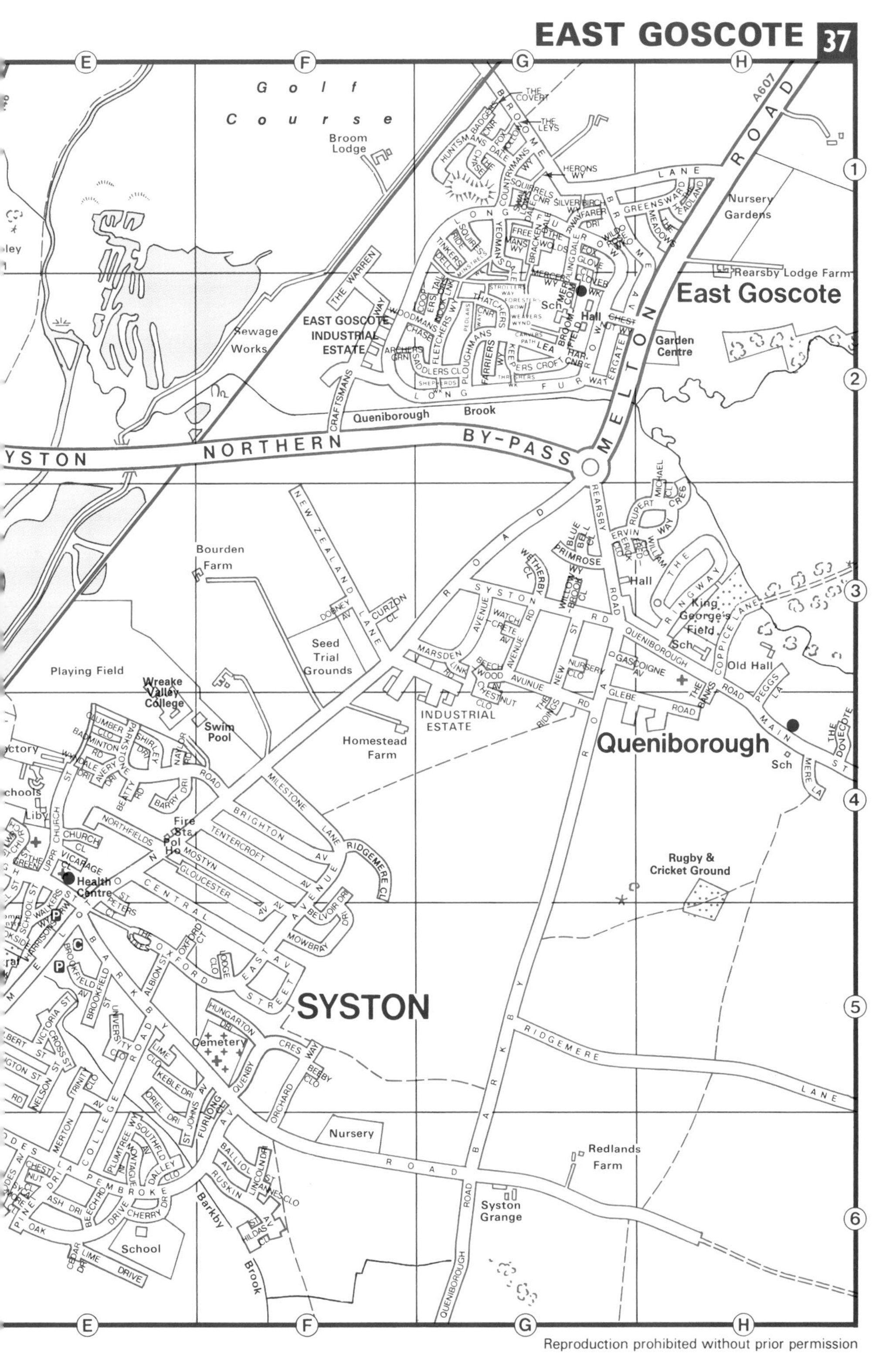
Golf Course
Broom Lodge
Sewage Works
EAST GOSCOTE INDUSTRIAL ESTATE
East Goscote
Garden Centre
Nursery Gardens
Rearsby Lodge Farm
Queniborough Brook
SYSTON NORTHERN BY-PASS
MELTON ROAD
A607
Bourden Farm
Seed Trial Grounds
Playing Field
Wreake Valley College
Swim Pool
Homestead Farm
INDUSTRIAL ESTATE
Queniborough
King George's Field
Old Hall
Rugby & Cricket Ground
SYSTON
Cemetery
Health Centre
Nursery
Redlands Farm
Syston Grange
School
Barkby Brook
RIDGEMERE LANE
BARKBY ROAD
QUENIBOROUGH ROAD

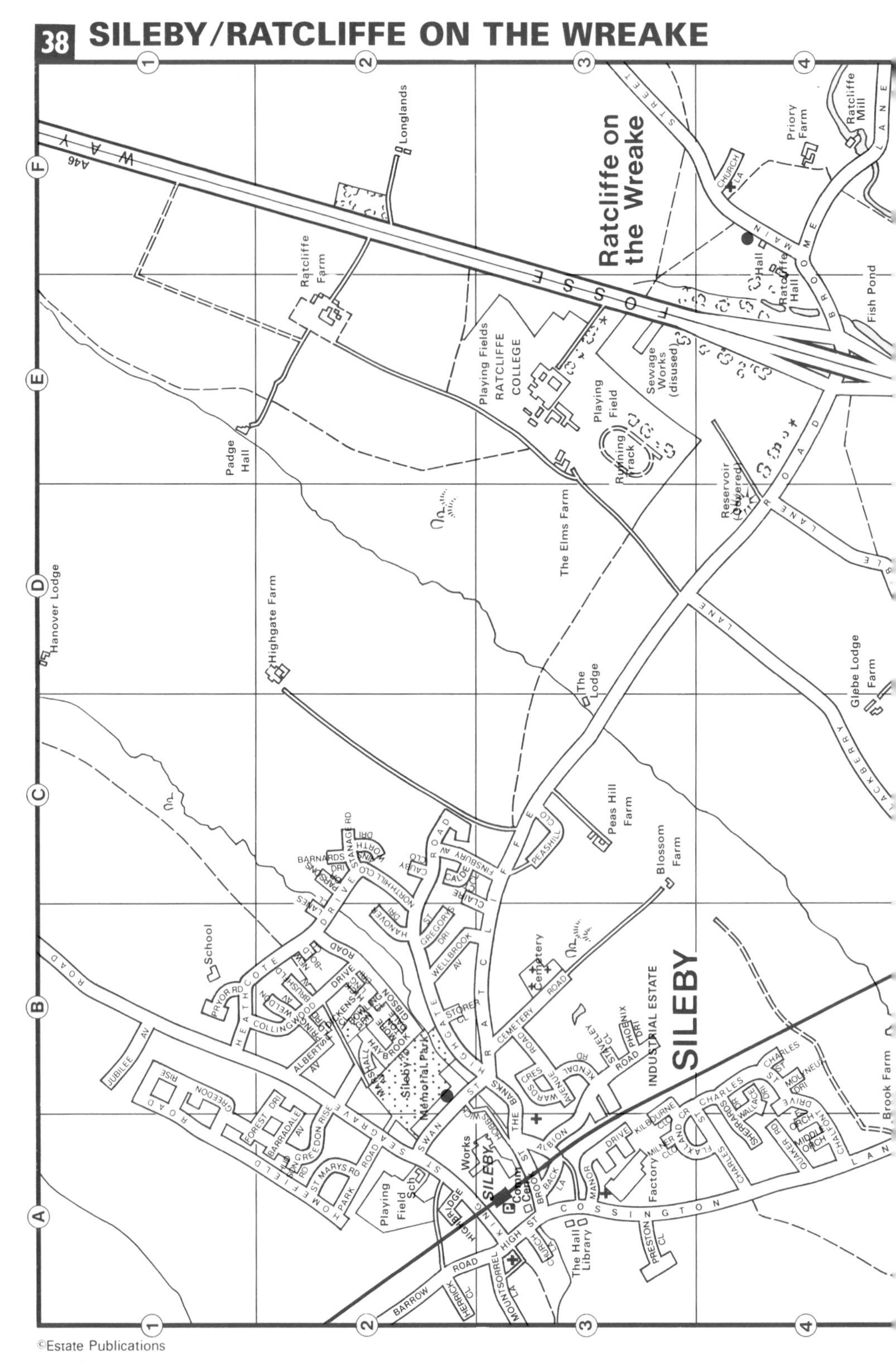

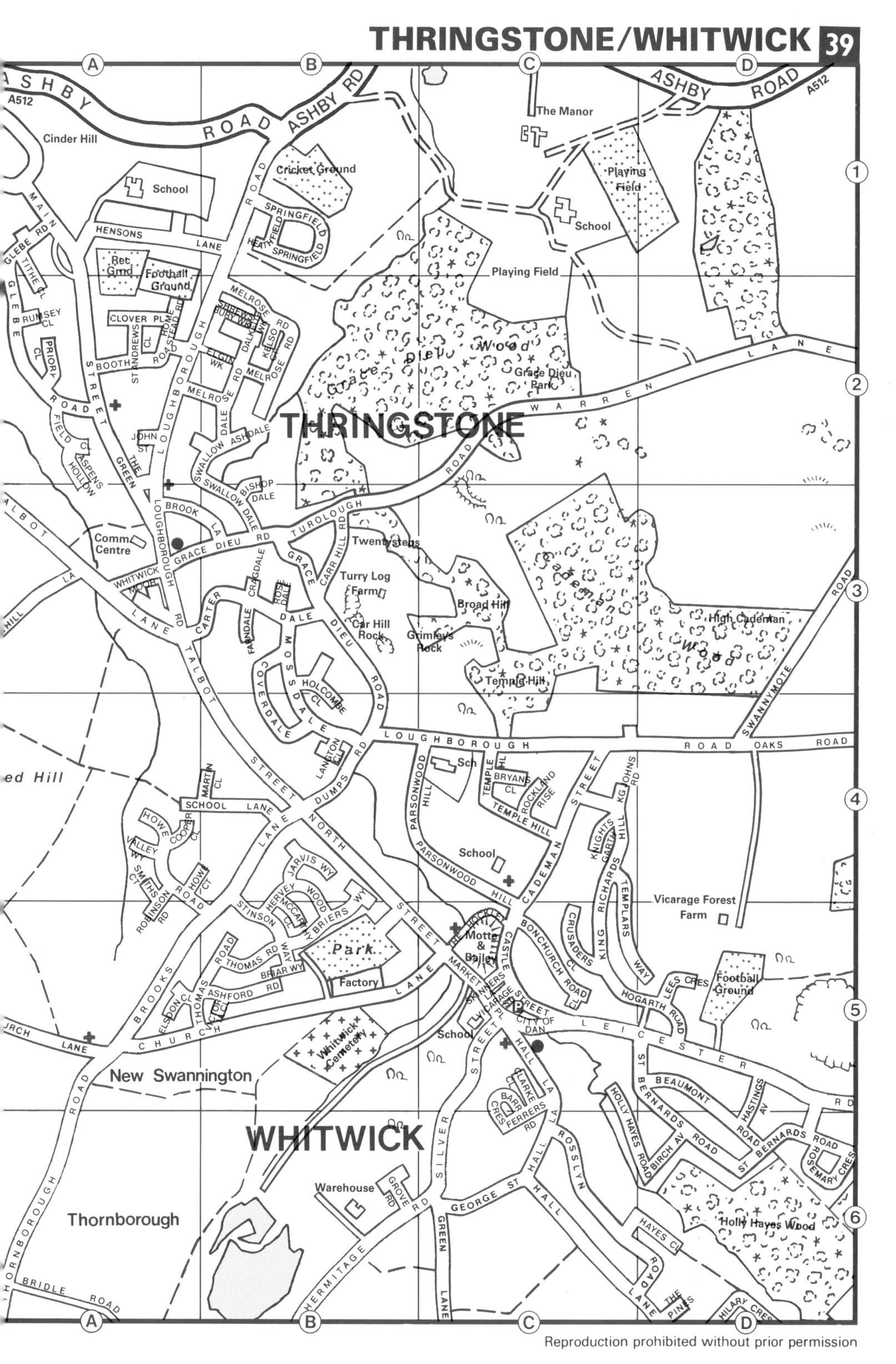
THRINGSTONE
WHITWICK
New Swannington
Thornborough
Cinder Hill
Grace Dieu Wood
Grace Dieu Park
Cademan Wood
High Cademan
Holly Hayes Wood
Broad Hill
Temple Hill
Twentysteps
Turry Log Farm
Car Hill Rock
Grimleys Rock
Vicarage Forest Farm
The Manor
Cricket Ground
Playing Field
Football Ground
Rec Grnd
Comm Centre
Park
Factory
Motte & Bailey
Whitwick Cemetery
Warehouse
School
ASHBY ROAD
A512
WARREN LANE
LOUGHBOROUGH ROAD
OAKS ROAD
LEICESTER RD
CHURCH LANE
TALBOT STREET
NORTH STREET
CADEMAN STREET
SILVER STREET
HERMITAGE RD
BRIDLE ROAD

A- Z INDEX TO STREETS

The Index includes some names for which there is insufficient space on the maps. These names are preceded by an * and are followed by the nearest adjoining thoroughfare.

Croft Clo. LE9 12 C5
Cumberland Way. LE9 12 B4
Dadlington La. LE9 12 A1
Dawsons La. LE9 12 C5
Derwent Clo. LE9 13 F3
Doctor Cookes Clo. LE9 12 B5
Doctors Fields. LE9 13 E4
Dovecote Way. LE9 12 C5
Earl St. LE9 13 H2
East Green. LE9 12 B4
Edinburgh Rd. LE9 13 E4
Elmdale Rd. LE9 13 E4
Elmesthorpe La. LE9 13 E5
Elwell Av. LE9 12 C2
Equity Rd. LE9 13 F4
Equity Rd East. LE9 13 F4
Fair Acre Rd. LE9 12 B5
Farm Dri. LE9 12 D3
Field Way. LE9 13 E3
Fir Tree Clo. LE9 12 C2
Forest View Rd. LE9 12 C4
Frank Booton Clo. LE9 13 H2
Frisby Rd. LE9 12 C3
Friswell La. LE9 12 B4
Galloway Clo. LE9 12 A4
Gartree Cres. LE9 13 E3
George Foster Clo. LE9 13 G2
George Geary Clo. LE9 12 D3
George St. LE9 12 C4
George Ward Clo. LE9 12 C4
Glyn Clo. LE9 12 B4
Goose La. LE9 12 B5
Green La. LE9 13 F2
Greenhill Dri. LE9 12 C4
Hallam Clo. LE9 13 H2
Harrison Clo. LE9 13 G2
Hastings Dri. LE9 12 C4
Hawthorne Way. LE9 12 C5
Hazel Way. LE9 12 B4
Heath Ct. LE9 13 E4
Heath La. LE9 12 D3
Heath La Sth. LE9 13 E3
Hereford Clo. LE9 12 A4
High St, Barwell. LE9 12 B5
High St, Earl Shilton. LE9 13 G3
High Tor East. LE9 13 F2
High Tor West. LE9 13 F2
Highfield St. LE9 13 E4
Hill St. LE9 12 C5
Hill Top. LE9 13 G2
Hinckley Rd, Barwell. LE9 12 A5
Hinckley Rd, Earl Shilton. LE9 13 E4
Hinckley Rd, Stapleton. LE9 12 A2
Holly La. LE9 12 C4
Hollydene Cres. LE9 13 E3
Howard Clo. LE9 12 B3
Hurst Rd. LE9 13 F4
INDUSTRIAL ESTATES:
Mill St Ind Est. LE9 12 B5
Oaks Ind Est. LE9 13 F3
Station Rd Ind Est. LE9 13 F3
Ivydene Clo. LE9 13 G3
James St. LE9 13 F3
Jersey Way. LE9 12 B5
Keats Clo. LE9 13 G2
Keats La. LE9 13 F2
Kerry Clo. LE9 12 B4
King Richards Hill. LE9 13 H2
King St. LE9 12 C4
Kings Row. LE9 13 F3
Kings Walk. LE9 13 F3
Kingsfield Rd. LE9 12 C4
Kirkby Rd, Barwell. LE9 12 B4
Kirkby Rd, East Shilton. LE9 13 F1
Knights Link. LE9 13 H2
Laburnum Dri. LE9 13 E4
Land Society La. LE9 13 F3
Leicester Rd, Barwell. LE9 12 C6
Leicester Rd, Earl Shilton. LE9 13 G2
Leighton Cres. LE9 13 G6
Lime Gro. LE9 13 E4
Lincoln Rd. LE9 12 B5
Lovelace Cres. LE9 13 G6
Lucas Way. LE9 13 F4
Lyndene Clo. LE9 13 F3
Main St. LE9 12 A1
Mallory St. LE9 12 D3
Malt Mill Bank. LE9 12 B4
Manor Cres. LE9 12 A1
Maple Way. LE9 13 E4
Mary St. LE9 13 G2
Maryland Clo. LE9 12 A5
Masefield Clo. LE9 12 C3
Mayfield Way. LE9 12 D4
Meadow Court Rd. LE9 13 G3
Meadow Rd. LE9 12 D4
Melton St. LE9 13 E3
Metcalfe St. LE9 13 F3
Mill La. LE9 13 H2
Mill St. LE9 12 B6
Moat Way. LE9 12 B5
Mona St. LE9 13 F4
Montgomery Rd. LE9 13 H3
Moore Rd. LE9 12 C3
Mount Av. LE9 12 C4
Mountfield Rd. LE9 13 F3
Myrtle Clo. LE9 12 B4
New St. LE9 13 E3
Newlands Rd. LE9 12 C3
Nock Verges. LE9 13 H2
Normandy Way. LE9 12 A6
Northleigh Way. LE9 13 G3
Norton Rd. LE9 12 D3
Notley Clo. LE9 12 D3
Notley Manor Dri. LE9 12 D3
Nursery Gdns. LE9 13 E4
Oakdale Rd. LE9 13 E4
Oaks Way. LE9 13 F3
Ormond Clo. LE9 12 B3
Oxford St, Barwell. LE9 12 C4
Oxford St, East Shilton. LE9 13 G3
Park Clo. LE9 13 F2
Park Rd. LE9 13 F2
Peartree Clo. LE9 12 C2
Peckleton Grn. LE9 12 C3
Peggs Clo. LE9 13 G3
Penny La. LE9 12 B4
Powers Rd. LE9 12 A6
Prospect Way. LE9 13 F2
Queen St. LE9 12 C5
Queensway. LE9 12 C4
Red Hall Dri. LE9 12 C4
Red Hall Rd. LE9 12 D3
Regent St. LE9 12 C4
Roman Clo. LE9 13 H2
Ronald Toon Rd. LE9 13 H3
Rossendale Rd. LE9 13 E3
Saffron Clo. LE9 12 D3
St Martins. LE9 12 A1
St Marys Av. LE9 12 A6
St Marys Ct. LE9 12 B5
Sandringham Av. LE9 13 E4
School La. LE9 12 A1
Shenton Rd. LE9 12 C4
Shilton Rd. LE9 12 C5
Shoesmith Clo. LE9 12 B5
Shrewsbury Clo. LE9 12 B3
Spring Gdns. LE9 13 G2
Stafford St. LE9 12 B4
Stanley St. LE9 12 B5
Stapleton La. LE9 12 A2
Station Rd, Earl Shilton. LE9 13 F4
Station Rd, Elmesthorpe. LE9 13 F5
Stoneycroft Rd. LE9 13 F4
The Barracks. LE9 12 B5
The Beeches. LE9 13 G2
The Cloisters. LE9 13 F3
The Close. LE9 12 C3
The Common. LE9 12 C5
The Crescent. LE9 13 E6
The Drive. LE9 12 C3
The Grange. LE9 13 F4
The Hollow. LE9 13 F3
The Leecroft. LE9 13 G3
The Poplars. LE9 13 H2
The Roundhills. LE9 13 G6
Thurlaston La. LE9 13 H2
Tom Eatough Ct. LE9 13 H3
Tower Rd. LE9 13 F2
Townend Rd. LE9 12 B4
Twyford Ct. LE9 12 C4
Ullswater Clo. LE9 13 G3
Vicarage Ct. LE9 13 G3
Vicarage St. LE9 13 G2
Washington Clo. LE9 12 B5
Waterfall Way. LE9 12 B6
Waters End. LE9 12 B6
Waughan St. LE9 13 G2
Weaver Rd. LE9 13 G3
Wensley Clo. LE9 12 B6
Wensleydale Av. LE9 12 B6
West St. LE9 13 G2
Wightman Rd. LE9 12 D4
Wilemans Clo. LE9 13 F4
Wilf Bown. LE9 13 H2
Wilkinson La. LE9 13 F5
Willow Tree Clo. LE9 12 C3
Willowdene Way. LE9 12 C5
Windermere Clo. LE9 13 F3
Wood St. LE9 13 F3
Worcester Clo. LE9 12 B3
Yew Tree Clo. LE9 12 C2

CASTLE DONINGTON

Ambassador Rd. DE74 16 C6
Anson Rd. DE74 16 C5
Apiary Gate. DE74 16 C2
Aston Av. DE74 16 B3
Back La. DE74 16 B1
Bakewell. DE74 16 C3
Barn Clo. DE74 16 C3
Barroon. DE74 16 C2
Bentley Rd. DE74 16 A1
Bondgate. DE74 16 C2
Borough St. DE74 16 C2
Bosworth Rd. DE74 16 A2
Campion Hill. DE74 16 B1
Carrs Clo. DE74 16 C2
Castle Hill. DE74 16 C2
Cavendish Clo. DE74 16 C3
Cedar Rd. DE74 16 C3
Charnock Hill. DE74 16 C6
Charnwood Av. DE74 16 D2
Cheribough Rd. DE74 16 B3
Church La. DE74 16 C1
Clapgun St. DE74 16 C2
Cordwell Clo. DE74 16 B2
Crabtree Clo. DE74 16 B3
Dakota Rd. DE74 16 C6
Darsway. DE74 16 B1
Delven La. DE74 16 C2
Diseworth Rd. DE74 16 B4
Dove Cote. DE74 16 C2
Eastway. DE74 16 C2
Eaton Rd. DE74 16 C3
Ferrers Clo. DE74 16 B2
Fosbrook Dri. DE74 16 A2
Fox Rd. DE74 16 A2
Garden Cres. DE74 16 C2
Gasny Av. DE74 16 C1
Grange Dri. DE74 16 B2
Grays Clo. DE74 16 C2
Grimes Gate. DE74 16 D6
Hall Farm Clo. DE74 16 C3
Hallam Fields. DE74 16 C3
Harcourt Pl. DE74 16 C2
Harvey Ct. DE74 16 C2
Harvey Rd. DE74 16 C3
Hastings St. DE74 16 C3
Haulton Dri. DE74 16 C2
Hawthorn Rd. DE74 16 C1
Hazelrigg Clo. DE74 16 B1
Hemington Hill. DE74 16 D2
High St. DE74 16 B4
Hill Top. DE74 16 B4
Hillside. DE74 16 C2
Huntingdon Dri. DE74 16 B2
Kirkland Clo. DE74 16 B2
Little Hill. DE74 16 C2
Lothian Pl. DE74 16 B2
Loudoun Pl. DE74 16 B2
Market Pl. DE74 16 C2
Market St. DE74 16 C2
Meadow Cres. DE74 16 C3
Minton Rd. DE74 16 A2
Moira Dale. DE74 16 D2
Montford Mews. DE74 16 D2
Montieth Pl. DE74 16 C2
Mount Pleasant. DE74 16 C3
Orchard Av. DE74 16 B2
Orly Av. DE74 16 C3
Paddock Clo. DE74 16 A2
Park Av. DE74 16 B2
Park La. DE74 16 A2
Peartree Clo. DE74 16 B2
Queensway. DE74 16 B2
Rawdon Clo. DE74 16 B1
Roby Lea. DE74 16 A2
Routh Av. DE74 16 C3
St Annes La. DE74 16 C2
St Edwards Rd. DE74 16 C3
Salina Clo. DE74 16 B2
Salters Clo. DE74 16 B2
School La. DE74 16 B2
Shield Cres. DE74 16 B3
Shirley Clo. DE74 16 B1
Short La. DE74 16 A1
Spital Hill. DE74 16 B1
Starkie Av. DE74 16 A2
Station Rd. DE74 16 C1
Staunton Clo. DE74 16 B2
Stone Hill. DE74 16 C3
Studbrook Clo. DE74 16 A2
Swan River. DE74 16 C5
Sycamore Rd. DE74 16 C1
Tanyard Clo. DE74 16 C1
The Biggin. DE74 16 C2
The Birches. DE74 16 D6
The Green. DE74 16 B2
The Hollow. DE74 16 C2
The Moat. DE74 16 C2
The Spinney. DE74 16 B2
The Spital. DE74 16 B1
Tipnall Rd. DE74 16 B2
Towles Pastures. DE74 16 B3
Trent La. DE74 16 C1
Vanguard Rd. DE74 16 C5
Victoria St. DE74 16 C1
Viscount Rd. DE74 16 D6
Walton Hill. DE74 16 B1
William Rd. DE74 16 C1
Windmill Clo. DE74 16 C3

COALVILLE

Abbey Rd. LE67 15 H1
Abbotts Oak Dri. LE67 15 F2
Agar Nook La. LE67 15 H2
Albert Rd. LE67 14 C2
Ashburton Rd. LE67 14 A5
Ashby Rd. LE67 14 A2
Ashtree Rd. LE67 14 A5
Atlas Rd. LE67 14 C1
Avenue Rd. LE67 14 B4
Baker St. LE67 14 B2
Bakewell St. LE67 14 C3
Balmoral Rd. LE67 15 E3
Bardon Clo. LE67 15 F5
Bardon Rd. LE67 14 D3
Barganey Clo. LE67 15 E3
Beacon Cres. LE67 15 G4
Bedale Clo. LE67 14 A4
Beech Rd. LE67 15 E4
Belgrave Clo. LE67 15 H2
Belton Clo. LE67 15 G2
Belvoir Rd. LE67 14 B2
Belvoir Shopping Centre. LE67 14 B2
Berrisford St. LE67 14 B3
Berryhill La. LE67 14 A6
*Blackbrook Ct, Bradgate Dri. LE67 15 G4
Blackbrook Dri. LE67 15 F4
Blackwood. LE67 15 F2
Botts Way. LE67 15 E4
Bracken Clo. LE67 14 B5
Bradgate Dri. LE67 15 G4
Brambles Rd. LE67 14 A5
Breach Rd. LE67 14 B4
Briar Clo. LE67 14 A5
Bridge Rd. LE67 14 B3
Bridle Rd. LE67 14 C1
Brindley Rd. LE67 14 A1
Broad St. LE67 14 B4
Broom Leys Av. LE67 14 D3
Broom Leys Rd. LE67 14 D3
Broughton St. LE67 14 B4
Brunel Way. LE67 14 A1
Buckingham Rd. LE67 15 E3
Burgess Rd. LE67 14 B3
Cambridge St. LE67 14 D3
Camelford Rd. LE67 14 B5
Castle Rock Dri. LE67 15 G1
Cavendish Cres. LE67 14 A5
Central Rd. LE67 14 B4
Charnborough Rd. LE67 15 G3
Charnwood Ct. LE67 14 C3
Charnwood St. LE67 14 D3
Chestnut Gro. LE67 15 F3
Clarence Ct. LE67 15 E3
Clarke Rd. LE67 15 G3
College Clo. LE67 14 B3
Comet Way. LE67 14 B1
Convent Dri. LE67 14 C4
Copse Clo. LE67 14 B5
Crescent Rd. LE67 14 B4
Cromore Clo. LE67 15 G3
Cropston Dri. LE67 15 F4
Curlew Clo. LE67 15 E4
Dauphine Clo. LE67 15 H3
Degens Way. LE67 14 A5
Dennis St. LE67 14 B6
Devana Av. LE67 14 D3
Deveron Clo. LE67 15 H3
Dove Rd. LE67 15 E4
Drome Clo. LE67 15 H3
Dunbar Rd. LE67 15 G3
Durris Clo. LE67 15 H3
Fairfield Rd. LE67 14 B5
Farm La. LE67 14 A6
Fordyce Rd. LE67 14 B5
Forest Rd. LE67 14 B5
Foxglove Rd. LE67 15 E4
Frearson Fields. LE67 14 A5
Garden Rd. LE67 14 C2
Garendon Rd. LE67 15 G4
Garfield Rd. LE67 14 B5
Gillamore Dri. LE67 15 E1
Glen Way. LE67 15 E4
Goliath Way. LE67 14 B1
Gorse Rd. LE67 14 B5
Grange Rd. LE67 14 C5
Grasmere. LE67 15 G2
Green La. LE67 14 D2
Greenfields Dri. LE67 15 F2
Greenhill Rd. LE67 15 F3
Gutteridge St. LE67 14 B3
Hall Gate. LE67 15 G3
Hall La. LE67 15 E1
Hamilton Rd. LE67 15 G3
Haslyn Walk. LE67 15 F3
Hawley Clo. LE67 14 C5
Hawthorn Clo. LE67 14 C2
Hector Rd. LE67 14 C2
Hedge Row. LE67 14 A5
Helmsdale Clo. LE67 15 H3
Hermitage Rd. LE67 14 C1
Heron Way. LE67 15 E4
High St. LE67 14 B2
Highfield St. LE67 14 A5
Hilary Cres. LE67 15 E1
Holly Bank. LE67 14 B5
Holts La. LE67 14 A6
*Honeysuckle Clo, Foxglove Rd. LE67 15 E4
Hotel St. LE67 14 B3
INDUSTRIAL ESTATES:
The Scotlands Ind Est. LE67 14 C3
Whitwick Business Park. LE67 14 D2
Jacks Walk. LE67 14 A5
Jackson St. LE67 14 B3
Jacque Mart Clo. LE67 15 H3
James St. LE67 14 B3
Kane Clo. LE67 14 A2
Kenmoor Cres. LE67 15 G3
King St. LE67 14 C4
Kingfisher Clo. LE67 15 F2
Kirkhill Clo. LE67 15 H3
Kirton Rd. LE67 15 H3
Lancaster Clo. LE67 15 H2
Launceston Dri. LE67 14 B5
Leicester Rd. LE67 15 G1
Linford Cres. LE67 15 F2
Links Clo. LE67 14 C5
London Rd. LE67 14 C3
Long La. LE67 14 C2
Longcliff Rd. LE67 15 G4
Lords Clo. LE67 15 E5
Mammoth St. LE67 14 C2
Manor Rd. LE67 14 A6
Mantle La. LE67 14 B2
Maplewell. LE67 15 F3
Margaret St. LE67 14 A2
Market St. LE67 14 B2
Marlborough Clo. LE67 14 B3
Meadow La. LE67 15 F2
Meadow View. LE67 14 A6
Melbourne St. LE67 14 B3
Memorial Sq. LE67 14 B2
Merbanster Way. LE67 15 E4
Mickledon Grn. LE67 15 E1
Mill Dam. LE67 14 C5
Mill Pond. LE67 14 C5
Muscovy Rd. LE67 15 E4
Nelson Fields. LE67 15 F2
Nene Way. LE67 15 E4
Neville Dri. LE67 15 F2
New St, Coalville. LE67 14 C4
New St, Hugglescote. LE67 14 A5
North Av. LE67 14 B4
Northfields Dri. LE67 15 F3
Oak Clo. LE67 15 E4

Oakham Dri. LE67 15 G2
Oaktree Rd. LE67 14 A5
Old Station Clo. LE67 14 B2
Owen St. LE67 14 A2
Oxford St. LE67 14 C3
Park Rd. LE67 14 C3
Peggs Grange. LE67 14 B5
Peldar Pl. LE67 15 G3
Perran Av. LE67 15 E2
Peterfield Rd. LE67 15 E1
Prince St. LE67 14 C4
Queen St. LE67 14 C4
Quelch Clo. LE67 14 B5
Quorn Cres. LE67 15 F3
River Sence Way. LE67 14 C5
Robin Rd. LE67 15 E4
Rochdale Cres. LE67 15 H2
Romans Cres. LE67 15 H3
Rowan Av. LE67 15 F3
St Clares Ct. LE67 14 C4
St Davids Cres. LE67 15 G2
St Faiths Rd. LE67 14 A4
St Ives. LE67 15 F4
St Johns Clo. LE67 14 B6
St Marys Av. LE67 14 A5
St Saviours Rd. LE67 14 A4
St Vincents Clo. LE67 14 A4
Samson Rd. LE67 14 B1
Sandringham Rd. LE67 15 E3
Scotlands Dri. LE67 14 C4
Scotlands Rd. LE67 14 B3
Seagrave Clo. LE67 15 H2
Sharpley Av. LE67 15 E2
Smith Cres. LE67 15 G3
Snipe Clo. LE67 14 A5
Speedwell Clo. LE67 14 C2
Stainsdale Grn. LE67 15 E1
Stamford Dri. LE67 15 H2
Standard Hill. LE67 14 A4
Station Rd. LE67 14 B6
Stenson Rd. LE67 14 C2
Stephenson Way. LE67 14 A1
Stone Row. LE67 14 C2
Stonehaven Clo. LE67 15 H3
Strathmore Clo. LE67 15 H3
Stretton Dri. LE67 15 H2
Swan Way. LE67 15 E4
Swithland Rd. LE67 15 G3
Sycamore Rd. LE67 15 E4
Tavistock Rd. LE67 14 B5
Teal Clo. LE67 15 E4
Telford Way. LE67 14 A1
The Green. LE67 14 B6
The Oval. LE67 15 E4
The Spinney. LE67 14 A5
Thirlmere. LE67 15 G2
Thornborough Rd. LE67 14 B2
Thornton Clo. LE67 15 G3
Tiverton Av. LE67 15 E1
Torrington Av. LE67 15 E1
Totnes Rd. LE67 14 B5
Townsend La. LE67 14 A6
Tressall Rd. LE67 15 E1
Tween Town. LE67 14 A6
Twyford Clo. LE67 15 H2
Vaughan St. LE67 14 B3
Vercor Clo. LE67 15 H3
Verdon Cres. LE67 15 F2
Victoria Rd. LE67 14 C2
Vulcan Way. LE67 14 B1
Wainwright Rd. LE67 14 C5
Warren Hills Rd. LE67 15 H1
Waterworks Rd. LE67 15 E4
Welland Clo. LE67 15 E4
Wentworth Rd. LE67 14 A4
Whetstone Dri. LE67 14 C2
Whitwick Rd. LE67 14 C2
Willm Clo. LE67 15 F4
Willow Grn. LE67 15 G2
Windsor Clo. LE67 15 F3
Wolsey Rd. LE67 14 B2
Woodhouse Rd. LE67 15 F3
Woods Clo. LE67 14 B5
Wortley Clo. LE67 14 C3
Wyatt Rd. LE67 14 C2
Wyggeston Rd. LE67 14 B4
York Pl. LE67 15 H2
Zetland Clo. LE67 14 B3

HINCKLEY/ BURBAGE

Abbotts Grn. LE10 20 D1
Albert Rd. LE10 18 D4
Aldin Way. LE10 18 B2
Aldridge Rd. LE10 20 B1
Alesworth Dri. LE10 20 D2
Alexander Gdns. LE10 18 C2
Alfreton Clo. LE10 20 D1
Alma Rd. LE10 18 D4
Ambion Way. LE10 19 F5
Applebee Rd. LE10 20 A1
Argents Mead Way. LE10 18 D4
Argentsmead. LE10 18 D5
Armadale Clo. LE10 18 A4
Armour Clo. LE10 20 B2
Aran Way. LE10 18 B4
Ashburton Clo. LE10 19 G6
Ashby Ct. LE10 19 E2
Ashby Rd. LE10 18 D3
Ashford Rd. LE10 18 B5
Aster Clo. LE10 20 B1
Aster Way. LE10 20 B1
Aston La. LE10 20 E1
Atkins Way. LE10 19 E6
Aulton Cres. LE10 18 B3
Aulton Way. LE10 18 B3
Avon Walk. LE10 18 A5
Azalea Clo. LE10 20 C2
Azalea Dri. LE10 20 C2
Azalea Walk. LE10 20 C1
Baines La. LE10 18 D4
Balfour Clo. LE10 19 E6
Balliol Rd. LE10 20 D1
Banky Meadow. LE10 19 G6
Baptist Walk. LE10 18 D4
Bar Mead. LE10 20 C3
Bardsey Clo. LE10 18 B4
Barlestone Dri. LE10 18 A4
Barleyfield. LE10 18 C1
Barrie Rd. LE10 18 D2
Barwell La. LE10 19 E2
Battledown Clo. LE10 18 B3
Bearsdon Cres. LE10 18 C3
Beatty Clo. LE10 18 D1
Beaumont Av. LE10 18 B6
Bedale Av. LE10 19 F2
Bedford Clo. LE10 19 E1
Beechwood Av. LE10 20 B3
Begonia Clo. LE10 20 C1
Begonia Dri. LE10 20 C1
Benbow Clo. LE10 18 D1
Beryl Av. LE10 18 A2
Blake Clo. LE10 18 D1
Blenheim Clo. LE10 19 F1
*Blockleys Yd, Regent St. LE10 18 D5
Bodmin Clo. LE10 19 F1
Bosworth Clo. LE10 18 A4
Bowling Grn Rd. LE10 19 E4
Bowman Grn. LE10 20 D1
Boyslade Rd. LE10 20 C1
Boyslade Rd East. LE10 20 D2
Bradgate Rd. LE10 19 F2
Bramcote Clo. LE10 19 F2
Brame Rd. LE10 18 C3
Brandon Clo. LE10 18 C5
Brascote Rd. LE10 18 A4
Brechin Clo. LE10 18 B4
Brenfield Dri. LE10 18 B4
Briar Clo. LE10 19 F6
Bridge Clo. LE10 18 D6
Britannia Centre. LE10 18 D4
Britannia Rd. LE10 20 E2
Broadsword Way. LE10 20 B2
Brockhurst Av. LE10 20 B3
Brodick Clo. LE10 18 A4
Brodick Rd. LE10 18 A5
Brookdale. LE10 18 B5
Brookfield Rd. LE10 18 C6
Brookside. LE10 18 D6
Brosdale Dri. LE10 18 B4
Browning Dri. LE10 18 C4
Brunel Rd. LE10 18 C5
Buckingham Clo. LE10 19 F1
Bullfurlong La. LE10 20 D2
Burbage Common Rd. LE10 19 H1
Burbage Rd. LE10 19 F5
Burleigh Rd. LE10 18 C2
Burnsway. LE10 18 C4
Bute Clo. LE10 18 C3
Butt La. LE10 19 E4
Butt La Clo. LE10 19 E4
Caldon Clo. LE10 18 B5
Cambourne Rd. LE10 19 G6
Campton Clo. LE10 19 E6
Canning St. LE10 18 C4
Carpenters Clo. LE10 20 D1
Castle Ct. LE10 18 D6
Castle St. LE10 18 D4
Castlemaine Dri. LE10 19 E2
Charles St. LE10 19 E4
Charnwood Rd. LE10 19 E3
Chatsworth Clo. LE10 20 D1
Cherwell Clo. LE10 18 A5
Chesser St. LE10 18 C4
Church Clo. LE10 20 E1
Church St. LE10 20 E1
Church Walk. LE10 18 D4
Clarence Rd. LE10 19 E5
Clarendon Rd. LE10 18 C5
Cleveland Rd. LE10 18 C4
Clifton Way. LE10 18 A3
Clivesway. LE10 18 C3
Cloverfield. LE10 18 C1
Coldstream Clo. LE10 18 A4
Coley Clo. LE10 18 D5
College La. LE10 19 E4
Colts Clo. LE10 20 B3
Coppice Clo. LE10 19 F2
Coral Clo. LE10 20 D2
Cornfield. LE10 18 C1
Cornwall Way. LE10 19 E1
Cosford Dri. LE10 18 A4
Cotes Rd. LE10 20 D2
Cotman Dri. LE10 18 B2
Council Rd. LE10 18 D4
Coventry Rd, Burbage. LE10 20 C2
Coventry Rd, Hinckley. LE10 18 A6
Cowper Rd. LE10 20 B1
Crammond Clo. LE10 18 B4
Cromarty Dri. LE10 18 A4
Crosskirk Clo. LE10 18 A4
Crossland Row. LE10 20 E1
Crossways. LE10 20 D2
Crownhill Rd. LE10 20 B3
Cumbrae Dri. LE10 18 B3
Curzon Clo. LE10 19 F6
Dahlia Clo. LE10 20 C1
Dale End Clo. LE10 18 A5
Damson Ct. LE10 18 B5
*Dares Walk, Albert Rd. LE10 18 D4
Darley Rd. LE10 20 C1
Dart Clo. LE10 18 B5
Darwin Clo. LE10 19 E1
Davenport Ter. LE10 19 E4
De Montfort Rd. LE10 19 E3
De-la-Bere Cres. LE10 20 F1
Dean Ct. LE10 19 E3
Dean Rd. LE10 19 E3
Denis Rd. LE10 20 A1
Denmore Dri. LE10 18 B3
Derby Rd. LE10 18 D3
Deveron Way. LE10 18 B3
Dorchester Rd. LE10 19 H6
Dove Clo. LE10 18 A5
Drake Way. LE10 18 D1
Druid Pl. LE10 18 D4
Druid St. LE10 18 D4
Dudley Rise. LE10 18 D6
Dunblane Way. LE10 18 B3
Duport Rd. LE10 19 F5
East Clo. LE10 18 D6
Eastwoods Rd. LE10 19 F3
Edale Grn. LE10 20 D1
Edendale Dri. LE10 19 E1
Edward Rd. LE10 18 C2
Elizabeth Rd. LE10 18 D2
Elm Tree Dri. LE10 19 F5
Embleton Clo. LE10 18 B4
Erskine Clo. LE10 18 A3
Eskdale Rd. LE10 18 A5
Fabius Clo. LE10 18 C5
Factory Rd. LE10 18 D3
Fairways Ct. LE10 19 G2
Falconers Grn. LE10 20 D1
Falmouth Dri. LE10 19 E1
Far Lash. LE10 19 F6
Farm Rd. LE10 20 C1
Farneway. LE10 18 B4
Farriers Way. LE10 20 D1
Featherston Dri. LE10 18 D6
Ferneley Av. LE10 18 B2
Ferness Clo. LE10 18 B3
Ferness Rd. LE10 18 B3
Field Clo. LE10 19 F1
Flamville Rd. LE10 20 F2
Fletcher Rd. LE10 19 E6
Forest Rd. LE10 19 F5
Forresters Clo. LE10 20 D1
Forresters Rd. LE10 20 D1
Forryan Rd. LE10 19 F6
Frederick Av. LE10 18 B2
Freemans La. LE10 20 E2
Freswick Clo. LE10 18 A3
Friary Clo. LE10 19 E4
Frith Way. LE10 18 A2
Frobisher Clo. LE10 18 D1
Gabden Rd. LE10 18 D3
Gainsborough Av. LE10 18 A2
Garden Clo. LE10 18 D6
George St. LE10 18 D5
Gladstone Clo. LE10 19 E1
Gladstone Ter. LE10 19 E4
Glebe Rd. LE10 19 F4
Glen Bank. LE10 19 E4
Glenbarr Clo. LE10 18 A4
Glenbarr Dri. LE10 18 A4
Goosehills Rd. LE10 20 C2
Gopal Rd. LE10 18 D3
Gowrie Clo. LE10 18 B3
Granby Clo. LE10 18 C5
Granby Rd. LE10 18 C5
Grange Dri. LE10 20 C2
Granville Gdns. LE10 18 C5
Greenmoor Rd. LE10 20 B1
Grosvenor Cres. LE10 20 E1
Grove Park. LE10 20 E1
Grove Rd. LE10 20 E1
Gwendoline Av. LE10 18 A2
Halbert Clo. LE10 20 B2
Hall Rd. LE10 20 B1
Hamilton Clo. LE10 18 B3
Hangmans La. LE10 19 E1
Hanover Ct. LE10 20 C1
Hansom Ct. LE10 18 D4
Hanson Rd. LE10 19 F3
Hardy Clo. LE10 19 D1
Hartington Grn. LE10 20 C1
Harwood Dri. LE10 19 F1
Hawkins Clo. LE10 18 D1
Hawley Rd. LE10 18 D6
Hawthorn Cres. LE10 20 C2
Hays La. LE10 18 B5
Henry St. LE10 18 A2
Herald Way. LE10 20 B2
Hereford Way. LE10 19 F6
Higham Way. LE10 19 E6
Highfields Rd. LE10 19 E4
Hill St. LE10 19 E4
Hillrise. LE10 19 F5
Hillside Rd. LE10 20 B1
Hinckley Rd. LE10 19 G6
Hogarth Clo. LE10 18 A2
Hogarth Dri. LE10 18 A2
Holliers Walk. LE10 18 D4
Holly Clo. LE10 20 C2
Hollycroft. LE10 18 C3
Hollycroft Cres. LE10 18 C3
Holt Rd. LE10 19 E6
Horsepool. LE10 20 E1
Hurst Rd. LE10 18 D5
Hyacinth Way. LE10 20 B1
Ilminster Clo. LE10 19 H6
INDUSTRIAL ESTATES:
Nutts La Trading Est. LE10 18 A6
Sapcote Rd Ind Est. LE10 19 G5
Sketchley La Ind Est. LE10 20 A2
Sketchley Meadows Business Pk. LE10 20 A2
Iris Clo. LE10 20 C2
Island Clo. LE10 19 E3
Jarvis Clo. LE10 18 D1
Jefferies Clo. LE10 19 E3
Jelicoe Way. LE10 18 D1
John Nichols St. LE10 18 B6
John St. LE10 19 E3
Johns Clo. LE10 20 B2
Kent Dri. LE10 19 E1
Kestrel Clo. LE10 20 D1
Kilberry Clo. LE10 18 A3
Kilby Grn. LE10 20 D1
Kilmarie Clo. LE10 18 A4
King Georges Way. LE10 18 B6
King Richard Rd. LE10 18 C3
King St. LE10 18 D4
Kingston Dri. LE10 19 E1
Kinross Way. LE10 18 A4
Kintyre Clo. LE10 18 B3
Kirfield Dri. LE10 19 F2
Knapton Clo. LE10 18 A2
Knights Clo. LE10 20 B2
Lancaster Rd. LE10 18 D5
Lance Clo. LE10 20 B2
Landseer Dri. LE10 18 B2
Laneside Clo. LE10 19 F1
Laneside Dri. LE10 19 F2
Langdale Rd. LE10 18 A5
Lash Hill Path. LE10 19 F6
Lawns Wood. LE10 18 A5
Lawton Clo 18 A4
Leicester Rd. LE10 19 E4
Leven Clo. LE10 18 B4
Leysmill Clo. LE10 18 A4
Library Clo. LE10 20 E2
Lilac Clo. LE10 20 C1
Linden Rd. LE10 18 C4
Linwood Clo. LE10 18 B3
Lismore Dri. LE10 18 C3
Lobelia Clo. LE10 20 C1
Lochmore Clo. LE10 18 A4
Lochmore Dri. LE10 18 A4
Lochmore Way. LE10 18 A4
Lodge Clo. LE10 20 E2
Lomond Clo. LE10 18 B4
London Rd. LE10 19 E4
Lossiemouth Rd. LE10 18 A4
Love La. LE10 20 E1
Lower Bond St. LE10 18 D4
Lucas Rd. LE10 20 B1
Lundy Clo. LE10 18 B4
Lupin Clo. LE10 20 B1
Lutterworth Rd. LE10 20 E2
Lychgate Clo. LE10 20 E2
Lychgate La. LE10 20 E2
Lyndhurst Clo. LE10 19 G6
Lyneham Clo. LE10 18 B4
Magee Clo. LE10 18 D2
Maizefield. LE10 18 C1
Manor Clo. LE10 20 A2
Manor Pl. LE10 18 D4
Manor St. LE10 18 D4
Manor Way. LE10 20 B2
Mansion St. LE10 18 D4
Maple Clo. LE10 20 C2
Marchant Rd. LE10 18 C5
Marigold Dri. LE10 20 C2
Market Pl. LE10 18 D4
Marlborough Clo. LE10 19 G6
Marywell Clo. LE10 18 A4
Mason Ct. LE10 18 C5
Meadow Dri. LE10 19 G6
Melrose Clo. LE10 18 B4
Merevale Av. LE10 18 C5
Merrick Ct. LE10 20 D2
Merrifield Gdns. LE10 20 C2
Middlefield Clo. LE10 18 D3
Middlefield Ct. LE10 18 D3
Middlefield La. LE10 18 D2
Middlefield Pl. LE10 18 D2
Mill Hill Rd. LE10 18 C4
Mill View. LE10 19 E4
Millais Rd. LE10 18 B2
Millers Grn. LE10 20 D1
Milton Clo. LE10 18 C4
Mistral Clo. LE10 19 F5
Moray Clo. LE10 18 B4
Morland Dri. LE10 18 B2
Mount Rd. LE10 18 D5
Munnings Dri. LE10 18 B2
Nelson Dri. LE10 19 D1
Netherley Rd. LE10 18 D2
New Bldgs. LE10 18 D4
New Rd. LE10 20 E1
New St. LE10 18 D3
Newquay Clo. LE10 19 E1
Newstead Av. LE10 20 B3
Norfolk Clo. LE10 20 C3
Normandy Way. LE10 18 A2
North Clo. LE10 20 C1
Northfield Rd. LE10 18 C5
Norwood Clo. LE10 19 F1
Nutts La. LE10 18 A6
Oaks Clo. LE10 20 C2
Oban Rd. LE10 18 A6
Orchard Clo. LE10 20 E2
Orchard St. LE10 19 E4
Orkney Clo. LE10 18 C4
Osbaston Clo. LE10 19 F2
Outlands Dri. LE10 18 A3
Paddock La. LE10 20 D2
Palmer Rd. LE10 18 B3
Park Rd. LE10 19 E5
Parsons La. LE10 19 E5
Pennant Rd. LE10 20 B2
Pentland Clo. LE10 18 B4
Penzance Clo. LE10 19 E1

Pike Clo. LE10	20 B2	Swains Grn. LE10	20 D1	Beech Way. LE67	17 A2	Mill La. DE74	17 C5
Pilgrims Gate. LE10	20 E1	Swinburne Rd. LE10	18 C4	Bernard Clo. LE67	17 B3	Moore Av. DE74	17 C4
Portland Dri. LE10	19 E1	Sycamore Clo. LE10	20 C2	Brick Kiln La. LE67	17 B3	New Brickyard La.	
Preston Rd. LE10	18 B2	Tame Way. LE10	18 A5	Brookside Cres. LE67	17 B2	DE74	17 B6
Priesthills Rd. LE10	18 D5	Teign Bank Clo. LE10	18 D2	Cedar Dri. LE67	17 A2	New St. DE74	17 C4
Primrose Dri. LE10	20 C1	Teign Bank Rd. LE10	18 D2	Central Av. LE67	17 B2	Nine Acres. DE74	17 A5
Princess Rd. LE10	19 E5	Tennyson Rd. LE10	18 C4	Chapel St. LE67	17 B2	Norman Ct. DE74	17 B6
Priory Walk. LE10	19 E4	The Borough. LE10	18 D4	Chestnut Clo. LE67	17 A2	Nottingham Rd. DE74	17 B4
Pughes Clo. LE10	20 E1	The Butwoods. LE10	19 F5	Christopher Clo. LE67	17 B1	Oldershaw Av. DE74	17 B5
Pyeharps Rd. LE10	20 C2	The Coppice. LE10	19 F5	Church View. LE67	17 A3	Packington Hill. DE74	17 A4
Queens Park Ter. LE10	19 E4	The Fairway. LE10	19 F5	Copson St. LE67	17 B3	Peppers Dri. DE74	17 A5
Queens Rd. LE10	19 E5	The Grove. LE10	18 C5	Costello Clo. LE67	17 C1	Pleasant Pl. DE74	17 B5
Radmore Rd. LE10	18 D2	The Horse Fair. LE10	18 D5	Curzon St. LE67	17 B2	Plummer La. DE74	17 B5
Raleigh Clo. LE10	18 D1	The Lawns. LE10	19 E4	Deepdale Clo. LE67	17 B2	Queens Rd. DE74	17 B5
Ramsey Clo. LE10	18 B4	The Meadow. LE10	19 F5	Douglas Dri. LE67	17 B3	Roberts Clo. DE74	17 B6
Rannoch Clo. LE10	18 B4	The Meadows. LE10	19 G6	Dryer Clo. LE67	17 B3	Ropewalk. DE74	17 B5
Ratcliffe Rd. LE10	20 D1	*The Narrows,		East Walk. LE67	17 B2	St Andrews Rd. DE74	17 B6
Reeves Rd. LE10	20 D1	Hill St. LE10	19 E4	Elizabeth Av. LE67	17 B1	Shepherd Walk. DE74	17 B6
Regency Ct. LE10	19 G6	The Ridgeway. LE10	20 B1	Elm Clo. LE67	17 A2	Sibson Dri. DE74	17 A5
*Regent Ct,		The Rills. LE10	19 E3	Fairfield. LE67	17 B3	Side Lea. DE74	17 B4
Regent St. LE10	18 D5	The Spindles. LE10	20 D2	Ferndale. LE67	17 A2	Springfield. DE74	17 A5
Regent St. LE10	18 D5	Thirlmere Rd. LE10	18 A5	Gamble Clo. LE67	17 B1	Staffords Acres. DE74	17 B5
Reynolds Clo. LE10	18 B2	Thornfield Way. LE10	19 E5	Gladstone St. LE67	17 B3	Station Rd. DE74	17 C4
Ribblesdale Av. LE10	19 E2	Thorny Croft Rd. LE10	19 E5	Glen Av. LE67	17 B3	Stone Hills. DE74	17 A5
Richmond Rd. LE10	18 C2	Three Pots Rd. LE10	20 C3	Grange Rd. LE67	17 B3	Suthers Rd. DE74	17 A5
Riddon Dri. LE10	18 B4	Tilton Rd. LE10	20 C1	Hall St. LE67	17 A3	Sutton Rd. DE74	17 B6
Robinson Way. LE10	20 D2	Torridon Way. LE10	18 B3	Harrats Clo. LE67	17 B3	The Croft. DE74	17 B5
Rodney Clo. LE10	18 D1	Trafford Rd. LE10	19 F3	Hawthorne Dri. LE67	17 A3	The Osiers. DE74	17 C5
Romney Clo. LE10	18 A2	Trent Av. LE10	18 A5	Heatherdale. LE67	17 A2	Thomas Rd. DE74	17 B6
Rosemary Way. LE10	18 B5	Trent Rd. LE10	18 A5	Hextall Dri. LE67	17 B3	Walton Ct. DE74	17 A2
Rosewood Clo. LE10	19 F6	Trevor Rd. LE10	19 F4	High St. LE67	17 A3	West Bank Mws. DE74	17 A5
Roston Dri. LE10	18 A4	Trinity La. LE10	18 C5	Hinckley Rd. LE67	17 A3	Whatton Rd. DE74	17 A6
Royal Ct. LE10	18 D5	Trinity Vicarage Rd.		Jacques Rd. LE67	17 B1	Windmill Way. DE74	17 A5
Rufford Clo. LE10	20 B3	LE10	18 C4	Laud Clo. LE67	17 A3	Wyvelle Cres. DE74	17 B4
Rugby Rd. LE10	18 C5	Truro Clo. LE10	19 E1	Legion Dri. LE67	17 B3		
Rutland Av. LE10	18 C6	Tudor Rd. LE10	18 C2	Leicester Rd. LE67	17 B2		
Rydale Clo. LE10	18 A5	Turner Dri. LE10	18 A2	Linden Clo. LE67	17 A2	LEICESTER	
Saddlers Clo. LE10	20 D1	Tweedside Clo. LE10	19 F1	Maple Dri. LE67	17 A2	CITY CENTRE	
St Catherine Clo. LE10	19 F6	Twycross Rd. LE10	20 D1	Meadow Walk. LE67	17 B2		
St Georges Av. LE10	18 C4	Upper Bond St. LE10	18 D4	Melbourne Rd. LE67	17 A3		
St James Clo. LE10	20 B2	Victoria Rd. LE10	20 D2	Oak Dri. LE67	17 A2	Abbey St. LE1	21 B2
St Martins. LE10	20 B1	Victoria St. LE10	19 E3	Orchard St. LE67	17 B3	Abbey Walk. LE1	21 B1
St Marys Rd. LE10	18 D5	Villa Clo. LE10	20 D2	Paget Rd. LE67	17 B1	Albion St. LE1	21 C4
St Pauls Gdn. LE10	18 C4	Walney Clo. LE10	18 B3	Parkdale. LE67	17 A2	Alfred Pl. LE1	21 B1
Salem Rd. LE10	20 D2	Warwick Gdns. LE10	19 E1	Penistone St. LE67	17 B1	All Saints Open. LE1	21 A2
Salisbury Rd. LE10	19 G6	Waterfield Way. LE10	20 A2	Pretoria Rd. LE67	17 C2	All Saints Rd. LE3	21 A3
Sandford Clo. LE10	19 F4	Waterloo Rd. LE10	18 D5	Ravenstone Rd. LE67	17 B1	Andover St. LE2	21 D5
Sandy Cres. LE10	18 C4	Watling Clo. LE10	20 A2	Redlands Est. LE67	17 C1	Ann St. LE1	21 D3
Sandy Walk. LE10	18 B3	Watling St. LE10	20 A3	Reform St. LE67	17 A3	Apple Gate. LE1	21 A4
Sapcote Rd. LE10	19 G5	Waveney Clo. LE10	18 B5	Rowan Dri. LE67	17 A2	Archdeacon La. LE1	21 C1
Saville Clo. LE10	19 E2	Welbeck Av. LE10	20 B3	St Denys Cres. LE67	17 A3	Arnhem St. LE1	21 D5
School Clo. LE10	20 E1	Well La. LE10	18 D4	Slaybarns Way. LE67	17 B2	Ashwell St. LE1	21 D5
Seaforth Dri. LE10	18 A3	Welwyn Rd. LE10	19 F4	Spring Rd. LE67	17 C2	Atkins St. LE2	21 B6
Seaton Clo. LE10	19 G6	Wendover Dri. LE10	19 E1	Springfield Clo. LE67	17 B2	Bath La. LE3	21 A4
Severn Av. LE10	18 B5	Wensum Clo. LE10	18 B5	Station Rd. LE67	17 A2	Bay St. LE1	21 B1
Shakespeare Dri. LE10	18 C4	Wentworth Clo. LE10	19 E2	Sunnyside. LE67	17 A3	Bedford St Nth. LE1	21 C1
Sharpless Rd. LE10	18 E6	Wesley Walk. LE10	20 E1	Swifts Clo. LE67	17 B3	Bedford St Sth. LE1	21 C1
Sheepy Clo. LE10	19 F4	West Clo. LE10	18 D6	Sycamore Clo. LE67	17 A2	Belgrave Gate. LE1	21 C1
Shelley Gdns. LE10	19 E2	Westfield Ct. LE10	18 C6	The Hastings. LE67	17 B2	Belvoir St. LE1	21 C4
Sherborne Rd. LE10	19 H6	Westfield Rd. LE10	18 C6	The New Row. LE67	17 B3	Berkley St. LE1	21 A2
Sisley Way. LE10	18 B2	Westminster Dri. LE10	20 D2	Thomas St. LE67	17 B3	Berridge St. LE1	21 B4
Sketchley Hall Gdns.		Weston Clo. LE10	18 B4	Thorndale. LE67	17 A3	Bishop St. LE1	21 C4
LE10	20 A2	Westray Dri. LE10	18 C4	Thornham Gro. LE67	17 B2	Blake St. LE1	21 B2
Sketchley La. LE10	20 A2	Wheatfield Way. LE10	18 C1	Valley Rd. LE67	17 A3	Bonners La. LE1	21 B5
Sketchley Manor La.		William Iliffe St. LE10	18 B6	Victoria Rd. LE67	17 B1	Bowling Green St. LE1	21 C4
LE10	20 B2	Willow Clo. LE10	20 C2	West Walk. LE67	17 B2	Bowmars La. LE1	21 A1
Sketchley Meadows.		Willowbank Clo. LE10	18 C5	Willow Way. LE67	17 A2	Britannia St. LE1	21 C1
LE10	20 A2	Willowdale. LE10	18 A5	Winchester Ct. LE67	17 B1	Brougham St. LE1	21 D2
Sketchley Old Village.		Winchester Dri. LE10	19 G6			Burgess St. LE1	21 A2
LE10	20 A2	Windrush Dri. LE10	18 A5			Burleys Flyover. LE1	21 B2
Sketchley Rd. LE10	20 C2	Windsor Ct. LE10	20 E2	KEGWORTH		Burleys Way. LE1	21 B2
Soarway. LE10	18 A5	Windsor St. LE10	20 E2			Burton St. LE1	21 D3
Southfield Rd. LE10	18 D6	Woburn Clo. LE10	19 E1			Butt Clo La. LE1	21 B2
Spa Clo. LE10	18 A5	Wolvey Rd. LE10	20 C3	Bedford Clo. DE74	17 B6	Byron St. LE1	21 C3
Spa La. LE10	19 E4	Wood St. LE10	18 D4	Borough St. DE74	17 B5	Calais Hill. LE1	21 C5
Spencer St. LE10	18 D4	Wood St Clo. LE10	19 E4	Borrowell. DE74	17 B4	Calais St. LE1	21 C5
Spinney Rd. LE10	20 A1	Woodfield Rd. LE10	20 A1	Bridge Fields. DE74	17 C5	Calgary Rd. LE1	21 D1
Springfield Rd. LE10	18 D5	Woodgate Rd. LE10	19 F5	Broadhill Rd. DE74	17 B4	Camden St. LE1	21 C3
Squires Grn. LE10	20 D1	Woodland Av. LE10	19 G6	Bulstode Pl. DE74	17 B5	Campbell St. LE1	21 D4
Stanley Rd. LE10	18 C2	Woodland Rd. LE10	19 F3	Burley Rise. DE74	17 B6	Cank St. LE1	21 B4
Station Rd. LE10	18 D5	Woodstock Clo. LE10	20 E1	Citrus Gro. DE74	17 B4	Canning Pl. LE1	21 B1
Stirling Av. LE10	18 A4	Woolbank. LE10	19 G6	Derby Rd. DE74	17 A4	Canning St. LE1	21 B1
Stockwell Head. LE10	18 D4	Workhouse La. LE10	20 E2	Dragwell. DE74	17 B5	Careys Clo. LE1	21 A4
Stoke Rd. LE10	18 B1	Wye Clo. LE10	18 A5	Foxhills. DE74	17 A6	Carlton St. LE1	21 C4
Stoneygate Dri. LE10	19 E2	Wykin Rd. LE10	18 A2	Frederick Av. DE74	17 B4	Carts La. LE1	21 B4
Strathmore Rd. LE10	18 A6	York Rd. LE10	18 D2	Gerrard Cres. DE74	17 B6	Castle La. LE1	21 A4
Stretton Clo. LE10	20 B1	Zealand Clo. LE10	19 F1	Heafield Dri. DE74	17 B5	Castle View. LE1	21 A5
Strutt Rd. LE10	20 E2			High St. DE74	17 A5	Castle Yard. LE1	21 A4
Sunnydale Cres. LE10	18 A5			Hillside. DE74	17 B6	Causeway La. LE1	21 A3
Sunnydale Rd. LE10	18 A5	IBSTOCK		Kingston La. DE74	17 D4	Chancery St. LE1	21 B4
Sunnyhill. LE10	19 F6			Kirby Dri. DE74	17 B6	Charles St. LE1	21 C3
Sunnyhill Sth. LE10	19 F6			Kirk Av. DE74	17 C5	Charter St. LE1	21 C1
Sunnyside. LE10	19 E2	Albert St. LE67	17 B1	Langley Dri. DE74	17 A5	Chatham St. LE1	21 C5
Sunnyside Park. LE10	19 E2	Argyle St. LE67	17 B1	Leatherlands. DE74	17 B5	Cheapside. LE1	21 B4
Surrey Clo. LE10	20 C3	Ashby Rd. LE67	17 A1	London Rd. DE74	17 C6	Christow St. LE1	21 D2
Sutton Clo. LE10	19 F2	Ashdale. LE67	17 A2	Long La. DE74	17 B4	Church Gate. LE1	21 B2

Church St. LE1	21 D4	
Clarence St. LE1	21 C3	
Clarendon St. LE2	21 A6	
Clyde St. LE1	21 D2	
Colton St. LE1	21 C4	
Conduit St. LE2	21 D5	
Constitution Hill. LE1	21 D4	
Crafton St East. LE1	21 D2	
Crafton St West. LE1	21 D2	
Crane St. LE1	21 B2	
Craven St. LE1	21 A1	
Crescent St. LE1	21 C6	
Cumberland St. LE1	21 A2	
Darker St. LE1	21 B2	
De Montfort Mws. LE1	21 D6	
De Montfort Pl. LE1	21 D6	
De Montfort Sq. LE1	21 D6	
De Montfort St. LE1	21 D6	
Deacon St. LE2	21 A6	
Dover St. LE1	21 C5	
Duns St. LE1	21 C2	
Duke St. LE1	21 B5	
Dunkirk St. LE1	21 C5	
Earl St. LE1	21 C3	
East Bond St. LE1	21 B2	
East Gates. LE1	21 B3	
East St. LE1	21 C5	
Eastern Blvd. LE2	21 A6	
Edmonton Rd. LE1	21 D2	
Elbow La. LE1	21 A2	
Eldon St. LE1	21 C3	
Erskine St. LE1	21 D3	
Every St. LE1	21 C4	
Fleet St. LE1	21 C2	
Foundry La. LE1	21 C1	
Fox La. LE1	21 C3	
Fox St. LE1	21 D4	
Fraser Clo. LE1	21 D1	
Free La. LE1	21 C3	
Freeschool La. LE1	21 A3	
Friar La. LE1	21 A4	
Friars Causeway. LE1	21 A3	
Friday St. LE1	21 A1	
Gallowtree Gate. LE1	21 B3	
Garden St. LE1	21 C2	
Gas St. LE1	21 C1	
Gateway St. LE2	21 A5	
George St. LE1	21 C1	
Gladstone St. LE1	21 D2	
Glebe St. LE2	21 D4	
Gosling St. LE2	21 A5	
Gower St. LE1	21 C2	
Grafton Pl. LE1	21 B1	
Granby Pl. LE1	21 C4	
Granby St. LE1	21 C4	
Grange La. LE2	21 B5	
Grape St. LE1	21 B2	
Grasmere St. LE2	21 A6	
Gravel St. LE1	21 B2	
Gray St. LE2	21 A5	
Great Central St. LE1	21 A2	
Greyfriars. LE1	21 B4	
Grosvenor St. LE1	21 C1	
Guildhall La. LE1	21 A4	
Halford St. LE1	21 C4	
Hannah Ct. LE1	21 C3	
Harding St. LE1	21 A1	
Harveys Walk. LE1	21 A4	
Havelock St. LE2	21 A6	
Haymarket. LE1	21 B3	
Heanor St. LE1	21 A1	
Henshaw St. LE2	21 B6	
High St. LE1	21 A3	
Highcross St. LE1	21 A2	
Hill St. LE1	21 C3	
Holy Bones. LE1	21 A3	
Horsefair St. LE1	21 B4	
Hotel St. LE1	21 B4	
Humberstone Gate.		
LE1	21 B3	
Humberstone Rd. LE5	21 D3	
Infirmary Clo. LE1	21 B6	
Infirmary Rd. LE1	21 B6	
Infirmary Sq. LE1	21 B6	
Jarrom St. LE2	21 A6	
Johnson St. LE1	21 A1	
Jubilee Rd. LE1	21 C2	
Junction Rd. LE1	21 D1	
Junior St. LE1	21 A2	
Kamloops Cres. LE1	21 D1	
Kildare St. LE1	21 C3	
King St. LE1	21 B5	
Labrador Clo. LE1	21 D2	
Langton St. LE1	21 C2	
Lee Circle. LE1	21 C2	
Lethbridge Clo. LE1	21 D2	

43

Lichfield St. LE1 21 B2
London Rd. LE2 21 D5
Long La. LE1 21 A2
Loseby La. LE1 21 B4
Lower Brown St. LE1 21 B5
Lower Free La. LE1 21 C3
Lower Garden St. LE1 21 C2
Lower Hastings St. LE1 21 C6
Lower Hill St. LE1 21 C2
Lower Lee St. LE1 21 C2
Mackenzie Way. LE1 21 D1
Malcolm Arc. LE1 21 B3
Manitoba Rd. LE1 21 D2
Mansfield St. LE1 21 B2
Marble St. LE1 21 B4
Market Pl. LE1 21 B4
Market Pl App. LE1 21 C4
Market Pl Sth. LE1 21 B4
Market St. LE1 21 B4
Marlborough St. LE1 21 B5
Marquis St. LE1 21 C5
Melton St. LE1 21 C1
Memory La. LE1 21 C1
Midland St. LE1 21 D3
Mill La. LE2 21 A6
Mill St. LE1 21 B5
Millstone La. LE1 21 B4
Monckton Clo. LE1 21 D1
Montreal Rd. LE1 21 D1
Morgan Ct. LE1 21 A3
Morledge St. LE1 21 D3
Museum Sq. LE1 21 C5
Navigation St. LE1 21 C1
Needlegate. LE1 21 A2
Nelson St. LE1 21 D5
New Bond St. LE1 21 B3
New Parliament St. LE1 21 C2
New Rd. LE1 21 B2
New St. LE1 21 B4
New Walk. LE1 21 C5
Newarke Clo. LE2 21 A5
Newarke St. LE1 21 B5
Newport Pl. LE1 21 C4
Newtown St. LE1 21 C6
Nichols St. LE1 21 D3
Northampton Sq. LE1 21 C4
Northampton St. LE1 21 C4
Northgate St. LE3 21 A2
Northgates. LE1 21 A2
Northumberland St. LE1 21 A2
Norton St. LE1 21 B5
Odeon Arc. LE1 21 B4
Old Mill La. LE1 21 A2
Old Milton St. LE1 21 C2
Ontario Clo. LE1 21 D1
Orchard St. LE1 21 D2
Ottawa Rd. LE1 21 D2
Oxford St. LE1 21 B5
Park St. LE1 21 C5
Pasture La. LE1 21 A2
Peacock La. LE1 21 A4
Pelham St. LE1 21 B6
Pelham Way. LE1 21 B6
Pocklingtons Walk. LE1 21 B4
Potter St. LE1 21 D3
Prebend St. LE1 21 D5
Princess Rd East. LE1 21 D6
Princess Rd West. LE1 21 C5
Quebec St. LE1 21 D2
Queen St. LE1 21 D3
Rawson St. LE1 21 C6
Regent Rd. LE1 21 B5
Regent St. LE1 21 D5
Richmond St. LE2 21 A5
Royal Arc. LE1 21 B3
Royal East St. LE1 21 C2
Rupert St. LE1 21 B4
Russell Sq. LE1 21 D1
Rutland St. LE1 21 C4
Rydal St. LE1 21 A6
St Augustine Rd. LE3 21 A4
St George St. LE1 21 D4
St Georges Way. LE1 21 D4
St James St. LE1 21 C3
St John St. LE1 21 B1
St Margarets St. LE1 21 B2
St Margarets Way. LE1 21 A1
St Mark St. LE1 21 C1
St Martins. LE1 21 B4
St Martins East. LE1 21 A4
St Martins West. LE1 21 A4
St Matthews Way. LE1 21 C2
St Nicholas Circle. LE1 21 A4
St Nicholas Pl. LE1 21 A4

St Peters La. LE1 21 A3
Samuel St. LE1 21 D3
Sandacre St. LE1 21 B2
Sanvey Gate. LE1 21 A2
*Shackleton St,
  Woodboy St. LE1 21 C1
Shires La. LE1 21 B3
Short St. LE1 21 B2
Silver Arc. LE1 21 B3
Silver St. LE1 21 B3
Slate St. LE2 21 D5
Slater St. LE3 21 A1
Soar La. LE3 21 A2
South Albion St. LE1 21 C5
South Church Gate.
  LE1 21 B1
Southampton St. LE1 21 D3
Southgates. LE1 21 A4
Stamford St. LE1 21 C4
Station St. LE1 21 D5
Swain St. LE1 21 D4
Talbot La. LE1 21 A4
Taylor Rd. LE1 21 D1
Thames St. LE1 21 C1
The Crescent. LE1 21 C5
The Gateway. LE2 21 A5
The Newarke. LE2 21 A5
The Oval. LE1 21 D6
Thornton Walk. LE1 21 A4
Toronto Clo. LE1 21 D1
Tower St. LE1 21 C6
Trinity La. LE1 21 C6
Turner St. LE1 21 C6
Ullswater St. LE2 21 A6
Upper Brown St. LE1 21 B5
Upper George St. LE1 21 D1
Upper King St. LE1 21 C6
Upper Nelson St. LE1 21 D6
Vaughan Way. LE1 21 A3
Vestry St. LE1 21 C3
Victoria Par. LE1 21 B3
Vine St. LE1 21 A2
Wanlip St. LE1 21 D1
Waterloo Way. LE1 21 C6
Watling St. LE1 21 B1
Welford Pl. LE1 21 B5
Welford Rd. LE1 21 B5
Welles St. LE1 21 A3
Wellington St. LE1 21 C5
West St. LE1 21 C6
West Walk. LE1 21 D6
Wharf St Nth. LE1 21 D2
Wharf St Sth. LE1 21 C2
Wheat St. LE1 21 D2
Wigston St. LE1 21 A2
William St. LE1 21 D3
Willow St. LE1 21 C1
Wilton St. LE1 21 C2
Wimbledon St. LE1 21 D3
Winifred St. LE2 21 A6
Wood St. LE1 21 C2
Woodboy St. LE1 21 C1
Wycliffe St. LE1 21 B4
Yarmouth St. LE1 21 C1
Yeoman La. LE1 21 C3
Yeoman St. LE1 21 C3
York Rd. LE1 21 B5
York St. LE1 21 C3
Yukon Way. LE1 21 D1

LOUGHBOROUGH

Abberton Way. LE11 22 A4
Acer Clo. LE11 23 F6
Afton Clo. LE11 22 B3
Alan Moss Rd. LE11 22 C2
Albany St. LE11 22 D1
Albert Pl. LE11 23 F3
Albert Prom. LE11 23 G3
Albert St. LE11 23 F3
Alfred St. LE11 23 F3
Allsops La. LE11 23 H2
Althorpe Dri. LE11 22 B2
Ambleside Clo. LE11 22 C5
Amis Clo. LE11 22 B1
Angus Dri. LE11 22 D3
Annies Wharf. LE11 23 G1
Archer Clo. LE11 23 E2
Armitage Clo. LE11 23 E2
Arthur St. LE11 23 F3
Ashby Cres. LE11 22 C3
Ashby Rd. LE11 22 C3
Ashby Sq. LE11 23 F2
Ashdown Clo. LE11 22 C2

Ashleigh Dri. LE11 22 D4
Aspen Av. LE11 23 F6
Atherstone Rd. LE11 23 E6
Aumberry Gap. LE11 23 G3
Avon Vale Rd. LE11 23 G4
Badger Ct. LE11 22 D6
Bailey Clo. LE11 22 D6
Bainbridge Rd. LE11 23 G5
Bampton St. LE11 23 F3
Barden Clo. LE11 22 B3
Barrack Row. LE11 23 G2
Barrow St. LE11 23 G3
Barsby Dri. LE11 22 D1
Baxter Gate. LE11 23 F2
Beacon Av. LE11 23 E5
Beacon Clo. LE11 23 E5
Beacon Dri. LE11 23 F5
Beacon Rd. LE11 23 E6
Beaufort Av. LE11 23 E6
Beaumont Rd. LE11 23 F6
Bedford St. LE11 23 F3
Beeches Rd. LE11 23 G4
Beehive La. LE11 23 F3
Belmont Way. LE11 22 A4
Belton Rd. LE11 23 E1
Belton Rd West. LE11 23 E1
Belvoir Dri. LE11 23 E6
Benscliffe Dri. LE11 22 D4
Berkeley Rd. LE11 22 C6
Biggin St. LE11 23 F2
Bishop St. LE11 23 G2
Blackbrook Ct. LE11 22 D1
Blackbrook Rd. LE11 22 C3
Blackham Rd. LE11 23 F5
Blake Dri. LE11 22 D1
Blenheim Clo. LE11 22 C2
Blithfield Av. LE11 22 D3
Bluebell Clo. LE11 23 E5
Bond Clo. LE11 23 G5
Borrowdale Way. LE11 22 C5
Bottleacre La. LE11 23 F1
Boyer St. LE11 23 G2
Braddon Rd. LE11 22 C1
Bradgate Rd. LE11 22 D6
Bridge St. LE11 23 F2
*Bridgeside Cotts,
  Canal Bank. LE11 23 F2
Brisco Av. LE11 23 E1
Broad St. LE11 23 F2
Broadway. LE11 23 F6
Bromhead St. LE11 23 G2
Brook La. LE11 22 C6
Brookfield Av. LE11 22 D5
Brookside Rd. LE11 22 D6
Browning Rd. LE11 22 C2
Browns La. LE11 23 F3
Buckingham Dri. LE11 22 B2
Buckingham Sq. LE11 23 G2
Burbage Clo. LE11 22 D1
Burder St. LE11 23 G1
Burfield Av. LE11 23 E3
Burleigh Rd. LE11 23 E3
Burns Rd. LE11 22 C2
Burton St. LE11 23 F4
Burton Walks. LE11 23 G4
Butterley Dri. LE11 22 B4
Byland Way. LE11 22 A1
Byron St. LE11 23 F2
Byron St Extension.
  LE11 22 D1
Cabin Leas. LE11 23 F1
Caldwell St. LE11 23 F3
Cambridge St. LE11 23 F2
Canal Bank. LE11 23 F2
Carington St. LE11 23 E1
Cartwright St. LE11 23 G1
Castledine St. LE11 23 G4
Castledine St Extension.
  LE11 23 G4
Cattlemarket. LE11 23 F3
Cedar Rd. LE11 23 H5
Chainbridge Clo. LE11 23 F1
Chapman St. LE11 23 G2
Charles St. LE11 23 F1
Charley Dri. LE11 22 D4
Charnwood Rd. LE11 23 F4
Charteris Clo. LE11 22 C1
Chatsworth Rd. LE11 22 C2
Chelker Way. LE11 22 B3
Chester Clo. LE11 23 E3
Chestnut St. LE11 23 E2
Chichester Clo. LE11 22 C6
Chiswick Dri. LE11 22 B2
Church Gate. LE11 23 F2
Church Lands. LE11 23 F1
Clarence St. LE11 23 G2

Cleeve Mount. LE11 22 B2
Cleveland Rd. LE11 23 E6
Cliff Av. LE11 23 E1
Clifford Rd. LE11 23 E1
Clowbridge Dri. LE11 22 B3
Cobden St. LE11 23 G3
Coe Av. LE11 22 B2
Colgrove Rd. LE11 23 E4
Compton Clo. LE11 22 B6
Coniston Cres. LE11 22 C5
*Connaught House,
  Victoria Pl. LE11 23 G3
Conway Clo. LE11 22 B2
Cookson Pl. LE11 22 C1
Cooper Ct. LE11 23 H4
Cothelstone Av. LE11 22 B2
Cotswold Clo. LE11 22 D3
Cottesmore Dri. LE11 23 E6
Cowdray Clo. LE11 23 F4
Craddock St. LE11 23 G2
Craven Clo. LE11 23 E6
Cricket La. LE11 22 D6
Croome Clo. LE11 23 G5
Cropston Av. LE11 22 A4
Cross Hill La. LE11 23 E5
Cross St. LE11 23 G2
Crosswood Clo. LE11 22 B3
Cumberland Rd. LE11 23 E2
Curzon St. LE11 23 F3
Cypress Clo. LE11 23 F6
De Lisle Ct. LE11 22 B4
De Montfort Clo. LE11 22 C1
Dead La. LE11 23 F2
Deane St. LE11 22 D1
Deanside Dri. LE11 22 D1
Deer Acre. LE11 23 F1
Derby Rd. LE11 22 D1
Derby Sq. LE11 23 F2
Derwent Dri. LE11 22 C5
Devonshire La. LE11 23 F3
*Devonshire Sq,
  Cattle Market. LE11 23 F3
Doyle Clo. LE11 22 C1
Duke St. LE11 23 G2
Dulverton Clo. LE11 22 C6
Duncan Way. LE11 22 B1
Dunholme Av. LE11 22 B2
Dunsmore Clo. LE11 22 C6
Durham Rd. LE11 22 D1
Easby Clo. LE11 22 B1
Edelin Rd. LE11 23 F5
Eden Clo. LE11 22 C1
Edward St. LE11 23 E1
Eliot Clo. LE11 22 B1
Elms Gro. LE11 23 G3
Empress Rd. LE11 23 G2
Epinal Way. LE11 22 C1
Exmoor Clo. LE11 22 C5
Eyebrook Clo. LE11 22 B4
Factory St. LE11 23 G3
Fairmount Dri. LE11 22 D4
Falcon St. LE11 23 G2
Farndale Dri. LE11 23 E6
Farnham Rd. LE11 23 F5
Fearon St. LE11 23 E2
Fennel St. LE11 23 F2
Finsbury Av. LE11 23 G3
Fleming Clo. LE11 22 C1
Forest Rd. LE11 22 D5
Forsyth Clo. LE11 22 B1
Fox Covert. LE11 23 F1
Foxcote Dri. LE11 22 A4
Frederick St. LE11 23 F3
Freehold St. LE11 23 G2
Gallico Clo. LE11 22 C1
Garendon Grn. LE11 22 C5
Garendon Rd. LE11 22 C2
Garton Rd. LE11 23 F3
Gavin Dri. LE11 22 C1
George St. LE11 23 E2
George Yd. LE11 23 F2
Gisboro Way. LE11 22 A1
Gladstone Av. LE11 23 F1
Gladstone St. LE11 23 F1
Glebe St. LE11 23 G1
Golding Clo. LE11 22 B1
Gordon Rd. LE11 23 G1
Grace-Dieu Rd. LE11 22 C3
Granby St. LE11 23 F3
Grange St. LE11 23 E3
Granville St. LE11 23 E3
Grasmere Rd. LE11 22 C5
Gray St. LE11 23 F3
Grassholme Dri. LE11 22 A4
Great Central Rd. LE11 23 G3
Green Clo La. LE11 23 F2

Gregory St. LE11 23 G3
Griggs Rd. LE11 23 F5
Grove Rd. LE11 22 D3
Guildford Way. LE11 22 B6
Hailey Av. LE11 22 B1
Hambledon Cres. LE11 23 E6
Hanford Way. LE11 23 G1
Hanover Ct. LE11 22 C1
Hardwick Dri. LE11 22 C2
Harlech Clo. LE11 22 D1
Havelock St. LE11 23 E2
Haydon Rd. LE11 22 D3
Hayward Av. LE11 23 H4
Hazel Rd. LE11 23 F6
Heathcote St. LE11 23 F3
Herbert St. LE11 23 F1
Hermitage Rd. LE11 22 B4
Herrick Rd. LE11 23 F4
Herriot Way. LE11 22 C1
High St. LE11 23 F2
Highfields Dri. LE11 22 D4
Hill Top Rd. LE11 22 D5
Hodson Ct. LE11 23 F4
Holbein Clo. LE11 23 G2
Holmfield Av. LE11 23 E1
Holt Dri. LE11 23 E4
Holywell Dri. LE11 22 C5
Hospital Way. LE11 22 D2
Howard Clo. LE11 22 C2
Howard St. LE11 23 F1
Howden Clo. LE11 22 A4
Howe Rd. LE11 23 F5
Hudson St. LE11 23 G2
Hume St. LE11 23 G2
Humphrey Clo. LE11 23 G4
Hurstwood Rd. LE11 22 B3
Huston Ct. LE11 23 F3
INDUSTRIAL ESTATES:
Belton Rd Ind Est.
  LE11 23 F1
James Av. LE11 22 B1
Japonica Clo. LE11 23 F6
Jetcott Av. LE11 23 E6
Johns Lee Clo. LE11 23 E5
Jordon Clo. LE11 22 D5
Jubilee Dri. LE11 23 E1
Judges St. LE11 23 H3
Keats Way. LE11 22 C1
Kenilworth Av. LE11 22 B2
Kensington Av. LE11 22 B2
Keswick Av. LE11 22 B2
King Edward Rd. LE11 23 G3
King George Av. LE11 23 H4
King George Rd. LE11 23 H4
King St. LE11 23 G3
Kingfisher Way. LE11 23 F6
Kings Av. LE11 23 E1
Kingswood Av. LE11 22 A1
Kinross Cres. LE11 22 C1
Kirkstone Dri. LE11 22 C5
Knightthorpe Rd. LE11 22 C2
Knipton Dri. LE11 22 B4
Ladybower Rd. LE11 22 B2
Lamport Clo. LE11 22 B2
Lanesborough Ct. LE11 23 F4
Laneshaw Clo. LE11 22 A4
Lansdowne Dri. LE11 23 F5
Leckhampton Rd. LE11 22 B2
Leconfield Rd. LE11 22 B6
Ledbury Rd. LE11 23 E6
Leicester Rd. LE11 23 G3
Leighton Av. LE11 22 B3
Lemyngton St. LE11 23 F2
Leopold St. LE11 23 F2
Lewis Rd. LE11 22 D1
Lilac Clo. LE11 23 F6
Lilleshall Way. LE11 22 B2
Lime Av. LE11 23 G3
Limehurst Av. LE11 23 F2

Linden Rd. LE11 23 F2
Lindisfarne Dri. LE11 22 A1
Linford Rd. LE11 22 D5
Ling Av. LE11 23 G5
Ling Rd. LE11 23 F5
Lisle St. LE11 23 H3
Little Moor La. LE11 23 H3
Longcliffe Gdns. LE11 22 A6
Lorrimer Way. LE11 22 D1
Lower Cambridge St.
  LE11 23 F1
Lower Gladstone St.
  LE11 23 F1
Lower Green. LE11 22 B6
Loweswater Dri. LE11 22 C5

Lowther Way. LE11 23 G5
Ludlow Clo. LE11 22 C6
Manor Dri. LE11 23 G6
Manor Rd. LE11 23 G6
Maple Rd. LE11 23 F6
Maple Rd North. LE11 23 F6
Maple Rd South. LE11 23 F6
Mardale Way. LE11 22 C5
Market Pl. LE11 23 F3
Market St. LE11 23 F2
Martindale Clo. LE11 22 D5
Maxwell Dri. LE11 22 B1
Mayfield Dri. LE11 23 F4
Mayo Clo. LE11 23 E6
Meadow Av. LE11 23 G1
Meadow La. LE11 23 G2
Melbreak Av. LE11 22 D6
Melville Clo. LE11 22 B1
Middle Av. LE11 23 E1
Middleton Pl. LE11 23 F4
Mildenhall Rd. LE11 22 B2
Mill La. LE11 23 G2
Milton St. LE11 22 D1
Mitchell Dri. LE11 22 B1
Moat Rd. LE11 22 D6
Moira St. LE11 23 G3
Monsarrat Way. LE11 22 C1
Montague Dri. LE11 22 B6
Moor La. LE11 23 G3
Morley St. LE11 23 G1
Morris Clo. LE11 23 H2
Mortimer Way. LE11 22 B1
Mount Grace Rd. LE11 22 B1
Mountfields Dri. LE11 22 D4
Nanpantan Rd. LE11 22 B6
Naseby Dri. LE11 22 A4
Navigation Way. LE11 23 F1
Naylor Av. LE11 23 H4
New Ashby Rd. LE11 22 A5
New King St. LE11 23 G3
New St. LE11 23 F3
Newbon Clo. LE11 22 D3
Nicolson Rd. LE11 22 B6
North Rd. LE11 23 G1
Nottingham Rd. LE11 23 G2
Nursery End. LE11 22 C6
Nutkin Clo. LE11 23 E4
Oakham Clo. LE11 22 D1
Oakhurst Ct. LE11 22 C2
Oaklands Av. LE11 23 E4
Oakley Dri. LE11 23 E5
Old Ashby Rd. LE11 22 A4
Oliver Rd. LE11 23 F4
Orchard St. LE11 23 F2
Orwell Clo. LE11 22 D1
Osborne Rd. LE11 22 C1
Osterley Clo. LE11 22 C2
Outwoods Av. LE11 23 E5
Outwoods Dri. LE11 23 E4
Outwoods Rd. LE11 23 E6
Oxburgh Clo. LE11 22 C2
Oxford St. LE11 23 E2
Packe St. LE11 23 F3
Pack Horse La. LE11 23 F3
Paget St. LE11 23 E2
Palmer Av. LE11 23 E1
Pantain Rd. LE11 22 D5
Park Av. LE11 23 F5
Park Ct. LE11 23 F4
Park Rd. LE11 23 E6
Park St. LE11 23 F3
Parklands Dri. LE11 23 E6
Patterdale Dri. LE11 22 C5
Peel Dri. LE11 23 G2
Perry Gro. LE11 23 G5
Petworth Dri. LE11 22 B2
Pevensey Rd. LE11 22 D1
Pinfold Gate. LE11 23 G3
Piper Clo. LE11 23 E5
Pitsford Dri. LE11 22 A4
Pleasant Clo. LE11 23 E2
Pocket End. LE11 22 D6
Poplar Rd. LE11 23 F6
Prestbury Rd. LE11 22 B2
Prince William Rd. LE11 23 F1
Prince William Way. LE11 23 F1
Princess St. LE11 23 F3
Priory Rd. LE11 22 D6
Pulteney Av. LE11 23 G5
Pulteney Rd. LE11 23 F5
Pytchley Dri. LE11 23 E6
Queens Rd. LE11 23 G2
Quorn Clo. LE11 23 H4
Radmoor Rd. LE11 23 E3
Railway Ter. LE11 23 H1
Ralph Clo. LE11 22 C6
Ratcliffe Rd. LE11 23 G1
Ravensthorpe Dri. LE11 22 D3
Raymond Av. LE11 22 C1
Raynham Dri. LE11 22 C2
Rectory Pl. LE11 23 F2
Rectory Rd. LE11 23 G2
Redmires Clo. LE11 22 B3
Redwood Rd. LE11 23 F6
Regent St. LE11 23 E2
Rendell St. LE11 23 F1
Rivington Dri. LE11 22 B4
Rockingham Rd. LE11 22 D1
Rosebery St. LE11 23 E2
Rosehill. LE11 22 B2
Roundhill Way. LE11 22 B3
Rowbank Way. LE11 22 B3
Royal Way. LE11 23 E1
Royland Rd. LE11 23 F3
Rudyard Clo. LE11 22 B4
Rufford Clo. LE11 22 B1
Rupert Brooke Rd. LE11 22 C2
Russell St. LE11 23 G3
Rutland St. LE11 23 G3
Rydal Av. LE11 22 C5
St Marys Clo. LE11 23 E2
St Olaves Clo. LE11 22 B2
Salisbury St. LE11 23 G2
Sandalwood Rd. LE11 22 D5
Sandringham Dri. LE11 22 C2
Schofield Rd. LE11 22 C4
School St. LE11 23 G3
Selbourne St. LE11 23 G3
Seward St. LE11 23 E3
Seymour Clo. LE11 22 B1
Shakespeare St. LE11 23 F2
Sharpley Rd. LE11 22 B4
Sheldon Clo. LE11 22 B1
Shelley St. LE11 22 D1
Shelthorpe Av. LE11 23 G5
Shelthorpe Rd. LE11 23 F5
Shepherds Clo. LE11 22 D5
Silverton Rd. LE11 23 E6
*Sir Robert Martin Ct, Windsor Rd. LE11 22 C1
Skevington Av. LE11 22 D3
Snells Nook La. LE11 22 A5
South St. LE11 23 F3
Southdown Rd. LE11 23 F6
Southfield Rd. LE11 23 F3
Sparrow Hill. LE11 23 G2
Speedspingle. LE11 23 E2
Spinney Hill Dri. LE11 22 C4
Springfield Clo. LE11 22 D6
Spruce Av. LE11 23 E6
Squirrel Way. LE11 23 E4
Stanford Hill. LE11 23 F1
Stanley St. LE11 23 F4
Station Av. LE11 23 E2
Station St. LE11 23 E2
Steeple Row. LE11 23 F2
Stewart Dri. LE11 22 B1
Stirling Av. LE11 22 C2
Stonebow Clo. LE11 22 A1
Storer Rd. LE11 23 E2
Sunnyhill Rd. LE11 23 E5
Swan St. LE11 23 F2
Swithland Clo. LE11 22 B1
Sycamore Way. LE11 23 F6
Sywell Av. LE11 22 B3
Tatmarsh La. LE11 23 F2
Tennyson Rd. LE11 22 C2
The Coneries. LE11 23 G2
The Osiers. LE11 23 F6
The Rushes. LE11 23 F2
The Widon. LE11 22 D6
Thirlmere Dri. LE11 22 C5
Thomas St. LE11 23 H3
Thorpe Acre Rd. LE11 22 C2
Thorpe Hill. LE11 22 C3
Toothill Rd. LE11 23 F2
Tow Path Clo. LE11 23 G1
Trelissick Clo. LE11 22 B2
Trinity St. LE11 23 G3
Tuckers Clo. LE11 23 H4
Tuckers Rd. LE11 23 H4
Turner Av. LE11 23 F4
Tyler Av. LE11 23 E1
Tynedale Rd. LE11 22 B6
Ulverscroft Rd. LE11 22 D6
Ulverton Clo. LE11 22 C6
Upper Green. LE11 22 D6
Valley Rd. LE11 22 D5
Victoria Pl. LE11 23 G3
Victoria St. LE11 23 F3
Wallace Rd. LE11 23 E4
Walnut Rd. LE11 23 F6
Wards End. LE11 23 F3
Warner Pl. LE11 23 G3
Warners La. LE11 23 F2
Warwick Way. LE11 22 C1
Watermead La. LE11 22 C6
Waterside Clo. LE11 23 G1
Waverley Clo. LE11 22 B2
Weaver Clo. LE11 23 G5
Wellington St. LE11 23 G3
Wesley Clo. LE11 22 B1
Westfield Dri. LE11 23 E3
Westmorland Av. LE11 22 C5
Whaddon Dri. LE11 23 G5
Wharncliffe Rd. LE11 23 G3
Wheatland Dri. LE11 23 G4
Whitby Clo. LE11 22 A1
White Gate. LE11 23 G2
Whitehouse Av. LE11 23 G4
William St. LE11 23 E3
Willow Rd. LE11 23 F6
Wilmington Ct. LE11 23 H4
Wilstone Clo. LE11 22 B3
Wilton Av. LE11 23 G4
Windleden Ct. LE11 22 B4
Windmill Rd. LE11 23 H3
Windsor Rd. LE11 22 C1
Winterburn Way. LE11 22 B4
Woburn Clo. LE11 22 C2
Wollaton Av. LE11 22 C2
Wolsey Way. LE11 23 H2
Wood Gate. LE11 23 F3
Woodbrook Rd. LE11 22 D5
Woodgate Dri. LE11 23 E4
Woodlands Dri. LE11 23 F4
Woodthorpe Av. LE11 23 G5
Woodthorpe Rd. LE11 23 G5
Wordsworth Rd. LE11 22 C2
Wyndham Rd. LE11 22 B1
Wythburn Clo. LE11 22 C5
York Rd. LE11 23 E3

LUTTERWORTH

Acacia Av. LE17 24 B3
Alder Cres. LE17 24 B4
Alexander Dri. LE17 24 B5
Almond Way. LE17 24 A3
Ashby La. LE17 24 B1
Ashleigh Dri. LE17 24 A3
Aspen Way. LE17 24 B3
Atlee Clo. LE17 24 A5
Avery Clo. LE17 24 B4
Azalea Clo. LE17 24 A4
Baker St. LE17 24 C4
Bank St. LE17 24 C4
Beech Av. LE17 24 A4
Bell St. LE17 24 C4
Bill Crane Way. LE17 24 B2
Bilton Way. LE17 24 C2
Bitteswell Rd. LE17 24 B2
Blackthorn Clo. LE17 24 A3
Boundary Rd. LE17 24 C4
Brookfield Way. LE17 24 A4
Burrough Way. LE17 24 B1
Byron Clo. LE17 24 B2
Canada Flds. LE17 24 C2
Carlson Gdns. LE17 24 C4
Cedar Av. LE17 24 A4
Central Av. LE17 24 C2
Chapel St. LE17 24 C4
Cherrytree Av. LE17 24 A4
Cheshire Clo. LE17 24 A5
Chestnut Av. LE17 24 A4
Church Clo. LE17 24 C4
Church Gate. LE17 24 C4
Church St. LE17 24 C4
Churchill Clo. LE17 24 A5
Conifer Clo. LE17 24 B3
Council Ct. LE17 24 C3
Coventry Rd. LE17 24 A4
Crescent Rd. LE17 24 C3
Cunningham Dri. LE17 24 A4
De Verdon Rd. LE17 24 A4
Deacon Clo. LE17 24 A2
Dempsey Clo. LE17 24 B2
Denbigh Pl. LE17 24 C2
Dunleyway. LE17 24 C2
Dyson Clo. LE17 24 B2
Elizabethan Way. LE17 24 C3
Elm Av. LE17 24 B4
Elmhirst Rd. LE17 24 B4
Faringdon Av. LE17 24 D4
Ferrers Rd. LE17 24 A4
Fieldingway. LE17 24 C3
Fir Tree Av. LE17 24 A4
George St. LE17 24 C4
Gibson Way. LE17 24 A5
Gilmorton Rd. LE17 24 C3
Gladstone St. LE17 24 C3
Goscote Dri. LE17 24 C3
Greenacres Dri. LE17 24 A3
Guthlaxton Av. LE17 24 C3
Hazel Dri. LE17 24 A3
High St. LE17 24 C4
Hill Dri. LE17 24 C5
Holly Dri. LE17 24 B3
Holmfield Clo. LE17 24 A4
Honeysucioe Clo. LE17 24 A3
Hunters Dri. LE17 24 B4
INDUSTRIAL ESTATES:
Bilton Way Ind Est. LE17 24 C1
Oaks Ind Est. LE17 24 D3
Wycliffe Ind Est. LE17 24 C3
Juniper Clo. LE17 24 A3
Ken Mackenzie Clo. LE17 24 C1
Kings Way. LE17 24 B4
Laburnum Av. LE17 24 A4
Ladywood Ct. LE17 24 C2
Larch Dri. LE17 24 B3
Lavender Clo. LE17 24 A4
Leicester Rd. LE17 24 C1
Leyton Clo. LE17 24 C4
Linden Dri. LE17 24 A4
Lower Leicester Rd. LE17 24 C3
Lutterworth Rd. LE17 24 B1
Macaulay Rd. LE17 24 B2
Magnolia Dri. LE17 24 B3
Maino Cres. LE17 24 A4
Manor Rd. LE17 24 B1
Maple Dri. LE17 24 A3
Market St. LE17 24 C4
Marylebone Dri. LE17 24 D4
Mazeland Ct. LE17 24 C3
Meriton Rd. LE17 24 A4
Midland Ct. LE17 24 C2
Mill Gro. LE17 24 C5
Misterton Way. LE17 24 C4
Montgomery Clo. LE17 24 A5
Moorbarns Rd. LE17 24 A6
Mulberry Clo. LE17 24 B3
New St. LE17 24 C3
Oakberry Rd. LE17 24 C1
Oakfield Av. LE17 24 A4
Orange Hill. LE17 24 C4
Orchard Rd. LE17 24 B4
Palmer Dri. LE17 24 B4
Pear Tree Clo. LE17 24 A3
Pine Clo. LE17 24 A3
Poplar Av. LE17 24 A4
Ramsey Clo. LE17 24 C4
Regent Ct. LE17 24 C4
Regent St. LE17 24 C4
Riverside Rd. LE17 24 C5
Robinia Clo. LE17 24 A4
Rowan Dri. LE17 24 B4
Rugby Rd. LE17 24 C5
Ryderway. LE17 24 B5
Rye Hill Rd. LE17 24 C4
St Johns Clo. LE17 24 B5
St Marys Rd. LE17 24 B4
*Shambles Ct, Bell St. LE17 24 C4
Shelley Dri. LE17 24 B2
Sherrierway. LE17 24 C2
Southern By-Pass. LE17 24 A5
Spencer Rd. LE17 24 C3
Spring Clo. LE17 24 B5
Spruce Way. LE17 24 B3
Station Rd. LE17 24 C4
Stoney Hollow. LE17 24 C4
Swiftway. LE17 24 C3
Swinford Rd. LE17 24 D6
Sycamore Dri. LE17 24 A3
Tedder Clo. LE17 24 A5
Tennyson Rd. LE17 24 B2
The Hawthorns. LE17 24 B3
The Nook. LE17 24 B1
*The Terrace, Rugby Rd. LE17 24 C5
Turnpike Clo. LE17 24 D2
Ullesthorpe Rd. LE17 24 A1
Valley La. LE17 24 B2
Walker Manor Ct. LE17 24 C4
Wetherby Ct. LE17 24 A5
Wheeler Clo. LE17 24 B4
Whittle Rd. LE17 24 B4
Wiclif Way. LE17 24 C3
Willowtree Cres. LE17 24 A4
Woodbine Cres. LE17 24 C4
Woodby La. LE17 24 A1
Woodlea Av. LE17 24 A3
Woodmarket. LE17 24 B5
Woodway Rd. LE17 24 A4
Wycliffe Ter. LE17 24 C3
Yew Tree Clo. LE17 24 A3

MARKET HARBOROUGH

Abbey St. LE16 27 C5
Adam & Eve St. LE16 27 C5
Adamswood Clo. LE16 27 A5
Albany Rd. LE16 26 D4
Albert Rd. LE16 27 D5
Althorp Clo. LE16 27 F5
Alvington Way. LE16 26 C3
Andrew Macdonald Clo. LE16 27 D5
Angel Ct. LE16 27 C5
Arden Clo. LE16 26 E4
Ardenway. LE16 26 D3
Argyle Park. LE16 27 C7
Ashfield Rd. LE16 26 C4
Ashley Way. LE16 27 F6
Astley Clo. LE16 27 B6
Audley Clo. LE16 27 F5
Auriga St. LE16 27 D6
Austins Clo. LE16 26 B4
Balfour Gdns. LE16 27 B7
Balmoral Clo. LE16 27 F5
Bamburgh Clo. LE16 27 F5
Bankfield Dri. LE16 26 E3
Barnard Gdns. LE16 27 B7
Bates Clo. LE16 26 C3
Bath St. LE16 27 C7
Bellfields La. LE16 27 E5
Bellfields St. LE16 27 E6
Berry Clo. LE16 26 E3
Birch Tree Gdns. LE16 26 D4
Birtley Coppice. LE16 26 B4
Bishop Clo. LE16 27 C7
Blenheim Way. LE16 26 C3
Bowden La. LE16 26 C4
Bowden Ridge. LE16 26 E3
Bramley Clo. LE16 26 D3
Braybrooke Rd. LE16 27 E6
Britannia Walk. LE16 27 D6
*Broadway Ter, The Crescent. LE16 26 D4
Brookfield Rd. LE16 27 A5
Brooklands Gdns. LE16 27 C5
Burghley Clo. LE16 27 E5
Burnmill Rd. LE16 26 C3
Butler Gdns. LE16 27 A7
Caxton St. LE16 27 D7
Charles St. LE16 27 B5
Chater Clo. LE16 26 E2
Chatsworth Dri. LE16 27 E5
Chiltern Clo. LE16 26 D3
Church Sq. LE16 27 C5
Church St. LE16 27 C5
Claremont Dri. LE16 27 E5
Clarence St. LE16 27 D5
Clarke St. LE16 27 B5
Clipstone St. LE16 27 D7
Coales Gdns. LE16 26 D3
Connaught Rd. LE16 26 D4
Court Yard. LE16 27 C5
Coventry Rd. LE16 27 B5
Crescent Clo. LE16 26 D4
Cromwell Cres. LE16 27 B7
Crosby Rd. LE16 27 D7
Cross St. LE16 27 D6
Dallison Clo. LE16 27 C7
Deacon Clo. LE16 26 B3
Deene Clo. LE16 27 E5
Delisle Clo. LE16 27 B6
Dingley Rd. LE16 26 F2
Dingley Ter. LE16 27 D5
Doddridge Rd. LE16 26 C4
Douglas Dri. LE16 26 D4
Dunslade Clo. LE16 27 E6
Dunslade Gro. LE16 27 E6
Dunslade Rd. LE16 27 E6
East St. LE16 27 B5
Edinburgh Clo. LE16 26 D4
Edward Rd. LE16 26 B4
Elm Dri. LE16 27 A6
Essex Gdns. LE16 27 B7

*Factory La, Adam & Eve St. LE16 — 27 C5
Fairfax Rd. LE16 — 27 C6
Fairfield Rd. LE16 — 26 B4
Fairway. LE16 — 26 B4
Farndale Vw. LE16 — 27 A6
Farndon Rd. LE16 — 27 A7
Fernie Rd. LE16 — 27 D5
Fieldhead Clo. LE16 — 27 A5
Fir Tree Walk. LE16 — 26 C4
Fleetwood Clo. LE16 — 27 B7
Fleetwood Gdns. LE16 — 27 B7
*Fox Yd, Adam & Eve St. LE16 — 27 C5
Gardiner St. LE16 — 27 A5
Gerrard Gdns. LE16 — 27 B7
Gladstone St. LE16 — 27 D6
Glebe Rd. LE16 — 27 E6
Goodwood Clo. LE16 — 27 F5
Gores La. LE16 — 27 E5
Goward St. LE16 — 27 C5
Granville St. LE16 — 27 C6
Great Bowden Rd. LE16 — 26 E4
Green La, Great Bowden. LE16 — 26 D2
Green La, Market Harborough. LE16 — 27 C7
Grenville Gdns. LE16 — 27 B7
Gunnsbrook Clo. LE16 — 26 E2
Hagley Clo. LE16 — 27 F5
Hammond Way. LE16 — 26 C4
Harborough Rd. LE16 — 26 A1
Harborough Rd, East Farndon. LE16 — 27 A8
Harborough Rd, Great Oxenden. LE16 — 27 D8
Harcourt St. LE16 — 27 B5
Harrison Clo. LE16 — 27 B7
Harrod Rd. LE16 — 26 D4
Hearth St. LE16 — 27 B5
Heygate St. LE16 — 26 C4
High St. LE16 — 27 C5
Highcross St. LE16 — 27 A5
Highfield St. LE16 — 27 B5
Hill Gdns. LE16 — 27 A5
Hillcrest Av. LE16 — 26 B4
Hillside Rd. LE16 — 26 D4
Holdenby Clo. LE16 — 27 F5
Holly Clo. LE16 — 26 C4
*Hollywell Ho, Leicester Rd. LE16 — 26 B4
Hopton Fields. LE16 — 27 B7
Horsefair Clo. LE16 — 26 B4
Horseshoe La. LE16 — 26 E2
Howard Way. LE16 — 27 B7
Huntingdon Gdns. LE16 — 27 B7
INDUSTRIAL ESTATES:
Euro Business Pk. LE16 — 26 F4
Riverside Ind Est. LE16 — 26 F4
Ireton Rd. LE16 — 27 B6
Jackson Clo. LE16 — 27 C7
Jerwood Way. LE16 — 27 D6
Jordan Clo. LE16 — 27 C5
Kingston Way. LE16 — 26 B3
Jubilee Gdns. LE16 — 26 D4
Kettering Rd. LE16 — 27 D5
Kings Rd. LE16 — 27 C5
Kingshead Pl. LE16 — 27 C5
Knights End Rd. LE16 — 26 F2
Knoll St. LE16 — 27 A5
Langton Rd. LE16 — 26 E1
Lathkill St. LE16 — 27 D6
Latimer Cres. LE16 — 27 D6
Launde Park. LE16 — 27 E6
Leicester La. LE16 — 26 A1
Leicester Rd. LE16 — 26 B4
Lenthall Sq. LE16 — 27 C7
Lincoln Ct. LE16 — 26 D3
Lindsey Gdns. LE16 — 27 B7
Little Bowden Manor. LE16 — 27 D5
*Little St, Church St. LE16 — 27 C5
Logan Ct. LE16 — 26 B4
Logan Cres. LE16 — 26 A4
Logan St. LE16 — 27 B5
Longleat Clo. LE16 — 27 F5
Lower Green Pl. LE16 — 26 E2
Lubenham Hill. LE16 — 27 A5
Madeline Clo. LE16 — 26 E3
Main St. LE16 — 26 D2
Manor Rd. LE16 — 26 E2
Manor Walk. LE16 — 27 C5

Market Harborough By-Pass. LE16 — 26 E1
Marlborough Way. LE16 — 26 C3
Maurice Rd. LE16 — 27 B7
Meadow Clo. LE16 — 26 D4
Meadow St. LE16 — 26 C4
Medway Clo. LE16 — 27 E5
Middledale Rd. LE16 — 27 E5
Mill Hill Rd. LE16 — 27 C5
Millers Yard. LE16 — 27 C5
Monroe Clo. LE16 — 26 B3
Montrose Clo. LE16 — 27 B7
Morley St. LE16 — 27 B5
Naseby Clo. LE16 — 27 C6
Naseby Sq. LE16 — 27 C6
Nelson St. LE16 — 27 B5
Newcombe St. LE16 — 27 C6
Nithsdale Av. LE16 — 27 C6
Nithsdale Cres. LE16 — 27 D6
Norbury Clo. LE16 — 27 B5
North Bank. LE16 — 27 C6
Northampton Rd. LE16 — 27 C5
Northleigh Gro. LE16 — 26 B4
Nunneley Way. LE16 — 26 D4
Oak Clo. LE16 — 26 D4
Oaklands Park. LE16 — 27 D6
Orchard St. LE16 — 26 C4
Overdale Clo. LE16 — 27 E5
Overfield Av. LE16 — 26 D3
Paddock Ct. LE16 — 26 C4
Park Dri. LE16 — 26 C4
Patrick St. LE16 — 27 D6
Perkins Clo. LE16 — 26 D4
Petworth Dri. LE16 — 27 C5
Pochin Dri. LE16 — 26 C3
*Poplars Ct, Leicester Rd. LE16 — 26 B4
Post Office La. LE16 — 27 D5
Pride Pl. LE16 — 27 B6
Queen St. LE16 — 27 E6
Rainsborough Gdns. LE16 — 27 B7
Rectory La. LE16 — 27 E6
*Redleigh Clo, Petworth Dri. LE16 — 27 F5
Rhodes Clo. LE16 — 27 A6
Ridgeway West. LE16 — 26 C3
Ripley Clo. LE16 — 27 F5
Ritchie Park. LE16 — 27 C8
Riverside. LE16 — 26 E4
Rochester Gdns. LE16 — 27 B7
Rockingham Rd. LE16 — 27 E5
Rolleston Clo. LE16 — 27 E5
Roman Way. LE16 — 26 C4
Rookwell Clo. LE16 — 27 D7
Rosemoor Clo. LE16 — 27 F5
Rowan Av. LE16 — 27 C7
Rugby Clo. LE16 — 27 B6
Rupert Rd. LE16 — 27 C7
Russet Clo. LE16 — 26 D3
Rutland Walk. LE16 — 26 D3
Ryelands Clo. LE16 — 27 F5
St Marys Rd. LE16 — 27 D5
St Nicholas Clo. LE16 — 27 D6
St Nicholas Way. LE16 — 27 D6
Saxon Clo. LE16 — 26 D4
School La. LE16 — 27 C5
Scotland Rd. LE16 — 27 D6
Scott Clo. LE16 — 26 C3
Selby Clo. LE16 — 27 C7
Sherrard Rd. LE16 — 26 C3
Shrewsbury Av. LE16 — 27 F6
Shropshire Clo Flats. LE16 — 26 C4
Shropshire Pl. LE16 — 26 C4
Skippon Clo. LE16 — 27 B6
Smyth Clo. LE16 — 26 C3
Southleigh Gro. LE16 — 26 B4
Spencer St. LE16 — 27 B5
Spinney Clo. LE16 — 27 A5
Springfield St. LE16 — 27 D6
Stablegate Way. LE16 — 27 E5
Stamford Clo. LE16 — 27 C6
Stanway Clo. LE16 — 27 E5
Station Rd. LE16 — 26 E3
Stevens St. LE16 — 27 B5
Stratton Rd. LE16 — 27 B7
Stuart Rd. LE16 — 27 B6
*Sulleys Yd, Adam & Eve St. LE16 — 27 C5
Sutton Rd. LE16 — 26 F2
Talbot Yd. LE16 — 27 C5
Thatch Meadow Dri. LE16 — 27 F5
The Broadway. LE16 — 26 C4
The Crescent. LE16 — 26 D4

The Firs. LE16 — 27 A5
The Furlongs. LE16 — 27 F5
The Green. LE16 — 26 E2
The Headlands. LE16 — 26 D4
The Heights. LE16 — 27 F6
The Oval. LE16 — 26 C4
The Pastures. LE16 — 27 A5
The Ridgeway. LE16 — 26 D3
The Square. LE16 — 27 C5
The Woodlands. LE16 — 26 A4
Thornborough Clo. LE16 — 27 E6
Timson Clo. LE16 — 26 B3
Turnpike Clo. LE16 — 26 B3
Tymecross Gdns. LE16 — 26 B3
Union Wharf. LE16 — 26 B4
Upper Green Pl. LE16 — 26 D2
Valley Way. LE16 — 26 F4
Vaughan Clo. LE16 — 27 C8
Victoria Av. LE16 — 26 B4
Walcot Rd. LE16 — 27 C6
Wartnaby St. LE16 — 27 A5
Warwick Clo. LE16 — 26 D3
Waterfield Pl. LE16 — 26 C3
Watson Av. LE16 — 27 A7
Welham Rd. LE16 — 26 E2
Welland Park Rd. LE16 — 27 B6
Western Av. LE16 — 27 B7
Westfield Clo. LE16 — 27 A5
Willow Cres. LE16 — 27 A6
Wilson Clo. LE16 — 27 E5
Windsor Ct. LE16 — 26 B4
Woburn Clo. LE16 — 27 E5
Woodbreach Dri. LE16 — 27 F5
Woodgate Clo. LE16 — 27 F6
Worcester Dri. LE16 — 26 C3
York St. LE16 — 27 D5

MEASHAM

Abney Cres. DE12 — 25 B2
Abney Dri. DE12 — 25 B3
Abney Walk. DE12 — 25 B3
Amersham Way. DE12 — 25 B1
Ash Dri. DE12 — 25 C1
Ashby Rd. DE12 — 25 C1
Atherstone Rd. DE12 — 25 B2
Blackthorne Way. DE12 — 25 B1
Bleach Hill. DE12 — 25 B3
Bosworth Rd. DE12 — 25 C1
Browning Dri. DE12 — 25 B3
Buckley Clo. DE12 — 25 C2
Burns Clo. DE12 — 25 B3
Burton Rd. DE12 — 25 A1
Buzzard Clo. DE12 — 25 B3
Byron Cres. DE12 — 25 B3
Chapel St. DE12 — 25 B1
Cophills Clo. DE12 — 25 B2
Dryden Clo. DE12 — 25 B3
Dysons Clo. DE12 — 25 A2
Eagle Clo. DE12 — 25 B2
Fenton Clo. DE12 — 25 B3
Fenton Cres. DE12 — 25 B3
Gallows La. DE12 — 25 D3
Grassy La. DE12 — 25 D1
Greenfield Rd. DE12 — 25 B1
Hawthorne Clo. DE12 — 25 B1
Hazel Clo. DE12 — 25 B1
High St. DE12 — 25 B2
Holly Rd. DE12 — 25 C1
Horses La. DE12 — 25 C2
Huntington Ct. DE12 — 25 A2
Huntington Way. DE12 — 25 A1
Iveagh Clo. DE12 — 25 B1
Jewsbury Av. DE12 — 25 D2
Kelso Clo.DE12 — 25 B1
Leicester Rd. DE12 — 25 C1
Lime Av. DE12 — 25 B1
Mallard Clo. DE12 — 25 A3
Mannings Ter. DE12 — 25 B2
Masefield Clo. DE12 — 25 B3
Meadow Gdns. DE12 — 25 B3
Mease Clo. DE12 — 25 B3
Milton Clo. DE12 — 25 B3
Navigation St. DE12 — 25 C2
New St. DE12 — 25 C1
Oak Clo. DE12 — 25 B1
Orchard Way. DE12 — 25 B1
Peggs Clo. DE12 — 25 C2
Pendale Clo. DE12 — 25 B1
Peregrine Clo. DE12 — 25 B1
Pipit Clo. DE12 — 25 B2
Poplar Dri. DE12 — 25 C1
Queens St. DE12 — 25 C1
Raven Clo. DE12 — 25 B2

Repton Rd. DE12 — 25 A2
Riverside Ct. DE12 — 25 A2
Rosebank Vw. DE12 — 25 B1
Rowan Clo. DE12 — 25 B1
Sandhill Clo. DE12 — 25 B2
Shackland Dri. DE12 — 25 D2
Shelley Clo. DE12 — 25 B3
Siskin Dri. DE12 — 25 A3
Skylark Clo. DE12 — 25 A3
Tamworth Rd. DE12 — 25 A3
Tennyson Clo. DE12 — 25 B3
The Croft. DE12 — 25 A2
Uplands Rd. DE12 — 25 C2
Wesley Hillman Ct. DE12 — 25 C2
Whitehouse Way. DE12 — 25 B1
Widgeon Dri. DE12 — 25 A3
Wilkes Av. DE12 — 25 B2
Willow Clo. DE12 — 25 C1
Wordsworth Way. DE12 — 25 B3
York Clo. DE12 — 25 B1

MELTON MOWBRAY

Abingdon Rd. LE13 — 28 B2
Acres Rise. LE13 — 28 F3
Adcock Clo. LE13 — 28 F2
Albert St. LE13 — 29 D6
Algernon Rd. LE13 — 28 E4
Alvaston Rd. LE13 — 28 B2
Ankle Hill Rd. LE13 — 29 D6
Arden Dri. LE13 — 28 A3
Ash Gro. LE13 — 28 C3
Ashfordby Rd. LE13 — 28 A4
Ashton Clo. LE13 — 29 C6
Avon Rd. LE13 — 29 C6
Baldocks La. LE13 — 29 D5
Balmoral Rd. LE13 — 28 C2
Banbury Dri. LE13 — 29 E7
Barker Cres. LE13 — 29 C7
Barngate Clo. LE13 — 28 D2
Bayswater Rd. LE13 — 28 B3
Beaconsfield Rd. LE13 — 28 B2
Beaumont Gdns. LE13 — 28 D2
Beck Hill Ct. LE13 — 28 D4
Beechwood Av. LE13 — 28 E2
Belvoir St. LE13 — 28 E3
Bentley St. LE13 — 28 D4
Bickley Av. LE13 — 28 D3
Birch Clo. LE13 — 28 C3
Bishop St. LE13 — 28 E4
Blakeney Cres. LE13 — 29 C7
Blenheim Walk. LE13 — 29 D6
Blythe Av. LE13 — 29 B5
Bowley Av. LE13 — 28 E2
Brampton Rd. LE13 — 28 A1
Branston Cres. LE13 — 29 E5
Brentingsby Clo. LE13 — 29 E5
Breward Way. LE13 — 28 D1
Brightside Av. LE13 — 28 B4
Brocklehurst Rd. LE13 — 28 F2
Brook La. LE13 — 29 D5
Brook St. LE13 — 28 D4
Brookfield Ct. LE13 — 28 B2
Brookfield St. LE13 — 28 B2
Browning Clo. LE13 — 28 C2
Brownlow Cres. LE13 — 29 C7
Buckminster Clo. LE13 — 29 E5
Burns Clo. LE13 — 28 C3
Burton Rd. LE13 — 29 D5
Burton St. LE13 — 29 D5
Byron Way. LE13 — 28 C2
Camomile Rd. LE13 — 29 B7
Cambridge Av. LE13 — 29 D7
Campion Pl. LE13 — 29 B7
Canterbury Dri. LE13 — 28 A1
Carnegie Cres. LE13 — 28 F2
Cedar Dri. LE13 — 28 C3
Celandine Dri. LE13 — 29 B7
Chadwell Clo. LE13 — 29 E5
Chalfont Clo. LE13 — 29 E7
Chalmondley Dri. LE13 — 28 D1
Chapel St. LE13 — 28 D4
Charlotte St. LE13 — 28 C3
Charnwood Dri. LE13 — 28 A3
Cheapside. LE13 — 28 C4
Chestnut Way. LE13 — 29 C6
Chetwynd Dri. LE13 — 28 A4
Cholmondley Dri. LE13 — 28 D1
Church St. LE13 — 28 C4
Churchill Clo. LE13 — 28 D2
Clark Dri. LE13 — 28 B1
Clumber St. LE13 — 28 C3

College Av. LE13 — 29 D6
Collingwood Cres. LE13 — 28 A4
Coltfoot Way. LE13 — 29 A7
Coniston Rd. LE13 — 28 A1
Conway Dri. LE13 — 28 C2
Copley Clo. LE13 — 28 E3
Cornwall Pl. LE13 — 29 C7
Cotswold Clo. LE13 — 29 E7
Cottesmore Av. LE13 — 28 C1
Cranmere Rd. LE13 — 28 D2
Craven St. LE13 — 29 D6
Crossfield Dri. LE13 — 28 F3
Dalby Rd. LE13 — 29 C5
De Montford. LE13 — 28 C2
Delamare Rd. LE13 — 28 D1
Denton Rise. LE13 — 29 E5
Derwent Dri. LE13 — 29 C6
Dickens Dri. LE13 — 28 C1
Dieppe Way. LE13 — 28 B2
Doctors La. LE13 — 28 E3
Dorian Rise. LE13 — 28 C3
Dorothy Av. LE13 — 28 B4
Dorset Dri. LE13 — 29 D7
Douglas Jane Clo. LE13 — 28 B3
Dovedale Clo. LE13 — 29 C6
Drive Dalby Rd. LE13 — 29 C6
Drummond Walk. LE13 — 28 C2
Duke St. LE13 — 28 E3
Dulverton Rd. LE13 — 28 B2
Eagles Dri. LE13 — 29 C7
East Av. LE13 — 28 C1
East Side Croft. LE13 — 28 D1
Eastfield Av. LE13 — 28 D3
Edendale Rd. LE13 — 28 B6
Egerton Rd. LE13 — 28 D4
Egerton View. LE13 — 29 C5
Elgin Dri. LE13 — 28 C3
Elmhurst Av. LE13 — 28 A2
Elms Rd. LE13 — 28 D4
Epping Dri. LE13 — 28 D2
Everest Dri. LE13 — 28 A2
Ewden Rise. LE13 — 29 C6
Fairfield Clo. LE13 — 28 D2
Faldo Dri. LE13 — 28 D1
Farmland Dri. LE13 — 28 C1
Ferneley Cres. LE13 — 28 E3
Fernie Av. LE13 — 28 C4
Field Clo. LE13 — 29 E6
Firwood Rd. LE13 — 28 E2
Forest Clo. LE13 — 28 D2
Freeby Clo. LE13 — 29 F5
Freshney Clo. LE13 — 29 B6
Garden La. LE13 — 28 B2
Garthorpe Dri. LE13 — 29 E5
Gartree Clo. LE13 — 29 D6
Gartree Dri. LE13 — 29 D6
Gaudaloupe Av. LE13 — 29 F6
George St. LE13 — 28 E4
Gilpin Clo. LE13 — 29 B6
Gladstone Av. LE13 — 28 B2
Gloucester Av. LE13 — 29 D7
Gloucester Cres. LE13 — 29 D7
Goldspink Clo. LE13 — 29 C7
Granby Rd. LE13 — 28 D1
Grange Dri. LE13 — 29 E5
Grantwood Rd. LE13 — 28 E2
Granville Rd. LE13 — 28 B2
Greaves Av. LE13 — 28 B4
Green Bank. LE13 — 28 E4
Greenhill Clo. LE13 — 28 D2
Greenslade. LE13 — 28 D4
Gretton Ct. LE13 — 28 B4
Hadfield Dri. LE13 — 28 D3
Hamilton Dri. LE13 — 29 C6
Harebell Dri. LE13 — 29 B7
Harlech Way. LE13 — 29 C6
Hartland Dri. LE13 — 28 C1
Hartopp Rd. LE13 — 29 C7
Hawthorn Dri. LE13 — 28 C2
Heather Cres. LE13 — 28 C3
High St. LE13 — 28 C4
Highfield Av. LE13 — 28 C3
Hilary Clo. LE13 — 28 E1
Hillside Av. LE13 — 28 B4
Honeysuckle Way. LE13 — 29 B6
Hollygate Clo. LE13 — 29 F5
Hudson Rd. LE13 — 28 F3
Humber Dri. LE13 — 29 C6
Hunt Dri. LE13 — 28 F2
Hunters Rd. LE13 — 28 D1
INDUSTRIAL ESTATES:
Hudson Rd Ind Est. LE13 — 28 F4
Irwell Clo. LE13 — 29 B6

James Lambert Dri. LE13
Jarvis Dri. LE13 28 B3
Johnson Clo. LE13 28 D3
Jubilee St. LE13 28 D4
Jubilee Way. LE13 28 E2
Kapelle Clo. LE13 28 F2
Keats Clo. LE13 28 C2
Kennet Way. LE13 29 B6
Kestrel Dri. LE13 29 C7
King St. LE13 28 D4
Kings Av. LE13 28 E3
Kings Rd. LE13 28 D4
Kipling Dri. LE13 28 B2
Kirby La. LE13 29 A7
Kirton Dri. LE13 28 B1
Lake Ter. LE13 29 B5
Lambert Clo. LE13 28 D2
Laura Davies Clo. LE13 28 D1
Laycock Av. LE13 28 C3
Leicester Rd. LE13 29 A6
Leicester St. LE13 28 C4
Lilac Way. LE13 28 C3
Limes Av. LE13 28 E3
Lincoln Dri. LE13 29 D7
Linnet Clo. LE13 29 B7
Loddon Clo. LE13 29 B6
Longate Rd. LE13 28 D2
Longfield Rd. LE13 28 D2
Longwill Av. LE13 28 D3
Lowesey Clo. LE13 29 F5
Loxley Dri. LE13 29 B6
Ludlow Dri. LE13 28 C2
Lyle Clo. LE13 28 D1
Lynton Rd. LE13 28 B2
Manners Dri. LE13 28 D1
Manor Clo. LE13 28 F2
Mansion House Gdns. LE13 28 D1
Maple Clo. LE13 28 C2
Market Pl. LE13 28 D4
Marteg Clo. LE13 29 B6
Mayfield St. LE13 28 B2
Meadow Way. LE13 29 E6
Medway Dri. LE13 29 C6
Melbourne Dri. LE13 28 A4
Melbray Dri. LE13 28 C1
Melton Spinney Rd. LE13 28 F2
Meynell Clo. LE13 29 C7
Mildmay Clo. LE13 28 D1
Mill La. LE13 29 D5
Mill St. LE13 29 D5
Milton Clo. LE13 28 C2
Morley St. LE13 28 A3
Mortimer Rd. LE13 28 D3
Mowbray Ct. LE13 29 B5
Needham Clo. LE13 28 D3
Nene Clo. LE13 29 B5
New St. LE13 28 D4
Newbury Av. LE13 28 A2
Newport Av. LE13 28 C3
Norfolk Dri. LE13 29 D7
Norman Way. LE13 28 C4
North St. LE13 28 D4
Northfield Clo. LE13 28 C3
Nottingham Rd. LE13 28 A1
Nottingham St. LE13 28 C4
Oak Rd. LE13 28 D4
Old Bridewell. LE13 28 D2
Owen Cres. LE13 28 D3
Oxbow Clo. LE13 29 B5
Oxford Dri. LE13 29 D7
Paddock Clo. LE13 29 D6
Pall Mall. LE13 28 F2
Palmerston Rd. LE13 28 B2
Park Av. LE13 28 B4
Park La. LE13 28 C4
Park Rd. LE13 28 C4
Pebble Bank La. LE13 28 F3
Petersfield Rd. LE13 28 B3
Pochin Clo. LE13 29 B5
Pollard Clo. LE13 28 F2
Princess Clo. LE13 29 C7
Queensway. LE13 29 C7
Quorn Av. LE13 28 B4
Raynes Walk. LE13 28 D3
Redbrook Cres. LE13 29 B6
Redwood Av. LE13 28 D2
Regent Pl. LE13 29 D5
Regent St. LE13 29 D5
Ribble Way. LE13 29 C6
Richmond Dri. LE13 29 E7
Riverside Rd. LE13 28 A4
Robin Cres. LE13 29 B7
Rockingham Dri. LE13 28 B3
Roseberry Av. LE13 28 D4

Ross Clo. LE13 28 E2
Rudbeck Av. LE13 28 B4
Rutland St. LE13 28 D4
Sage Cross St. LE13 28 D4
St Johns Clo. LE13 28 D4
St Johns Dri. LE13 28 D4
St Marys Clo. LE13 28 C4
Salisbury Av. LE13 28 E3
Sandy La. LE13 29 D6
Sapcote Dri. LE13 29 E6
Saxby Rd. LE13 28 E4
Scalford Rd. LE13 28 C1
Severn Hill. LE13 29 C6
Shelley Av. LE13 28 C2
Shepherds Croft. LE13 28 C2
Sherrard St. LE13 28 D4
Sherwood Dri. LE13 28 A4
Snow Hill. LE13 28 D4
Soar Clo. LE13 29 B6
Solway Clo. LE13 29 B6
Somerset Clo. LE13 29 D7
South Par. LE13 28 C4
Spinney Clo. LE13 28 F2
Springfield St. LE13 28 B3
Stafford Av. LE13 28 E4
Stanley St. LE13 28 D4
Staveley Rd. LE13 28 A3
Stirling Rd. LE13 28 B3
Suffolk Clo. LE13 29 E7
Sussex Av. LE13 29 D7
Swale Clo. LE13 29 C6
Swallowdale Rd. LE13 29 C7
Swan Clo. LE13 29 B7
Swift Clo. LE13 29 C7
Sycamore Clo. LE13 28 C3
Sysonby Grange La. LE13 28 A4
Sysonby St. LE13 28 B3
Tamar Rd. LE13 29 B6
Tennis Av. LE13 29 D6
Tennyson Way. LE13 28 C2
Thames Dri. LE13 29 B6
The Crescent. LE13 28 C3
The Uplands. LE13 29 C5
Thorpe End. LE13 28 D4
Thorpe Rd. LE13 28 E4
Thrush Clo. LE13 29 B7
Torrance Dri. LE13 28 D1
Trent Bank. LE13 29 B6
Tudor Hill. LE13 29 D7
Tweed Dri. LE13 29 C6
Valley Rd. LE13 29 B6
Victoria St. LE13 29 D6
Waltham Rise. LE13 29 E5
Warwick Rd. LE13 29 D6
Waverley Ct. LE13 29 D6
Weaver Grn. LE13 28 B3
Welby La. LE13 28 A2
Welland Rise. LE13 29 C6
West Av. LE13 28 A3
Westminster Clo. LE13 28 A1
Whitelake Clo. LE13 29 B6
Wicklow Av. LE13 29 D6
Willcox Dri. LE13 29 F6
Willoughby Clo. LE13 29 E5
Willow Dri. LE13 28 D3
Wilton Ct. LE13 28 B4
Wilton Rd. LE13 28 C4
Wilton Ter. LE13 28 C4
Winchester Dri. LE13 28 A1
Windsor St. LE13 28 D4
Winster Cres. LE13 29 B6
Witham Clo. LE13 29 C6
Woodcock Dri. LE13 29 C7
Woodland Av. LE13 29 D6
Worcester Dri. LE13 29 D7
Wren Clo. LE13 29 B7
Wycliffe Av. LE13 28 D3
Wycomb Gro. LE13 29 F5
Wyfordby Clo. LE13 29 E6
Wymondham Way. LE13 28 D1
Wyndham Av. LE13 29 D6
Wyvern Ter. LE13 28 D4
Yew Tree Cres. LE13 29 D2

NARBOROUGH/ENDERBY

Abbey Rd. LE9 31 F5
Acan Way. LE9 31 D6
Acer Clo. LE9 31 C6
Alexander Av. LE9 30 D3
Alexandra St. LE9 31 F6
Alyssum Way. LE9 31 C5

Aquitane Clo. LE9 30 D3
Ashlands Way. LE9 31 C5
Badgers Clo. LE9 31 D6
Bantlam La. LE9 30 E3
Barbara Clo. LE9 30 D3
Beechwood Rd. LE9 31 E7
Beggars La. LE9 30 C1
Bell La. LE9 31 E6
Belle View. LE9 31 E6
Bennett Rise. LE9 31 B6
Biddle Rd. LE9 31 E7
Bingley Ct. LE9 31 E7
Bingley Rd. LE9 31 E7
Blaby Rd. LE9 30 E3
Blake Ct. LE9 30 C3
Blakenhall Clo. LE9 31 C6
Boswell St. LE9 31 D5
Briers Clo. LE9 31 E6
Broad St. LE9 30 E3
Brook St, Enderby. LE9 30 D3
Brook St, Huncote. LE9 31 A6
Broom Way. LE9 31 C5
Broomhills Rd. LE9 31 C6
Browning St. LE9 31 D5
Burns St. LE9 31 D5
Burrows Clo. LE9 31 D7
Bushey Clo. LE9 31 E6
Buttercup Clo. LE9 31 D5
Byron Clo. LE9 30 D4
Callan Clo. LE9 31 D6
Camellia Clo. LE9 31 C5
Camelot Way. LE9 30 D4
Campion Clo. LE9 31 C5
Canons Clo. LE9 31 E6
Capers Clo. LE9 30 C3
Carey Rd. LE9 31 A6
Carlton Av. LE9 31 E6
Carter Clo. LE9 30 D3
Cedar Cres. LE9 31 E6
Chantry Clo. LE9 31 A6
Chapel St. LE9 30 D3
Chaucer St. LE9 31 D5
Cheney Ct. LE9 31 A6
Cheney End. LE9 31 A6
Cherrytree Gro. LE9 30 D3
Chestnut Clo. LE9 31 E7
Church La. LE9 31 E6
Church View. LE9 31 E6
Clover Clo. LE9 31 D5
Coleridge Dri. LE9 30 C4
Coltbeck Av. LE9 31 D6
Columbia Clo. LE9 30 D3
Compton Dri. LE9 31 A6
Conery La. LE9 30 D3
Cooper Clo. LE9 31 B6
Cooperation St. LE9 30 E3
Copt Oak Ct. LE9 31 D5
Copt Oak Rd. LE9 31 D5
Cornfield Clo. LE9 31 E7
Cornwall St. LE9 30 D3
Cosby Rd. LE9 31 F7
Coventry Rd. LE9 31 C8
Coventry Rd. LE9 31 E6
Cowslip Clo. LE9 31 C5
Critchlow Rd. LE9 31 A6
Cross St. LE9 30 D3
Cumberwell Dri. LE9 30 F4
Cutters Clo. LE9 31 D6
Denman La. LE9 31 A6
Desford Rd, Enderby. LE9 30 A1
Desford Rd, Narborough. LE9 31 E6
Dovecote Rd. LE9 31 A8
Drovers Way. LE9 31 D7
Drummond Rd. LE9 30 D3
Duncan Av. LE9 31 A6
Elmhurst Clo. LE9 31 C6
Enderby Rd. LE9 30 A3
Equity Rd. LE9 30 D4
Eunice Av. LE9 31 A6
Farm Clo. LE9 31 F7
Federation St. LE9 30 D4
Feldspar Clo. LE9 30 D2
Fern Lea. LE9 31 C5
Field Clo. LE9 31 F7
Finch Way. LE9 31 C6
Fletchers Clo. LE9 31 D7
Forest Rd, Enderby. LE9 30 C4
Forest Rd, Huncote. LE9 30 A4
Forest Rd, Narborough. LE9 31 D6
Foss Way. LE9 30 F4
Fosse Clo. LE9 30 F4
Foxglove Clo. LE9 31 D5

Fritchley Clo. LE9 31 B6
Froanes Clo. LE9 30 D2
Furrows Clo. LE9 31 F7
Gayton Heights. LE9 30 D3
Geary Clo. LE9 31 E6
George St. LE9 30 D3
Granite Clo. LE9 30 D2
Grays Ct. LE9 30 D3
Greenhill Clo. LE9 31 C6
Greenwich Clo. LE9 31 E6
Grizedale Gro. LE9 30 C4
Gumley Sq. LE9 30 D3
Gurney Cres. LE9 31 F7
Guthlaxton Gap. LE9 31 C8
Hall Walk. LE9 30 D3
Hampstead Clo. LE9 31 E6
Hardwicke Rd. LE9 31 C6
Harolds La. LE9 30 D2
Harvest Clo. LE9 31 F7
Haybarn Clo. LE9 31 F7
Hazel Clo. LE9 31 E7
Heighton Cres. LE9 31 E7
Hemlock Clo. LE9 31 C5
Herdsman Clo. LE9 31 F7
Heron Way. LE9 30 F4
Herrick Clo. LE9 30 D3
High St. LE9 30 D3
Hillberry Clo. LE9 31 D6
Hobill Clo. LE9 31 B6
Holland Way. LE9 31 E6
Holyoake St. LE9 30 D4
Homer Dri. LE9 30 C4
Honeycomb Clo. LE9 31 D5
Hornbeam Clo. LE9 31 C5
Huncote Rd. LE9 31 B6
Hyde Clo. LE9 31 E6

INDUSTRIAL ESTATES:
Mill Hill Ind Est. LE9 30 D2
Oaks Ind Est. LE9 31 D6
Regent St Ind Est. LE9 31 F6

Jacob Clo. LE9 30 D4
Jacques Clo. LE9 30 D3
Jarrett Clo. LE9 30 D3
Jasmine Ct. LE9 31 C5
John St. LE9 30 D4
Jubilee Cres. LE9 31 E6
Keats Clo. LE9 30 C4
Kielder Clo. LE9 30 C4
King Edward Av. LE9 30 D3
King St. LE9 30 D3
Kingsbridge Clo. LE9 31 D6
Kingsley Clo. LE9 31 D5
Kipling Dri. LE9 30 D4
Kirk La. LE9 30 E3
Langham Dri. LE9 31 D6
Langley Clo. LE9 31 B6
Lapwing Ct. LE9 31 C6
Leicester Rd, Enderby. LE9 30 E3
Leicester Rd, Narborough. LE9 31 E6
Linnett Clo. LE9 31 D6
Lobelia Clo. LE9 31 C5
Lodge Clo. LE9 31 A6
Lord Clo. LE9 31 D7
Mcdowell Way. LE9 31 E7
Main St. LE9 31 A6
Maple Tree Walk. LE9 31 F7
Marigold Way. LE9 31 C6
Masefield Av. LE9 30 D4
Masons Clo. LE9 31 E6
Meadow Ct. LE9 31 E6
Meadows Edge. LE9 30 D4
Mellier Clo. LE9 31 D6
Milford Clo. LE9 31 D6
Mill Hill. LE9 30 C2
Mill La. LE9 30 E4
Mill View. LE9 31 A6
Milton St. LE9 31 D5
Mitchell Rd. LE9 30 D3
Moores La. LE9 30 D3
Mortimer Rd. LE9 31 D7
Narborough Rd. LE9 31 A6
Needwood Way. LE9 30 C4
Oak Rd. LE9 31 E7
Orchid Clo. LE9 31 C5
Overfield Clo. LE9 31 D6
Park Rd. LE9 31 E6
Pimpernel Way. LE9 31 C5
Pope Cres. LE9 30 D3
Poplar Rd. LE9 31 E7
Primrose Clo. LE9 31 D5
Princess St. LE9 31 F6
Quarry La. LE9 31 C6
Queens Dri. LE9 30 F4
Radnor Ct. LE9 30 C4

Ratcliffe Dri. LE9 31 A6
Rawson St. LE9 30 D3
Red Hill Av. LE9 31 D6
Regent St. LE9 31 F6
Riddington Rd. LE9 31 E7
Ridgeway. LE9 31 F7
Riverside Way. LE9 31 E7
Robotham Clo, Huncote. LE9 31 B6
Robotham Clo, Littlethorpe. LE9 31 D7
Rossetti Rd. LE9 30 D3
Roy Clo. LE9 31 F5
Royal Ct. LE9 31 F6
St James Clo. LE9 31 A6
Salts Clo. LE9 30 D4
Sandhill Dri. LE9 30 F4
School La, Huncote. LE9 31 B6
School La, Narborough. LE9 31 E6
Seine La. LE9 30 C3
Sharpe Clo. LE9 31 E6
Shelley Rd. LE9 30 D4
Sheridan Clo. LE9 30 C4
Shortridge La. LE9 30 D3
Sloane Clo. LE9 30 D3
Snowdrop Clo. LE9 31 C5
Sorrel Way. LE9 31 C5
Southey Clo. LE9 30 D4
Speedwell Clo. LE9 31 C5
Spiers Clo. LE9 31 D7
Sportsfield Rd. LE9 31 A6
Spring Gdns. LE9 31 F7
Squirrel Clo. LE9 31 D6
Stable Clo. LE9 31 E7
Stainore Av. LE9 30 C4
Station Rd. LE9 31 E6
Stewart Av. LE9 30 D4
Strawberry Gdns. LE9 30 C3
Sycamore Way. LE9 31 E7
Teasel Clo. LE9 31 D5
Tennyson St. LE9 31 D5
The Burrows. LE9 31 C6
The Close. LE9 30 D4
The Coppice. LE9 31 D6
The Cross. LE9 30 D3
The Green. LE9 31 B6
The Meadows. LE9 31 F7
The Nook. LE9 31 F7
The Paddocks. LE9 31 F7
The Pastures. LE9 31 E6
The Rise. LE9 30 D4
The Square. LE9 31 E7
Thistle Clo. LE9 31 D5
Thornborough Clo. LE9 31 C6
Thornhills Gro. LE9 30 C4
Thornton Dri. LE9 31 E6
Thurlaston La. LE9 30 A3
Tiverton Clo. LE9 31 E6
Townsend Rd. LE9 30 D3
Vetch Clo. LE9 31 C5
Victoria St. LE9 31 E6
Wakeley Clo. LE9 31 C6
Warren Parkway. LE9 30 D2
Warren Rd. LE9 31 F5
Warwick Rd. LE9 31 F7
Waudby Clo. LE9 31 F7
West St. LE9 30 D4
Whitebeam Clo. LE9 31 D5
William St. LE9 31 E7
Williams Clo. LE9 31 E7
Willow Clo. LE9 31 E7
Woodfield Clo. LE9 31 E6
Woodhouse Rd. LE9 31 C6
Woodland Av. LE9 31 D5
Woodside Clo. LE9 31 C6
Wordsworth Cres. LE9 31 D5

OAKHAM

Alexander Cres. LE15 32 B3
Alpine Clo. LE15 32 B3
Alsthorpe Rd. LE15 32 E2
Ashfield. LE15 32 D1
Ashwell Rd. LE15 32 D2
Avon Clo. LE15 32 C4
Balmoral Rd. LE15 32 C3
Banff Clo. LE15 32 E3
Barleythorpe Rd. LE15 32 C2
Barlow Rd. LE15 32 D2
Beech Rd. LE15 32 E2
Bowling Grn Clo. LE15 32 E2
Braunston Rd. LE15 32 A4
Brooke Rd. LE15 32 C4

Browning Rd. LE15 32 B3
Buckingham Rd. LE15 32 C3
Bull La. LE15 32 D3
Bullfinch Clo. LE15 32 E1
Burley Pk Way. LE15 32 E1
Burley Rd. LE15 32 D2
Calder Clo. LE15 32 B4
Calgary Cres. LE15 32 E3
Camrose Clo. LE15 32 E3
Catmos St. LE15 32 D3
Catmose Park Rd. LE15 32 E3
Chaffinch Clo. LE15 32 E1
Chater Rd. LE15 32 C4
Chestnut Rd. LE15 32 D1
Cheviot Clo. LE15 32 B3
Chiltern Clo. LE15 32 A3
Church Pass. LE15 32 D2
Church St. LE15 32 D2
Churchill Rd. LE15 32 B3
Claresholme Clo. LE15 32 E3
Cold Overton Rd. LE15 32 A3
Cotswold Walk. LE15 32 A3
Cricket Lawns. LE15 32 D3
Crown Gdns. LE15 32 D3
Crown St. LE15 32 D3
Cunnington Clo. LE15 32 C3
Deans St. LE15 32 C2
Dee Clo. LE15 32 B4
Derwent Dri. LE15 32 C3
Digby Dri. LE15 32 B3
Don Clo. LE15 32 B4
Dove Clo. LE15 32 B4
Edmonton Way. LE15 32 E3
Elm Clo. LE15 32 E2
Fairview. LE15 32 E3
Ferrers Clo. LE15 32 A2
Finch Av. LE15 32 B3
Finkey St. LE15 32 C2
Forth Clo. LE15 32 C4
Foxfield Way. LE15 32 D1
Gaol St. LE15 32 D3
Glebe Way. LE15 32 A3
Glen Dri. LE15 32 C4
Grampian Way. LE15 32 A3
Greenfield. LE15 32 D1
Griffiths Clo. LE15 32 D1
Gunthorpe Clo. LE15 32 F2
Hanbury Way. LE15 32 A4
Hardwick Clo. LE15 32 F2
Harrington Way. LE15 32 B4
Heron Rd. LE15 32 E1
High St. LE15 32 D3
Hill Rd. LE15 32 B2
Hilltop Dri. LE15 32 A2
Holyrood Clo. LE15 32 C3
Horn Clo. LE15 32 F2
Hudson Clo. LE15 32 A3
Irwell Clo. LE15 32 B4
Jasper Rd. LE15 32 E3
Jay Clo. LE15 32 E1
John St. LE15 32 C3
Kennedy Clo. LE15 32 B3
Kestrel Rd. LE15 32 E1
Kilburn Rd. LE15 32 D2
Kingfisher Clo. LE15 32 E1
Kings Clo. LE15 32 B3
Kings Rd. LE15 32 C3
Ladywell. LE15 32 E2
Landsend Way. LE15 32 C1
Larchfield. LE15 32 D1
Lethbridge Clo. LE15 32 E3
Limefield. LE15 32 D1
Livingstone Clo. LE15 32 D1
Lodge Gdns. LE15 32 E3
Long Row. LE15 32 C3
Lonsdale Way. LE15 32 B3
Main Rd. LE15 32 A1
Malvern Walk. LE15 32 B3
Manor La. LE15 32 A1
Market Pl. LE15 32 D2
Market St. LE15 32 D2
Martin Clo. LE15 32 E1
Mayfield. LE15 32 D1
Meadowfield. LE15 32 D1
Melton Rd. LE15 32 C2
Mendip Rd. LE15 32 A3
Mill St. LE15 32 D3
Mountbatten Rd. LE15 32 B3
Nene Cres. LE15 32 C4
New St. LE15 32 C3
Nightingale Clo. LE15 32 E1
Noel Av. LE15 32 B4
Normanton Dri. LE15 32 E2
Northgate St. LE15 32 C2
Oakfield. LE15 32 D1
Park La. LE15 32 C2
Parkfield Rd. LE15 32 B2
Partridge Way. LE15 32 E1
Pasture La. LE15 32 A1
Penn St. LE15 32 D3
Pentland Ct. LE15 32 A3
Peterborough Av. LE15 32 E2
Pillings Rd. LE15 32 C1
Plover Clo. LE15 32 E1
Princess Av. LE15 32 B3
Queens Rd. LE15 32 D2
Redland Rd. LE15 32 A2
Redwing Clo. LE15 32 E1
Ribble Walk. LE15 32 B4
Robin Clo. LE15 32 E1
Ryefield. LE15 32 D1
St Albans Clo. LE15 32 E3
St Annes Clo. LE15 32 C3
St Peters Clo. LE15 32 D2
Sandringham Clo. LE15 32 B3
Schofield Rd. LE15 32 D1
School Rd. LE15 32 D2
Severn Clo. LE15 32 B4
Shannon Way. LE15 32 B4
Snelston Clo. LE15 32 E2
Snowdon Av. LE15 32 B3
South St. LE15 32 C3
Spey Dri. LE15 32 C4
Springfield Way. LE15 32 D1
Stables Ct. LE15 32 D3
Stamford Rd. LE15 32 D3
Station App. LE15 32 C2
Station Rd. LE15 32 C2
Summerfield. LE15 32 D1
Sunnyfield. LE15 32 D1
Tay Clo. LE15 32 B4
Tees Clo. LE15 32 C4
The Dell. LE15 32 D3
The Vale. LE15 32 D4
Trent Rd. LE15 32 B4
Tyne Rd. LE15 32 C4
Uppingham Rd. LE15 32 D3
Vicarage Rd. LE15 32 D2
Warn Cres. LE15 32 A3
Welland Way. LE15 32 B4
West Rd. LE15 32 C3
Westfield Av. LE15 32 B3
Westgate St. LE15 32 C3
Willoughby Gdns. LE15 32 C3
Willow Cres. LE15 32 E2
Windsor Dri. LE15 32 C3
Witham Av. LE15 32 C4
Woodland View. LE15 32 E2
Wreake Walk. LE15 32 B4
Wren Clo. LE15 32 E1

RATBY/ KIRBY MUXLOE

Armson Av. LE9 33 B5
Ash Ct. LE6 33 B1
Barns Clo. LE9 33 A5
Barons Clo. LE9 33 A5
Barton Clo. LE6 33 B3
Barwell Rd. LE9 33 B5
Beacon Clo. LE6 33 C1
Beaumont Grn. LE6 33 C1
Bedford Dri. LE6 33 C1
Beech Av. LE6 33 B1
Bell Clo. LE6 33 A3
Berrys La. LE6 33 A3
Bluebell Clo. LE9 33 C4
Bradgate Dri. LE6 33 A2
Bramley Ct. LE3 33 D2
Buckingham Clo. LE6 33 B1
Calverton Clo. LE6 33 A3
Cardinal Clo. LE6 33 A3
Carrow Rd. LE3 33 D6
Castle Rise. LE6 33 C1
Castle Rd. LE9 33 B5
Cedar Ct. LE6 33 C1
Centurion Ct. LE6 33 A3
Chapel La. LE6 33 A3
Charnwood Clo. LE3 33 D6
Chestnut Walk. LE6 33 C1
Church La. LE6 33 A2
Church Rd. LE9 33 B5
Cottage Clo. LE6 33 A2
Court Clo. LE9 33 B5
Crofters Clo. LE3 33 D3
Cufflin Clo. LE6 33 A3
Danehill. LE6 33 A2
Desford La. LE9 33 A5
Desford Rd. LE9 33 A5
East Walk. LE6 33 A2
Elm Clo. LE6 33 C1
Elm Tree Av. LE3 33 D3
Farley Way. LE9 33 C4
Farmers Clo. LE3 33 D3
Ferndale Dri. LE6 33 A3
Fishponds Clo. LE3 33 D3
Forest Dri. LE9 33 B6
Forge Clo. LE3 33 D3
Fox La. LE9 33 B5
Freemans Ct. LE6 33 B3
Garendon Way. LE6 33 B1
Garfit Rd. LE9 33 B5
Gillbank Dri. LE6 33 A3
Glebe Clo. LE3 33 D3
Glenfield La. LE9 33 C4
Grange Clo. LE3 33 D2
Grange Clo. LE6 33 A3
Greys Dri. LE6 33 B1
Groby Rd. LE3 33 A2
Gullet La. LE9 33 A5
Hastings Rd. LE9 33 C6
Heathbrook Dri. LE6 33 B3
Hedgerow La. LE9 33 A5
Hewitt Dri. LE9 33 C6
Highfield Rd. LE6 33 B1
Hill Dri. LE6 33 B3
Holmewood Dri. LE9 33 C6
Holt Dri. LE9 33 C6
INDUSTRIAL ESTATES:
Mill La Ind Est. LE3 33 D2
Ingle Dri. LE6 33 A3
Jordan Ct. LE6 33 B3
Journeymans Grn. LE6 33 A3
Kings Way. LE6 33 C1
Kirby Rd. LE3 33 D3
Ladysmith Rd. LE9 33 A5
Lancaster Ct. LE6 33 B1
Larchwood Av. LE6 33 C1
Laundon Clo. LE6 33 C1
Laundon Way. LE6 33 B1
Lee Rise. LE6 33 A3
Leicester Western By-Pass. LE3 33 C3
Lime Av. LE6 33 B1
Lime Gro. LE9 33 A6
Linden La. LE9 33 C6
Links Rd. LE9 33 A6
Lockley Clo. LE6 33 B3
Louise Av. LE6 33 C1
Main St. LE3 33 D2
Main St. LE9 33 B5
Main St. LE6 33 A3
Markfield Rd. LE6 33 A2
Martin Sq. LE6 33 B3
Meadow Clo. LE6 33 B3
Millers Clo. LE3 33 D3
Nicholas Dri. LE6 33 A3
Nook Clo. LE6 33 A2
Oakcroft Av. LE9 33 B5
Oakmeadow Way. LE6 33 B1
Old Hall Clo. LE6 33 C1
Overfield Clo. LE6 33 A2
Overfield Walk. LE6 33 A2
Packer Av. LE3 33 D6
Park Rd. LE6 33 A3
Parkfield Clo. LE6 33 B3
Pine Tree Av. LE6 33 C1
Portland Rd. LE9 33 B6
Preston Clo. LE6 33 B3
Pretoria Rd. LE9 33 B5
Primrose Way. LE9 33 C4
Princess Dri. LE9 33 B6
Pymm Ley La. LE6 33 C1
Queensmead Clo. LE6 33 C1
Quorndon Rise. LE6 33 B1
Ratby La. LE9 33 B4
Ratby Rd. LE6 33 B1
Robinsfield. LE6 33 B3
Rosendene Clo. LE9 33 C6
Round Hill. LE9 33 C6
Sacheverell Way. LE6 33 B1
St Peters Clo. LE3 33 D3
Saxons Rise. LE6 33 A2
Scudamore Rd. LE3 33 D5
Spinney Clo. LE6 33 B1
Spinney Side. LE6 33 B1
Spring Clo. LE6 33 B3
Stamford Dri. LE6 33 C1
Stamford Rd. LE9 33 C6
Stamford St. LE3 33 A2
Station Clo. LE9 33 B6
Station Dri. LE9 33 B6
Station Rd, Kirby Muxloe. LE9 33 B5
Station Rd, Ratby. LE6 33 A3
Sycamore Dri. LE6 33 C1
Sycamore Gro. LE6 33 C1
Taverner Dri. LE6 33 B3
The Close. LE9 33 A2
The Croft. LE9 33 B5
The Fairway. LE9 33 C6
The Huntings. LE9 33 A5
The Keep. LE9 33 B5
The Mill La. LE3 33 D2
The Oasis. LE3 33 D3
Timberwood Dri. LE6 33 B1
Towers Dri. LE9 33 B6
Tudor Gro. LE6 33 C1
Tyler Rd. LE6 33 B3
Ulverscroft Dri. LE6 33 C1
Vicarage Clo. LE9 33 C4
Victoria Dri. LE6 33 C1
Walton Clo. LE9 33 C6
Wanstead Rd. LE3 33 D5
Warrington Dri. LE6 33 B1
Wentworth Grn. LE9 33 B6
Wesley Clo. LE6 33 A3
Whitehouse Clo. LE6 33 B1
Whittington Dri. LE6 33 A2
Willow Dri. LE6 33 B1
Wilshere Clo. LE9 33 A6
Windmill Clo. LE6 33 B3
Windsor Av. LE6 33 C1
Wollaton Clo. LE3 33 D3
Wolsey Clo. LE6 33 C1
Woodlands La. LE9 33 B4
Woodley Rd. LE6 33 A2

ROTHLEY/ MOUNTSORREL

Anthony St. LE7 34 C6
Arundel Clo. LE12 34 A4
Ash Gro. LE12 34 C3
Babington Ct. LE7 34 C6
Babington Rd. LE7 34 C5
Badgers Bank. LE7 34 C5
Balmoral Rd. LE12 34 B3
Barley Way. LE7 34 C5
Barnard Way. LE12 34 B3
Barons Way. LE12 34 C2
Beaumaris Rd. LE12 34 B4
Beeches Av. LE12 34 C2
Belvoir Clo. LE12 34 B4
Berkeley Clo. LE12 34 C3
Blair Clo. LE12 34 B4
Bond La. LE12 34 A2
Boundary Rd. LE12 34 B3
Bradgate Clo. LE12 34 B1
Braemar Clo. LE12 34 B4
Breech Hedge. LE7 34 C5
Brookland Way. LE12 34 C4
Brownhill Cres. LE7 34 A6
Bulrush Clo. LE12 34 D3
Buttercup Clo. LE12 34 C2
Caenarvon Clo. LE12 34 B4
Carisbrooke Rd. LE12 34 B3
Castle Rd. LE12 34 B3
Cedar Gro. LE12 34 C3
Celandine Clo. LE12 34 D2
Church Hill Rd. LE12 34 B3
Church St. LE7 34 C6
Cloud Lea. LE12 34 C4
Clover La. LE12 34 D3
Conway Rd. LE12 34 B3
Cossington La. LE7 34 D6
Cromwell Rd. LE12 34 B4
Cross Green. LE7 34 C5
Cross Hedge. LE7 34 C5
Cross La. LE12 34 C4
Crown La. LE12 34 B2
Curlew Clo. LE12 34 B1
Danvers Rd. LE12 34 C3
Dover Clo. LE12 34 B3
Dunster Rd. LE12 34 B3
Edinburgh Way. LE12 34 B3
Elm Clo. LE12 34 C3
Fair Mead. LE12 34 C4
Farnham Clo. LE7 34 C5
Field Crest. LE12 34 B4
Flaxland. LE7 34 C5
Forge End. LE7 34 C6
Fort Rd. LE12 34 B3
Fowke St. LE7 34 C5
Foxglove Clo. LE12 34 D2
Furrow Clo. LE7 34 C5
Garland. LE7 34 C5
Gipsy La. LE12 34 A4
Glamis Clo. LE12 34 B4
Glebe Clo. LE12 34 B3
Glenfrith Clo. LE12 34 C3
*Glenfrith Gdns, Glenfrith Clo. LE12 34 C3
Grange La. LE12 34 B4
Grangefields Dri. LE7 34 D5
Granite Way. LE12 34 A1
Greenway Clo. LE7 34 C5
Hallfields La. LE7 34 C6
Halstead Rd. LE12 34 A3
Hawcliffe Rd. LE12 34 B1
Hawthorn Rd. LE12 34 C2
Heron Clo. LE12 34 C2
Highfields Rd. LE12 34 B3
Homefield La. LE7 34 D5
Horne Croft. LE7 34 C5
Howe La. LE7 34 C6
Iris Clo. LE12 34 C2
Johns Av. LE12 34 C3
Kenilworth Clo. LE12 34 B3
Kestrel La. LE12 34 D2
Kinchley La. LE12 34 A3
Kingfisher Rd. LE12 34 C2
Kirby Clo. LE12 34 B4
Knights Cres. LE7 34 C5
Laurel Clo. LE12 34 C2
Leicester Rd. LE12 34 C2
Linden Gro. LE12 34 C3
Linkfield Av. LE12 34 C3
Linkfield Rd. LE12 34 C3
Long Furlong. LE12 34 B4
Loughborough Rd, Mountsorell. LE12 34 D3
Loughborough Rd, North End. LE12 34 B1
Macaulay Rd. LE7 34 C5
Maitland Av. LE12 34 C3
Mallard Rd. LE12 34 D2
Marigold La. LE12 34 C2
Market Pl. LE12 34 C2
Marl Fields. LE12 34 D3
Marsh Rd. LE12 34 C3
Martin Av. LE12 34 B3
Meadow Rd. LE12 34 C4
Mere Clo. LE12 34 C4
Montsoreau Way. LE12 34 B4
Mountsorrel La, Rothley. LE7 34 C3
Mountsorrel La, Sileby. LE12 34 D1
Mountsorrell and Rothley By-Pass. LE12 34 C1
North St. LE7 34 C6
Oldfield La. LE12 34 C4
Orchard View. LE12 34 C4
Orchid Clo. LE12 34 C2
Otter La. LE12 34 C2
Paddock Clo. LE7 34 C6
Partridge Clo. LE12 34 D2
Peppers Clo. LE12 34 B1
Plain Gate. LE7 34 A4
Plough Clo. LE12 34 B4
Pott Acre. LE12 34 D3
Renning End. LE12 34 C4
Rochester Clo. LE12 34 B4
Rockhill Dri. LE12 34 B3
Rockingham Rd. LE12 34 B4
Rosslyn Av. LE12 34 A3
Rothley Rd. LE12 34 C2
Row Leyes Furlong. LE12 34 D3
Rowena Ct. LE12 34 C4
Rubicon Clo. LE12 34 C3
Rushey La. LE12 34 A2
School St. LE7 34 C6
Sheepcote. LE7 34 C5
Sileby Rd. LE12 34 C1
Skylark Av. LE12 34 C3
Slash La. LE12 34 D1
Speedwell Rd. LE12 34 C2
Stirling Clo. LE12 34 A4
Strachan Clo. LE12 34 C3
Swallow Clo. LE12 34 D2
Swan Clo. LE12 34 C2
Swithland La. LE12 34 A3
Templar Way. LE7 34 C5
The Green. LE12 34 C2
The Homestead. LE12 34 C2
The Osiers. LE12 34 A3
The Ridgeway. LE7 34 A6
The Ridings. LE7 34 A4
The Rise. LE7 34 D5
The Romans. LE12 34 C3
The Roods. LE7 34 C5
Town Green St. LE7 34 C6
Walkers La. LE7 34 C6
Walton Way. LE12 34 B4

Watling St. LE12 34 C2
Vaughs Dri. LE12 34 B4
Wellsic La. LE7 34 C6
West Cross La. LE12 34 A3
Westfield La. LE7 34 A6
Whatton Oaks. LE12 34 C3
Willow Gro. LE12 34 A3
Windmill Clo. LE12 34 C2
Windmill End. LE7 34 C5
Windsor Clo. LE12 34 B3
Wood La. LE12 34 A1
Woodfield Rd. LE7 34 C5
Woodgate. LE7 34 C6
York Clo. LE12 34 B4

SHEPSHED

Anson Rd. LE12 35 A3
Arbury Dale. LE12 35 D4
Arundel Gro. LE12 35 A5
Ashby Rd Central. LE12 35 B5
Ashby Rd East. LE12 35 D5
Ashby Rd West. LE12 35 A5
Balmoral Av. LE12 35 B4
Banbury Dri. LE12 35 A4
Beaumaris Cres. LE12 35 A4
Beech Clo. LE12 35 D3
Belton St. LE12 35 B2
Belvoir Way. LE12 35 A4
Beresford Ct. LE12 35 C3
Black Brook. LE12 35 A4
Blacksmiths Av. LE12 35 D2
Boundary Way. LE12 35 D1
Brendon Clo. LE12 35 D5
Brick Kiln La. LE12 35 A6
Bridge St. LE12 35 C2
Britannia St. LE12 35 C3
Brook St. LE12 35 C2
Brookside Clo. LE12 35 C4
Butthole La. LE12 35 C4
Caernarfon Clo. LE12 35 B4
Caistor Croft. LE12 35 A4
Cambridge St. LE12 35 C5
Carr La. LE12 35 A1
Central Av. LE12 35 C4
Challottee. LE12 35 C3
Chapel St. LE12 35 C2
Charnwood Rd. LE12 35 B5
Chatsworth Clo. LE12 35 A3
Chestnut Clo. LE12 35 D3
Cheviot Dri. LE12 35 D4
Chiltern Av. LE12 35 D3
Church Gate. LE12 35 C3
Church Side. LE12 35 C3
Church St. LE12 35 C2
Coach Rd. LE12 35 D3
Coachmans Ct. LE12 35 D2
Conway Dri. LE12 35 A4
Coombe Clo. LE12 35 C5
Cotton Croft. LE12 35 C4
Countrymans Way. LE12 35 C1
Cumbrian Way. LE12 35 D3
Danvers La. LE12 35 C3
Deacon Clo. LE12 35 C3
Domont Clo. LE12 35 B4
Dovecote. LE12 35 C2
Factory St. LE12 35 B2
Fairway Rd. LE12 35 C3
Fairway Rd Sth. LE12 35 C5
Field Av. LE12 35 C1
Field St. LE12 35 C1
Forest St. LE12 35 C2
Forman Rd. LE12 35 C4
Freehold St. LE12 35 C3
Garendon Clo. LE12 35 C3
Garendon Rd. LE12 35 C3
Gelders Hall Rd. LE12 35 B5
Glenfields. LE12 35 B3
Glenmore Av. LE12 35 B3
Grange La. LE12 35 B3
Grange Rd. LE12 35 A3
Griffin Clo. LE12 35 A4
Hall Croft. LE12 35 C3
Hallamford Rd. LE12 35 A1
*Harley Clo,
  Cotton Cft. LE12 35 C4
Harriman Clo. LE12 35 C2
Harrington Rd. LE12 35 D3
Hathern Rd. LE12 35 D1
Highfields Clo. LE12 35 C4
Holt Rise. LE12 35 C5
Homeway Clo. LE12 35 D4

Ingleberry Rd. LE12 35 C6
Iveshead Rd. LE12 35 B6
Jolly Farmers La. LE12 35 B6
Jubilee Path. LE12 35 A5
Kings Rd. LE12 35 B5
Kirkhill. LE12 35 C3
Lacey Ct. LE12 35 C3
Lambert Av. LE12 35 B3
Lansdowne Av. LE12 35 C1
Lansdowne Rd. LE12 35 C1
Leicester Rd. LE12 35 C3
Lindley Av. LE12 35 C4
Little Haw La. LE12 35 A3
Longcliffe Rd. LE12 35 A4
Loughborough Rd. LE12 35 C2
Ludlow Pl. LE12 35 A4
Malvern Av. LE12 35 C4
Manor Gdns. LE12 35 B2
Market Pl. LE12 35 C2
McCarthy Rd. LE12 35 B3
Mendip Clo. LE12 35 D4
Mill Clo. LE12 35 D1
Moorfield Pl. LE12 35 C3
Morley La. LE12 35 B6
Moscow La. LE12 35 A6
Nelson Clo. LE12 35 D3
Neville Clo. LE12 35 B3
New Walk. LE12 35 B2
Newark Clo. LE12 35 A4
Newlands Av. LE12 35 C5
Nook Clo. LE12 35 D5
Northwood Dri. LE12 35 C1
Norwich Clo. LE12 35 A4
Nursery Clo. LE12 35 C1
Oakley Av. LE12 35 B2
Oakley Clo. LE12 35 C2
Oakley Rd. LE12 35 B2
Old Station Clo. LE12 35 B5
Orchard Clo. LE12 35 B4
Oxford St. LE12 35 B4
Oxley Clo. LE12 35 B4
Park Av. LE12 35 C5
Park Clo. LE12 35 B3
Park Rise. LE12 35 B3
Patterson Pl. LE12 35 C2
Pear Tree Av. LE12 35 D3
Pennine Clo. LE12 35 D5
Penrith Av. LE12 35 A4
Pentland Av. LE12 35 D4
Pick St. LE12 35 B2
Piper Clo. LE12 35 C1
Ploughmans Dri. LE12 35 C2
Polden Clo. LE12 35 D5
Porlock Clo. LE12 35 D4
Pudding Bag La. LE12 35 A6
Purbeck Av. LE12 35 D4
Purley Clo. LE12 35 D4
Quantock Rise. LE12 35 D4
Queen St. LE12 35 C3
Radnor Dri. LE12 35 C1
Ring Fence. LE12 35 B4
Ringwood Rd. LE12 35 C1
Rockingham Clo. LE12 35 A5
Romway Clo. LE12 35 C4
St Bernards Clo. LE12 35 B4
St Botolph Rd. LE12 35 C4
St James St. LE12 35 C4
St Winifride Rd. LE12 35 C4
*Salmon Mews,
  Britannia St. LE12 35 C3
Sandringham Rise.
  LE12 35 A4
Shepherds Clo. LE12 35 C2
Smithy Way. LE12 35 D3
Snowden Clo. LE12 35 D5
Spring Clo. LE12 35 D3
Spring La. LE12 35 C5
Springfield Rd. LE12 35 B4
Sullington Rd. LE12 35 C4
Tamworth Clo. LE12 35 A4
Temple Clo. LE12 35 D5
Tetbury Dri. LE12 35 A4
The Inleys. LE12 35 D3
The Lant. LE12 35 C3
The Meadows. LE12 35 B4
Thorpe Rd. LE12 35 B4
Tickow La. LE12 35 A3
Trueway Dri. LE12 35 D4
Trueway Dri Sth. LE12 35 D4
Tyler Ct. LE12 35 C1
Wellyard Clo. LE12 35 D3
Westoby Clo. LE12 35 D3
Wicklow Clo. LE12 35 D4
Wightman Clo. LE12 35 C3
Windsor Dri. LE12 35 B4

Wood Clo. LE12 35 D3
Woodlands Dri. LE12 35 C1
Woodmans Way. LE12 35 C1
Wortley Clo. LE12 35 D1

SILEBY/RATCLIFFE ON THE WREAKE

Ainsworth Dri. LE12 38 C2
Albert Av. LE12 38 B2
Albion Rd. LE12 38 A3
Avenue Rd. LE12 38 B3
Back La. LE12 38 A3
Barnards Dri. LE12 38 C2
Barradale Av. LE12 38 A2
Barrow Rd. LE12 38 A2
Blackberry La. LE7 38 C4
Bowling Green Clo.
  LE12 38 B2
Brook St. LE12 38 A3
Broome La. LE7 38 E4
Brushfield Av. LE12 38 B2
Calde Clo. LE12 38 C2
Cauby Clo. LE12 38 C2
Cemetery Rd. LE12 38 B3
Chalfont Dri. LE12 38 A4
Charles St. LE12 38 A4
Church La,
  Ratcliffe. LE7 38 F4
Church La,
  Sileby. LE12 38 A3
Claire Ct. LE12 38 C2
Collingwood Dri. LE12 38 B2
Cossington La. LE12 38 A3
Dickens Clo. LE12 38 B2
East Orchard. LE12 38 A4
Finsbury Av. LE12 38 C3
Flaxland Cres. LE12 38 A4
Forest Dri. LE12 38 A2
Fosse Way. LE12 38 E3
Gibson Rd. LE12 38 A2
Greedon Rise. LE12 38 A2
Hanover Dri. LE12 38 B2
Haybrook Rd. LE12 38 B2
Heathcote Dri. LE12 38 B1
Herrick Clo. LE12 38 A2
Hickling Dri. LE12 38 B2
High St. LE12 38 A3
Highbridge. LE12 38 A2
Highgate Rd. LE12 38 B2
Hobbswick. LE12 38 A3
Homefield Rd. LE12 38 A3
Hudson Rd. LE12 38 A2
Humble La. LE7 38 D4
INDUSTRIAL ESTATES:
  Albion Rd
  Ind Est. LE12 38 B3
  Jubilee Av. LE12 38 B1
Kendal Rd. LE12 38 B3
Kilbourne Clo. LE12 38 B3
King St. LE12 38 A3
Lanes Clo. LE12 38 B2
Main St. LE7 38 F4
Manor Dri. LE12 38 A3
Marshall Av. LE12 38 B2
Middle Orchard. LE12 38 A4
Milner Clo. LE12 38 A3
Molyneux Dri. LE12 38 B4
Moreton Dale. LE12 38 B2
Mountsorrel La. LE12 38 A3
Newbold Ct. LE12 38 B2
North Hill Clo. LE12 38 C2
Park Rd. LE12 38 A2
Parsons Dri. LE12 38 C3
Peashill Clo. LE12 38 C3
Phoenix Dri. LE12 38 C3
Preston Clo. LE12 38 A3
Pryor Rd. LE12 38 B1
Quaker Rd. LE12 38 A4
Ratcliffe Rd. LE12 38 B3
St Gregorys Dri. LE12 38 A2
St Marys Rd. LE12 38 A2
Seagrave Rd. LE12 38 A2
Sherrards Dri. LE12 38 A4
Springfield Rd. LE12 38 C2
Stanage Rd. LE12 38 C2
Staveley Clo. LE12 38 B2
Storer Clo. LE12 38 B2
Swan St. LE12 38 A3
The Banks. LE12 38 A3
Wallace Dri. LE12 38 B4
Wards Cres. LE12 38 A3
Weldon Rd. LE12 38 B2
Wellbrook Av. LE12 38 B2

SYSTON/ EAST GOSCOTE

Abbots Clo. LE7 36 D5
Albert St. LE7 37 E5
*Albion Par,
  Albion St. LE7 37 E5
Albion St. LE7 37 E5
Anthony Clo. LE7 36 C6
Archdale St. LE7 36 C6
Archers Grn. LE7 37 F2
Ash Dri. LE7 37 E6
Augustus Clo. LE7 36 C6
Avenue Rd. LE7 37 G3
Avery Dri. LE7 37 E4
Back La. LE7 36 B2
Badgers Cnr. LE7 37 G1
Badminton Rd. LE7 37 E4
Balliol Av. LE7 37 F6
Barkby La. LE7 36 C6
Barkby Rd. LE7 37 E5
Barry Dri. LE7 37 E4
Bath St. LE7 37 E4
Beatty Rd. LE7 37 E4
Beeby Clo. LE7 37 F5
Beech Rd. LE7 37 E6
Beechwood Av. LE7 37 G3
Belvoir Dri. LE7 37 F5
Bennetts La. LE7 36 B1
Blackberry La. LE7 36 B1
Blackthorn Dri. LE7 36 C5
Bluebell Clo. LE7 37 G3
Bracken Dale. LE7 37 G1
Brighton Av. LE7 37 F4
Broad St. LE7 36 D5
Broad Way. LE7 36 D5
Brook St. LE7 37 E5
Brookfield Av. LE7 37 E5
Brookfield St. LE7 37 E5
Brookside. LE7 37 E5
Broome Av. LE7 37 G1
Broome La. LE7 37 G1
Broomfield. LE7 37 G2
Bruxby St. LE7 36 C6
Carvers Path. LE7 37 G2
Cedar Dri. LE7 37 E6
Central Av. LE7 37 E4
Chapel Clo. LE7 37 E4
Chapel St. LE7 37 E4
Chatsworth Dri. LE7 36 D5
Cherry Dri. LE7 37 E6
Chestnut Clo,
  Queniborough. LE7 37 G3
Chestnut Clo,
  Syston. LE7 37 E6
Chestnut Way. LE7 37 G2
Church Clo. LE7 37 E4
Church Rd. LE7 36 A6
Clover Walk. LE7 37 G2
Clumber Clo. LE7 37 E4
College Rd. LE7 37 E6
Coopers Nook. LE7 37 G2
Coplow Cres. LE7 36 D6
Coppice La. LE7 37 H3
Cossington La. LE7 36 C2
Countrymans Way. LE7 37 G1
Covert Clo. LE7 36 C5
Craftsmans Way. LE7 37 F2
Cranmer Dri. LE7 36 D5
Cross St. LE7 37 E4
Curlew Clo. LE7 36 C4
Curzon Clo. LE7 37 F3
Cygnet Clo. LE7 36 C5
Dalley Clo. LE7 37 E6
Dobney Av. LE7 37 F3
East Av. LE7 37 F5
Ervin Way. LE7 37 G2
Farriers Way. LE7 37 G2
Field Vw. LE7 36 C5
Fisher Clo. LE7 36 B1
Flatten Way. LE7 36 D4
Fletchers Way. LE7 37 G2
Foresters Row. LE7 37 G1
Fosse Way. LE7 36 C6
Foundry La. LE7 36 D6
Fox Hollow. LE7 37 G1
Foxglove Clo. LE7 37 G2
Frederick Clo. LE7 37 F5
Freemans Way. LE7 37 G1
Furlong Clo. LE7 37 F5
Gascoigne Av. LE7 37 G3
*George Toon Ct,
  Brook St. LE7 36 D5

Glebe Rd. LE7 37 G4
Glebe Way. LE7 36 C4
Gloucester Av. LE7 37 E4
Goodes Av. LE7 37 E6
Goodes La. LE7 37 E6
Gorse La. LE7 36 C5
Greensward. LE7 37 H1
Haddon Clo. LE7 36 D5
Hadrian Clo. LE7 36 C6
Halford St. LE7 36 D5
Hall Clo. LE7 36 A1
Harcourt Clo. LE7 36 D4
Hardwick Cres. LE7 36 D5
Harrisons Row. LE7 37 E5
Harvesters Cnr. LE7 37 G2
Heath Av. LE7 36 C5
Heron Way. LE7 36 C5
Herons Way. LE7 37 G1
High St. LE7 36 D4
Hollybush Clo. LE7 36 C5
Holmdale Rd. LE7 36 D6
Homestead Clo. LE7 36 A1
Humble La. LE7 36 B1
Hungarton Dri. LE7 37 F5
Huntsmans Dale. LE7 37 G1
INDUSTRIAL ESTATES:
  East Goscote
  Ind Est. LE7 37 F2
  Queniborough Ind Est.
    LE7 37 G4
Iona Rd. LE7 36 C5
Keble Dri. LE7 37 E5
Keepers Croft. LE7 37 G2
Kestrel Clo. LE7 36 C4
Kingfisher Clo. LE7 36 C4
Lime Clo. LE7 37 E5
Lime Dri. LE7 37 E6
Lincoln Dri. LE7 37 F6
Lindisfarne Rd. LE7 36 C5
Lindum Clo. LE7 36 C6
Ling Dale. LE7 37 G1
Link Rd. LE7 37 G3
Lodge Clo. LE7 37 F5
Long Furrow. LE7 37 G1
Lower Church St. LE7 37 E4
Maiden St. LE7 36 C5
Main St,
  Cossington. LE7 36 A1
Main St,
  Queniborough. LE7 37 H4
Mallard Dri. LE7 36 C5
Marcus Clo. LE7 36 C6
Marsden Av. LE7 37 G3
Martin Dri. LE7 36 C5
Meadow La. LE7 36 B4
Melton Rd. LE7 36 C6
Mercers Way. LE7 37 G2
Merchants Common.
  LE7 37 G2
Mere La. LE7 37 H4
Merton Av. LE7 37 E6
Michael Clo. LE7 37 H3
Middlefield Rd. LE7 36 B2
Milestone La. LE7 37 F4
Mill La. LE7 36 C3
Millers Clo. LE7 36 D6
Minstrels Walk. LE7 37 G1
Montague Av. LE7 37 E6
Moorland Rd. LE7 37 E6
Mostyn Av. LE7 37 E4
Mowbray Dri. LE7 37 F5
Naylor Rd. LE7 37 E4
Necton St. LE7 36 D5
Nelson St. LE7 37 E5
New St. LE7 37 G3
New Zealand La. LE7 37 H3
North St. LE7 36 D5
Northfields. LE7 37 E4
Nursery Clo. LE7 37 G3
Oak Dri. LE7 37 E5
Orchard Way. LE7 37 F5
Oriel Dri. LE7 37 E5
Oxford Ct. LE7 37 E5
Oxford St. LE7 37 E5
Paddock Vw. LE7 37 G1
Parkstone Rd. LE7 37 E4
Partridge Clo. LE7 37 G1
Pedlars Way. LE7 37 G2
Peggs La. LE7 37 H4
Pembroke Av. LE7 37 E6
Pine Dri. LE7 37 E6
Platts La. LE7 36 A2
Ploughmans Lea. LE7 37 G1
Plumtree Way. LE7 37 G3
Primrose Way. LE7 37 G3
Priory Clo. LE7 37 E6

ESTATE PUBLICATIONS

LOCAL RED BOOKS

ALFRETON, BELPER, RIPLEY
ASHFORD, TENTERDEN
BANGOR, CAERNARFON
BARNSTAPLE, ILFRACOMBE
BASILDON, BILLERICAY
BASINGSTOKE, ANDOVER
BATH, BRADFORD-ON-AVON
BEDFORD
BOURNEMOUTH, POOLE, CHRISTCHURCH
BRENTWOOD
BRIGHTON, LEWES, NEWHAVEN, SEAFORD
BRISTOL
BROMLEY (London Bromley)
BURTON-UPON-TRENT, SWADLINCOTE
BURY ST. EDMUNDS
CAMBRIDGE
CARDIFF
CARLISLE
CHELMSFORD, BRAINTREE, MALDON, WITHAM
CHESTER
CHESTERFIELD
CHICHESTER, BOGNOR REGIS
COATBRIDGE, AIRDRIE
COLCHESTER, CLACTON
CORBY, KETTERING
CRAWLEY & MID SUSSEX
CREWE
DERBY, HEANOR, CASTLE DONINGTON
EASTBOURNE, BEXHILL, SEAFORD, NEWHAVEN
EDINBURGH, MUSSELBURGH, PENICUIK
EXETER, EXMOUTH
FALKIRK, GRANGEMOUTH
FAREHAM, GOSPORT
FLINTSHIRE TOWNS
FOLKESTONE, DOVER, DEAL & ROMNEY MARSH
GLASGOW, & PAISLEY
GLOUCESTER, CHELTENHAM
GRAVESEND, DARTFORD
GRAYS, THURROCK
GREAT YARMOUTH, LOWESTOFT
GRIMSBY, CLEETHORPES
GUILDFORD, WOKING
HAMILTON, MOTHERWELL, EAST KILBRIDE
HARLOW, BISHOPS STORTFORD
HASTINGS, BEXHILL, RYE
HEREFORD
HERTFORD, HODDESDON, WARE
HIGH WYCOMBE
HUNTINGDON, ST. NEOTS
IPSWICH, FELIXSTOWE
ISLE OF WIGHT TOWNS
KIDDERMINSTER
KINGSTON-UPON-HULL
LANCASTER, MORECAMBE
LEICESTER, LOUGHBOROUGH
LINCOLN
LLANDUDNO, COLWYN BAY
LUTON, DUNSTABLE
MACCLESFIELD
MAIDSTONE
MANSFIELD, MANSFIELD WOODHOUSE
MEDWAY, GILLINGHAM
MILTON KEYNES
NEW FOREST TOWNS
NEWPORT, CHEPSTOW
NEWTOWN, WELSHPOOL
NORTHAMPTON
NORTHWICH, WINSFORD
NORWICH
NOTTINGHAM, EASTWOOD, HUCKNALL, ILKESTON
OXFORD, ABINGDON
PENZANCE, ST. IVES
PETERBOROUGH
PLYMOUTH, IVYBRIDGE, SALTASH, TORPOINT
PORTSMOUTH, HAVANT, WATERLOOVILLE
READING
REDDITCH, BROMSGROVE
REIGATE, BANSTEAD, LEATHERHEAD, DORKING
RHYL, PRESTATYN
RUGBY
ST. ALBANS, WELWYN, HATFIELD

SALISBURY, AMESBURY, WILTON
SCUNTHORPE
SEVENOAKS
SHREWSBURY
SITTINGBOURNE, FAVERSHAM, ISLE OF SHEPPEY
SLOUGH, MAIDENHEAD, WINDSOR
SOUTHAMPTON, EASTLEIGH
SOUTHEND-ON-SEA
STAFFORD
STEVENAGE, HITCHIN, LETCHWORTH
STIRLING
STOKE-ON-TRENT
STROUD, NAILSWORTH
SWANSEA, NEATH, PORT TALBOT
SWINDON, CHIPPENHAM, MARLBOROUGH
TAUNTON, BRIDGWATER
TELFORD
THANET, CANTERBURY, HERNE BAY, WHITSTABLE
TORBAY (Torquay, Paignton, Newton Abbot)
TRURO, FALMOUTH
TUNBRIDGE WELLS, TONBRIDGE, CROWBOROUGH
WARWICK, ROYAL LEAMINGTON SPA &
  STRATFORD UPON AVON
WATFORD, HEMEL HEMPSTEAD
WELLINGBOROUGH
WESTON-SUPER-MARE, CLEVEDON
WEYMOUTH, DORCHESTER
WINCHESTER, NEW ARLESFORD
WORCESTER, DROITWICH
WORTHING, LITTLEHAMPTON, ARUNDEL
WREXHAM
YORK

COUNTY RED BOOKS (Town Centre Maps)

BEDFORDSHIRE
BERKSHIRE
BUCKINGHAMSHIRE
CAMBRIDGESHIRE
CHESHIRE
CORNWALL
DERBYSHIRE
DEVON
DORSET
ESSEX
GLOUCESTERSHIRE
HAMPSHIRE
HEREFORDSHIRE
HERTFORDSHIRE
KENT
LEICESTERSHIRE & RUTLAND
LINCOLNSHIRE
NORFOLK
NORTHAMPTONSHIRE
NOTTINGHAMSHIRE
OXFORDSHIRE
SHROPSHIRE
SOMERSET
STAFFORDSHIRE
SUFFOLK
SURREY
SUSSEX (EAST)
SUSSEX (WEST)
WILTSHIRE
WORCESTERSHIRE

OTHER MAPS

KENT TO CORNWALL (1:460,000)
COUNTY MAP - DORSET
            - SOMERSET
            - WILTSHIRE
CHINA (1:6,000,000)
INDIA (1:3,750,000)
INDONESIA (1:4,000,000)
NEPAL (1,800,000)
SOUTH EAST ASIA (1:6,000,000)
THAILAND (1:1,600,000)

STREET PLANS

EDINBURGH TOURIST PLAN
ST. ALBANS

OFFICIAL TOURIST & LEISURE MAPS

SOUTH EAST ENGLAND (1:200,000)
KENT & EAST SUSSEX (1:150,000)
SUSSEX & SURREY (1:150,000)
SUSSEX (1:150,000)
SOUTHERN ENGLAND (1:200,000)
ISLE OF WIGHT (1:50,000)
WESSEX (1:200,000)
DORSET (1:150,000)
DEVON & CORNWALL (1:200,000)
CORNWALL (1:180,000)
DEVON (1:200,000)
DARTMOOR & SOUTH DEVON COAST (1:100,000)
EXMOOR & NORTH DEVON COAST (1:100,000)
GREATER LONDON M25 (1:80,000)
EAST ANGLIA (1:200,000)
CHILTERNS & THAMES VALLEY (1:200,000)
THE COTSWOLDS (1:110,000)
COTSWOLDS & WYEDEAN (1:200,000)
WALES (1:250,000)
CYMRU (1:250,000)
THE SHIRES OF MIDDLE ENGLAND (1:250,000)
STAFFORDSHIRE & SHROPSHIRE (1:200,000)
PEAK DISTRICT (1:100,000)
SNOWDONIA (1:125,000)
YORKSHIRE (1:200,000)
YORKSHIRE DALES (1:125,000)
NORTH YORKSHIRE MOORS (1:125,000)
NORTH WEST ENGLAND (1:200,000)
ISLE OF MAN (1:60,000)
NORTH PENNINES & LAKES (1:200,000)
LAKE DISTRICT (1:75,000)
BORDERS OF ENGLAND & SCOTLAND (1:200,000)
BURNS COUNTRY (1:200,000)
HEART OF SCOTLAND (1:200,000)
GREATER GLASGOW (1:150,000)
EDINBURGH & THE LOTHIANS (1:150,000)
ISLE OF ARRAN (1:63,360)
FIFE (1:100,000)
LOCH LOMOND & TROSSACHS (1:150,000)
ARGYLL THE ISLES & LOCH LOMOND (1:275,000)
PERTHSHIRE, DUNDEE & ANGUS (1:150,000)
FORT WILLIAM, BEN NEVIS, GLEN COE (1:185,000)
IONA (1:10,000) & MULL (1:115,000)
GRAMPIAN HIGHLANDS (1:185,000)
LOCH NESS & INVERNESS (1:150,000)
AVIEMORE & SPEY VALLEY (1:150,000)
SKYE & LOCHALSH (1:130,000)
ARGYLL & THE ISLES (1:200,000)
CAITHNESS & SUTHERLAND (1:185,000)
HIGHLANDS OF SCOTLAND (1:275,000)
WESTERN ISLES (1:125,000)
ORKNEY & SHETLAND (1:128,000)
ENGLAND & WALES (1:650,000)
SCOTLAND (1:500,000)
HISTORIC SCOTLAND (1:500,000)
SCOTLAND CLAN MAP (1:625,000)
BRITISH ISLES (1:1,100,000)
GREAT BRITAIN (1:1,100,000)

EUROPEAN LEISURE MAPS

EUROPE (1:3,100,000)
BENELUX (1:600,000)
FRANCE (1:1,000,000)
GERMANY (1:1,000,000
IRELAND (1:625,000)
ITALY (1:1,000,000)
SPAIN & PORTUGAL (1,1,000,000)
CROSS CHANNEL VISITORS' MAP (1:530,000)
WORLD (1:35,000,000)
WORLD FLAT

TOWNS IN NORTHERN FRANCE STREET ATLAS
BOULOGNE SHOPPERS MAP
CALAIS SHOPPERS MAP
DIEPPE SHOPPERS MAP

ESTATE PUBLICATIONS are also
Distributors in the UK for:

INTERNATIONAL TRAVEL MAPS, Canada
HALLWAG, Switzerland
ORDNANCE SURVEY

Catalogue and prices from:

ESTATE PUBLICATIONS
Bridewell House, Tenterden, Kent. TN30 6EP.

Tel: 01580 764225   Fax: 01580 763720